OMBUDSMEN COMPARED

OMBUDSMEN COMPARED

FRANK STACEY

CLARENDON PRESS . OXFORD
1978

Oxford University Press, Walton Street, Oxford OX2 6DP

OXFORD LONDON GLASGOW
NEW YORK TORONTO MELBOURNE WELLINGTON
IBADAN NAIROBI DAR ES SALAAM LUSAKA CAPE TOWN
KUALA LUMPUR SINGAPORE JAKARTA HONG KONG TOKYO
DELHI BOMBAY CALCUTTA MADRAS KARACHI

British Library Cataloguing in Publication Data
Stacey, Frank
Ombudsmen compared.
1. Ombudsman
I. Title
350'.0091 JF1525.045 78-40256
ISBN 0-19-827420-3

Printed in Great Britain by
Western Printing Services Ltd, Bristol

FOREWORD

FRANK Stacey died on 4 October 1977. On that day the copy-editor's comments on this book reached the University of Nottingham. With the help of his colleagues and in consultation with his files and sources which were at our house I have tried to do for him what he would have done in the final stages of the publication of *Ombudsmen Compared.* It is clear that he would have brought the work more up to date at the galley proof stage than I have been able to do. However, I have preferred to preserve his contribution as he left it where I have been unclear what amendments he might have made.

There were certain areas where it was clear that he had intended improvements. One in particular was with regard to the German military Ombudsman which, just before his death, he was discussing with David Childs. Dr. Childs has himself kindly written a contribution which I am sure Frank Stacey would have accepted and acknowledged.

It would not have been possible for me to complete this task without the help of Professor Pear and the Department of Politics at the University of Nottingham. In addition to David Childs, whom I have already mentioned, I would like to thank Peter Morris for his contribution. Special mention must be made of Peter James who worked as Frank Stacey's research assistant and who in addition to particular contributions was responsible for the comprehensiveness of the bibliography. Very special thanks are due to Ann Morris, Frank's secretary, who not only helped him so much, but who helped me to pick up the threads of his work. In addition I would like to thank Wyn Grant of the University of Warwick for his advice on the local commissioners and his contribution on the devolution bills.

The edges may be rougher than Frank Stacey would have left them, but with the help of these his friends and colleagues I have done my best to see that the volume is as nearly as possible as he would have wished it to be.

Husbands Bosworth
December 1977

MARGARET STACEY

PREFACE

In an earlier book, *The British Ombudsman*, published by the Clarendon Press in 1971, I discussed the campaign for an Ombudsman in Britain, the passage of the Parliamentary Commissioner Bill through Parliament, and the first four years of operation of the Parliamentary Commissioner's office. In the latter part of the book I made some comparisons between the Parliamentary Commissioner and Ombudsmen in other countries, but necessarily only briefly. I was keenly aware that to make any worthwhile comparisons it would be necessary to visit other countries with Ombudsmen systems, to interview the Ombudsmen and members of their staff, and to make a close analysis of their annual reports and other documentary material, where it was available.

This I resolved to do. But so rapid has been the development of the Ombudsman idea, and so rapid its implementation in countries throughout the world, that clearly I would not have been able to take in all the countries, and states in federal countries, since to visit them all would have meant going to more than twenty countries and places as far apart as Alaska, Fiji, Israel, and Australia. I decided therefore to take for comparison a group of countries which have much in common in their institutional and historical background. I visited Scandinavia first, choosing to go to Sweden because it is there that the Ombudsman idea originated, and Sweden has the most developed Ombudsman system in the world. Next I visited Denmark whose system was modelled on the Swedish Ombudsmen, but with some important differences, and Norway whose Ombudsman for Administration is similar in style to the Danish Ombudsman, while the Norwegian Ombudsman for the Armed Forces has features which are quite unique.

I then went to Canada which is the federal country in which there was the earliest, and most thorough, development of Ombudsmen systems at state level. Eight out of ten Canadian provinces now have Ombudsmen and whereas in Australia, by comparison, five out of six states now have Ombudsmen, the first Australian

Ombudsman was appointed as recently as 1972, while in Canada two provinces appointed Ombudsmen in 1967 (Alberta and New Brunswick), one in 1968 (Quebec), and two in 1969 (Manitoba and Nova Scotia). I decided to make a special study of the Quebec Protecteur du Citoyen (Public Protector) since Quebec is the most populous province in Canada to have a long-established Ombudsman. Out of the three prairie provinces, I chose to go to Manitoba, and from the maritime provinces, I chose New Brunswick. I am very grateful to the Nuffield Foundation which provided most of the finance which enabled me to visit Canada and conduct interviews there.

Next I visited France to interview the Médiateur. The developments in France are of interest in many ways, but there are two special reasons for studying the Médiateur. First, France has one of the most admired systems of administrative law in the world, and some critics of Ombudsman proposals in Britain had argued that an Ombudsman would be superfluous in France. Second, the Médiateur is, to some extent, modelled on the British Parliamentary Commissioner since he can only be approached through parliamentarians.

Finally, I have made an extended study of developments in the Parliamentary Commissioner's office in the ten years which it has now been in existence since 1967. I have also studied the Health Service Commissioner's office, set up in 1973, and the operation of the Local Commissioners for England, Wales, and Scotland who began to receive complaints against local authorities and water authorities in 1974 and 1975. This book is therefore a comparison of Ombudsmen systems in Britain, Scandinavia, Canada, and France and of the three forms of the British system which have developed since 1967.

I have found the research for this study not only fascinating but most enjoyable since all the Ombudsmen I have interviewed have co-operated fully in the research, and have received me with great courtesy and interest. In Stockholm I interviewed Mr. Ulf Lundvik, who is now the Chief Ombudsman in Sweden, Mr. Anders Wigelius, who is now one of the three other Ombudsmen and was then a Deputy Ombudsman, and Mr. Tor Sverne, who was the other Deputy Ombudsman. In Copenhagen I interviewed Mr. Nordskov Nielsen, the Danish Ombudsman, and in Oslo Mr. Ture Sinding-Larsen, the Head of Office of the Ombudsman for Administration, and Mr. Jack Helle, the Head of Office of the Ombudsman for the Armed Forces. In Quebec I interviewed Dr. Louis Marceau, who was Protecteur du Citoyen until 1976, and in Montreal his Deputy, M. Robert Lévèque. In Manitoba I interviewed the Ombudsman Mr. George Maltby and two of his investigators, Mr. Dick Glover and Mr. Max Regiedzinski. When I visited New Brunswick, the Ombudsman at that time, Mr. Charles Léger, was seriously ill, but I was fortunate to be able to interview the legal advisers to Mr. Ross Flemington, the first New Brunswick Ombudsman, Mr. Eric Appleby and Mr. David Olmstead. They were acting in the place of Mr. Léger during his terminal illness.

In Paris I interviewed the Médiateur, M. Aimé Paquet, his Délégué général (until November 1975), M. Jacques Legrand, and his Constitutional Adviser, M. Henri Desfeuilles. The co-operation I have received from Ombudsmen in the United Kingdom has been equally good. For my previous study I had interviewed the first Parliamentary Commissioner, Sir Edmund Compton. For the present book I interviewed the second Parliamentary Commissioner, Sir Alan Marre, and his successor Sir Idwal Pugh. I have interviewed his Deputy, as Parliamentary Commissioner, Mr. Henry McKenzie Johnston, on three occasions, and his Deputy, as Health Service Commissioner, Mr. Geoffrey Weston. The co-operation I have enjoyed with the Local Commissioners has been particularly close. Mr. Clifford Pearce, who was in charge, at that time, of the Local Government Division in the Department of the Environment, kindly suggested that I should meet the three Local Ombudsmen for England at an early stage. I had an excellent preliminary discussion with the chairman of the Commission, Lady Serota, the two other English Commissioners, Mr. Denis Harrison and Mr. Patrick Cook, and the Secretary to the Commission, Mr. Michael Hyde, in November 1975. I have since seen all of them again on several occasions, either together or individually, and I have been able to enjoy a continuing dialogue with them on the development of their office. I have also had valuable discussions with Mr. Dayfdd Jones-Williams, the Local Commissioner for Wales, and the Secretary of his Commission, Mr. Hywel F. Jones, as with the Scottish Local Commissioner, Mr. Robert Moore.

All the Ombudsmen have seen drafts of the chapters in this book and I am very grateful for the many helpful corrections and comments they, and their staffs, have sent to me. The responsibility for all the statements of fact and interpretation in this book is, however, entirely my own.

Department of Politics
University of Nottingham
May 1977

FRANK STACEY

CONTENTS

LIST OF TABLES

I

THE SWEDISH OMBUDSMEN

THE Swedish Ombudsmen are at once the longest established and the most powerful of all Ombudsmen. It is therefore logical to look at them first. In 1713 the Swedish King appointed an officer, who came to be known as the Chancellor of Justice, to investigate complaints against royal officials. When Sweden gained a democratic Constitution in 1809, Parliament appointed its own officer, the Justitieombudsman, to investigate complaints from citizens. In 1915 the office of Parliamentary Ombudsman, or Justitieombudsman, was modified by Parliament's decision to set up a second Ombudsman, known as the Militieombudsman, who took over from the Justitieombudsman the task of investigating complaints against the armed services.

After the Second World War, however, it became increasingly clear that the Justitieombudsman was overburdened with work while the number of complaints reaching the Militieombudsman was declining. Consequently, in 1968 Parliament decided to do away with a separate military Ombudsman and instead to establish three Ombudsmen in the office of Justitieombudsman. One of the Ombudsmen was to be concerned with complaints against the armed forces as well as against certain sectors of civil administration. The three Ombudsmen themselves determined how responsibility for investigating complaints against government agencies was divided. Also in 1968 Parliament decided to set up two Deputy Ombudsmen who were not formally allocated sectors of government, but gave general assistance to the three Ombudsmen. The Deputy Ombudsmen were not full-time members of the Ombudsmen's staff and, when not standing in for one of the Ombudsmen, they presided as judges in one of the common law or administrative courts. They were therefore 'reserve' Ombudsmen who could be called upon to take over the work of an Ombudsman when he was sick or on holiday, or to take on part of his case-load when he was engaged in one or more particularly difficult and time-consuming investigations. They did not 'understudy' specific Ombudsmen, indeed this would hardly have been possible with three Ombudsmen and only two Deputy Ombudsmen.

Another disadvantage of the organization in the Ombudsmen's Office, on the 1968 pattern, was that, formally speaking, all three Ombudsmen were of equal rank. Problems of co-ordination therefore had to be sorted out between them without any one of them having a designated role as mediator or chief co-ordinator. These difficulties, coupled with a steady rise in the volume of complaints to the Ombudsmen, led to a recognition that some kind of reorganization and expansion of the Ombudsmen's office was necessary. In 1972 Parliament (the Riksdag) appointed a Committee to look into the problem and in 1975 it recommended a new form of organization and a number of amendments to the statutes regulating the Ombudsmen's work. These were approved by Parliament in November 1975 and the new system came into effect in the spring of 1976.

Under the new organization there are four Ombudsmen and no Deputy Ombudsmen. One of the Ombudsmen is elected by Parliament to hold the office of Chief Ombudsman and Administrative Director of the Ombudsman's Office. He co-ordinates the work of the other Ombudsmen and, in consultation with them, decides on the areas of government for which they have responsibility in investigating complaints and initiating investigations.

Before we consider how the areas of government are now allocated between them, it is important to note how wide is the total area for which they are responsible. Between them, the four Ombudsmen cover all agencies of government, both central and local. This is a situation which seems remarkable to the British observer familiar with all those sectors of government from which the British Parliamentary Commissioner for Administration is excluded by the 1967 Act. These are some of the areas which are, in whole or part, exempted in Britain but not in Sweden: the Swedish Ombudsmen can investigate all kinds of complaints against the police, they can investigate complaints against all the activities of the Foreign Office and the security services. They can investigate complaints against nationalized industries, although not against industries which are wholly, or partly, state owned but are run as private companies. They can investigate complaints against administration by local authorities, they can investigate complaints which arise in the health service. Local authorities and the health service are now covered in Britain by Local Commissioners and the Health Service Commissioner but these Commissioners do not, in general, have such extensive powers as are possessed by the Swedish Ombudsmen. (See below in Chapters VIII and VII.)

The Swedish Ombudsmen are excluded from investigating the decisions of elected members, that is Members of Parliament and elected members of local authorities. They are also excluded from considering action taken by Cabinet Ministers. In this respect, then, the British Parliamentary Commissioner has a wider authority since he can investigate the actions of Ministers and has done so in a number of important cases, for example in the Sachsenhausen case in 1967, the Duccio painting case in 1969, and in the Court Line case in 1975.[1] Part of the rationale of Swedish Ministers being exempt from investigation by the Ombudsmen is that most areas of central government in Sweden are administered by boards and do not come under the direct control of Ministers. The conduct of administration by the boards is subject to investigation by the Ombudsmen.

In May 1976, when the new organization of Ombudsmen came into operation, Mr. Ulf Lundvik was elected Chief Ombudsman and Administrative Director of the Ombudsmen's Office. It was, in effect, a *de jure* recognition of a *de facto* leadership in the Ombudsmen's Office which he had long possessed. His experience is unrivalled. Before being appointed an Ombudsmen he was a Judge of the Supreme Court. Earlier in his career he had served as a Deputy Ombudsman and earlier again had worked in the Ombudsmen's Office as a legal assistant. He also contributed to one of the academic studies of Ombudsmen. He wrote part of the chapter on Sweden in the symposium on Ombudsmen edited by D. C. Rowat in 1965.[2]

The other three Ombudsmen elected in May 1976 were Mr. Anders Wigelius, who had been one of the two Deputy Ombudsmen under the old system, Mr. Karl-Erik Uhlin, who was previously Secretary of the Ombudsmen's Office, and Mr. Leif Ekberg, who had previously served as president of an Administrative Appeal

[1] See F. Stacey, *The British Ombudsman* (Clarendon Press, 1971), pp. 248–58 and 311. See also below, pp. 152–162, passim.

[2] See Ulf Lundvik, 'Comments on the Ombudsman for Civil Affairs', in D. C. Rowat (ed.), *The Ombudsman. Citizens' Defender* (Allen and Unwin, 1965), pp. 44–50.

Court. The division of responsibilities which Mr. Lundvik then arranged with the other Ombudsmen is as follows. Mr. Lundvik himself is responsible for oversight of the law which ensures access by members of the public to official documents at all levels of government. He is also concerned with problems caused by data processing and with personnel matters in central and local government. In addition, he investigates cases of special importance. Mr. Wigelius supervises the courts of justice, public prosecutors, the police, and prisons. Mr. Ekberg is concerned with taxation cases and social welfare. Mr. Uhlin supervises the armed forces and all matters in civil administration not allotted to the other Ombudsmen.[1]

The new legislation adopted in 1975 limits the role of Ombudsmen in prosecuting officials. It also places rather more emphasis on their right to institute disciplinary proceedings against officials rather than to prosecute.[2] It remains to be seen how far the Ombudsmen may decide to start disciplinary proceedings in cases where before they would have prosecuted. The number of prosecutions each year was anyway quite small in relation to the total number of cases investigated.[3] When I interviewed Mr. Lundvik I asked him to give me some examples of cases where the Ombudsman had prosecuted an official. One example which he gave me seemed of particular interest. A headmaster was prosecuted because it was claimed that he had behaved illegally in three respects. First, he was said to have suspended two boys from school because of their political (left-wing) sympathies. There was an election in the offing and he had told the boys not to come to school during the election period, the implication being that they would be a harmful influence at this time. Second, he was said to have cancelled the school sports day and given the whole school a day's holiday. Third, although he was bound by law to teach for three hours a week, he had not in fact been teaching for these three hours.

The court in which the headmaster was prosecuted found that all three allegations against him were true and fined him 1,800 kronor. This was then deducted from his salary. He also had to pay 1,500 kronor in costs. He therefore suffered a monetary penalty of 3,300 kronor of which the sterling equivalent was at that time about £290.

[1] The Swedish Parliamentary Ombudsman, Report for the period 1 January 1976 to 30 June 1976. Summary in English, p. 338.

[2] *The Swedish Parliamentary Ombudsmen* (Stockholm, 1976), p. 6 (pamphlet in English on the operation of the Ombudsmen's office).

[3] See below, p. 6.

This prosecution, and its outcome, seem doubly surprising to a British observer since public servants are not liable to prosecution by the Parliamentary Commissioner and, under the 1974 Local Government Act and the 1975 Local Government (Scotland) Act, the internal administration of schools is excluded from investigation by the Local Commissioners. The case well illustrates the Swedish system in which public servants are not entitled to behave in an arbitrary fashion or to exceed their powers which are, as far as possible, clearly defined. It should also be noted, that, in this case, the Ombudsman would not have prosecuted had it not been for the fact that the headmaster had been unwilling to accept that he had been at fault. The Ombudsman therefore concluded that he would be likely to continue in such arbitrary behaviour if he were not prosecuted.

I was also interested to establish with Mr. Lundvik just what are the powers of an Ombudsman in prosecuting, or admonishing, judges. He confirmed that it would generally be the behaviour of a judge in presiding over a case which would be the subject of complaint and investigation. The Ombudsman is not, however, confined to looking at procedural questions and sometimes, but not often, may need to scrutinize the judge's decision in the case.

A judge is always prosecuted by an Ombudsman in the court superior to the court over which he himself presides. Here I was able to get clarification of one point which had been obscure to me. Some of the literature on the Swedish Ombudsmen gives the impression that judges of the Supreme Court are not liable to prosecution by an Ombudsman. This is not strictly so, although such a prosecution would be extremely unlikely. An Ombudsman could, in law, prosecute a judge of the Supreme Court but, since there is no court superior to that court, he would have to resort to impeachment of the judge.

Some emphasis has been given here to the Ombudsmen's power to prosecute since it is somewhat unusual and does need clarification to the outside observer. Only in Finland, to my knowledge, does an Ombudsman have power to prosecute public servants in a similar way.[1] But prosecutions are very unusual in Sweden and in the

[1] The Danish Ombudsman in law has power to order prosecution of officials. In practice, this power is rarely, if ever, used. It was not used at all in the first nine years of operation of the Ombudsman's office. See I. M. Pedersen, 'Denmark's Ombudsmand', in D. C. Rowat (ed.), op. cit., p. 81.

great majority of cases the Ombudsmen are able to secure redress for the individual without resort to prosecution, or without undertaking disciplinary action against the public servant concerned. Thus in 1975, out of 2,293 cases investigated by the Ombudsmen, there were only 3 cases in which they found it necessary to prosecute the public servant or to recommend that disciplinary proceedings should be taken.[1] Mr. Lundvik told me that, in all his experience, he could recall no occasion when a central or local government agency had failed to act upon a recommendation of the Ombudsman. On the other hand, the Government did not always act on an Ombudsman's suggestion for changing the law.

The function of the Ombudsmen in initiating investigations is also important. In 1975 the Ombudsmen completed 400 cases which they had investigated on their own initiative. In 202 of these cases they admonished the government agency concerned and in 6 made prosposals to Parliament or the Government for legislative or policy changes. It is not surprising that the proportion of the cases they initiated in which they found fault with the government agency was much higher than in those cases which were investigated as a result of complaint from a member of the public.[2] The Ombudsmen often initiate investigations after reading press reports which give them cause to think that something has gone wrong in an administrative agency, and in a fairly high proportion of such cases their concern is found to be justified. Sometimes the cause for investigation may not be a press report but may still arise from study of the media. For example, a member of the Ombudsmen's staff recently found that a government agency was advertising in the press for employees in terms which appeared to contravene the law which forbids discrimination against women. He reported this to one of the Ombudsmen who then decided to initiate an investigation.

The Ombudsmen also have power to inspect courts, administrative agencies, hospitals, prisons, military units, etc. Before the 1975 reforms each Ombudsman used to spend about thirty working days a year on inspections. The increasing case-load has made it necessary to reduce the time spent on inspections. The new instructions to Ombudsmen indicate that each Ombudsman is authorized to undertake inspections whenever he wants to, but it is understood that he will only inspect an agency or institution where he has reason to

[1] The Swedish Parliamentary Ombudsmen, Annual Report for 1975. Summary in English, p. 612.

[2] See Table I, p. 7.

believe that the situation there is unsatisfactory.[1] The British Parliamentary Commissioner does not have power to initiate investigations or to carry out inspections and has a very limited power, in practice, to recommend changes in legislation.

TABLE I

The Swedish Ombudsmen in 1975

Complaints dealt with by the Ombudsmen during the year			*3,202*
They were handled in the following manner:			
Rejected (outside jurisdiction, etc.)			1,214
Referred to other state agencies			95
Investigated by the Ombudsmen			1,893
Cases initiated by the Ombudsmen			*400*
The results of investigations:			
	Investigated	Found justified*	Found justified %
Complaint cases	1,893	440	23·2
Ombudsmen's initiatives	400	208	52·0
Totals	2,293	648	28·7

Source: Derived from tables published by the Swedish Ombudsmen in their Annual Report for 1975, pp. 611 and 612.

* The category 'Found justified' is compiled from those investigations which resulted in either a prosecution or disciplinary proceedings, criticism of a government agency, or proposal to the Government or Parliament.

I was particularly interested to find out about the procedure followed by the Ombudsmen in making an investigation. It is clear that in the majority of cases the Ombudsmen and their staff make their recommendations on the basis of documentary material and do not interview the public servants who are the subject of complaint. Mr. Lundvik told me that in an increasing number of cases interviews are now being conducted. Such interviews are sometimes undertaken by the Ombudsmen, but more often by members of their staff, or by Public Prosecutors or Chiefs of Police, at the request of the Ombudsmen. The Ombudsmen's office also has a former police official on its staff who, Mr. Lundvik told me, had made some very valuable investigations on the instructions of the Ombudsmen.

The Ombudsmen can call for all the documents in the case from

[1] *The Swedish Parliamentary Ombudsmen*, p. 12.

government agencies, and no documents can be withheld from them. In drawing up their reports, however, the Ombudsmen will not quote documents which relate to matters of security. All the Ombudsmen's reports are open to inspection by the press, as are the original complaints to the Ombudsmen. This degree of access flows from the principle of public access to official documents which was established in Sweden as long ago as 1766, at the same time as freedom of the press was established by law. The reverse principle therefore applies to official documents as applies in Britain. Whereas in Britain all official documents are confidential unless a specific decision is taken to communicate them to the public and the press, in Sweden all official documents are open to scrutiny by the public and the press, unless special reasons can be given for keeping them confidential.

Journalists come to the office of the Justitieombudsman every morning to inspect the files of decisions by the Ombudsmen, and of newly lodged complaints. This provision for open access for the press has certain advantages over the system of strictly limited access which applies in Britain. The British Parliamentary Commissioner, when he has completed a case, sends his report to the Member of Parliament who raised the case with him as well as to the civil servant complained against, and to the Permanent Secretary of the Department concerned. It is then up to the M.P. to decide whether to communicate the Parliamentary Commissioner's report to the press; and in a high proportion of cases M.P.s do not do this. The Parliamentary Commissioner himself publishes reports only in an 'anonymized' form except on the rare occasions, in his special reports, where he gives names of the complainants. Each quarter he publishes a collection of his results reports. But their anonymity, and the absence of any comment by the Parliamentary Commissioner, makes these quarterly volumes disappointingly obscure.[1]

The result is that the British Parliamentary Commissioner hides his light under a bushel. The general public is insufficiently aware of his effectiveness because so little information about his activities filters through to the press. In Sweden, by contrast, the press can get information about all the Ombudsmen's cases and publish whatever details they choose. This free accessibility has undoubtedly played a part in informing the Swedish public about the Ombudsmen and has encouraged ordinary people to seek redress through them.

[1] See below, Ch. VII, p. 144.

Mr. Lundvik is not, however, fully satisfied with the present situation as regards publicity. He feels that the press tend to give greater coverage to the complaints than to the reports. This is understandable since the complaints are often more sensational. He also finds that his reports are often so mangled in the process of sub-editing that he sometimes finds it difficult to recognize them. This is a criticism, of course, of the press rather than of the principle of free access. It seems clear that the Ombudsmen's reports are given reasonable coverage in both the national and the local press, although the newspapers are not always as responsible in their handling of the material as the Ombudsmen would wish them to be. To a British observer, free access for the press to the Ombudsmen's reports seems wholly desirable. Whether there should also be free access to the original complaints is more open to question, but Mr. Lundvik assured me that, in the Swedish climate of opinion, free access for the press to the text of complaints could not be denied.

One of the most discussed features of the British Parliamentary Commissioner is that he is limited to reporting upon injustices caused to complainants 'in consequence of maladministration'.[1] It is sometimes claimed that this kind of limitation applies, in practice, to the Scandinavian Ombudsmen. This is certainly not true of the Swedish Ombudsmen. They are able to report not only upon the legality of a course of action taken by a government servant, but also on the question whether a decision was a reasonable one. Let us take an example of one field of administration which used to fall within Mr. Lundvik's purview. He used to be responsible for investigating complaints against the postal services. Until fairly recently, in Sweden every house had its own little post-box at the gate, in which the postman delivered letters, and from which he collected outgoing mail.

A few years ago the decision was taken that, in order to facilitate collection of letters, only certain houses would be allocated post-boxes. Mr. Lundvik then received many complaints from householders that their post-boxes had been withdrawn. An old lady, for example, would complain that she had to go out along frozen roads to collect her mail and that she should be given a post-box of her own. Mr. Lundvik told me that he sympathized with such complainants but, in general, he did not think it right to condemn the decision of the postal authorities, since with motorized collection

[1] See below, esp. pp. 130–134.

and delivery of mail it would be very time-consuming for the postmen to stop at every house. The point is, however, that it was open to the Ombudsman to say whether or not the decision was a reasonable one. He was not limited to procedural questions: to considering whether or not the decision had been properly made, whether there had been proper consultation with consumer representatives, etc.

What of some of the other limitations which the 1967 Act imposes on the British Parliamentary Commissioner? Do they have a parallel in Sweden? The British legislation provides, for example, that the Parliamentary Commissioner will not normally investigate a complaint where the complainant has a remedy in a court of law or administrative tribunal. The Act does give the Parliamentary Commissioner discretion to waive this limitation if it does not seem to him reasonable to expect a complainant to go to a court or tribunal, but the implication is that this will be exceptional.[1] In practice, the Parliamentary Commissioner frequently rejects cases, or discontinues them, if he finds that the complainant has a remedy in a court of law or administrative tribunal. For example, he has discontinued an inquiry into a complaint that the prison medical authorities had been negligent in the care of a prisoner, thereby causing his death, when it appeared that the prisoner's wife had a remedy in a court of law.[2]

The Swedish Ombudsmen are not limited in this way. If there is provision for appeal to a court or a higher authority in a case which has been sent to an Ombudsman, he may nowadays decline to investigate it because of the increasing volume of cases which come to the Ombudsmen. If, however, it seems likely that there has been a serious failure in the administration, or an important principle is involved, the Ombudsman will investigate at once without asking the complainant to exhaust the channels of appeal. If, after the Ombudsman's investigation, the complainant decides to take his case to court, he can make use of the Ombudsman's report in stating his case to the court. This seems to be a sensible arrangement. The British statute goes out of its way to try to ensure that the Parliamentary Commissioner does not trench upon the field of the courts and of administrative tribunals. The Com-

[1] See Parliamentary Commissioner Act, 1967, Sect. 5(2).

[2] This case was raised with Andrew Faulds when he was Labour M.P. for Smethwick, and quoted by him in the BBC television programme 'The Court of Last Resort' on 10 March 1970.

missioner can, for example, examine a complaint that a government department has not behaved properly towards a complainant before he took his case to an administrative tribunal, but the Commissioner may not investigate the conduct of the case by the tribunal. No such inhibition is placed upon the Swedish Ombudsmen. They can investigate a complaint that an administrative court has acted improperly or unfairly, just as they can investigate such complaints against the ordinary courts.

Since the Swedish Ombudsmen have such wide powers, covering all central services, since they are not limited to cases alleging maladministration, or in many of the other ways in which the British Parliamentary Commissioner is limited, and since the public has such ready access to the Ombudsmen, it is interesting to note what kind of staff is found necessary to deal adequately with the large volume of cases which they receive. The Ombudsmen must be lawyers, and most of them have been judges. This is logical since the Ombudsmen have such wide powers in relation to courts and administrative tribunals. But this does not mean that they were judges with a similar training and background to that of British judges. Whereas a British judge has begun his career as a barrister (or more rarely a solicitor), in private practice, the Swedish judge is a member of a career service and will normally have been recruited to the service from university. There is no equivalent of the British magistrates' courts in Sweden, manned by laymen: the local courts in Sweden are presided over by career judges. Therefore the Swedish judge is a public servant and is less of a stranger to matters of administration than a British judge is. Similarly, the training given to lawyers is broader in scope than is a legal training in Britain. A law degree in Sweden will include elements of social sciences which are not normally found in British law schools.

The Swedish Ombudsmen are appointed by Parliament for a four-year term. Their appointments are subject to renewal, and renewal for a second term is normal, but it would not be accurate to say that renewal is automatic until retiring age. Mr. Alfred Bexelius served as Ombudsman for sixteen years until 1972 but his long period of service should not be considered to have necessarily created a precedent. When Ombudsmen leave office they are quite often appointed judges of the Supreme Court. Mr. Bertil Wennergren was so appointed when he ceased to be an Ombudsman in

1975. But the other Ombudsman who retired at this time, Mr. Gunnar Thyresson, became a legal adviser to Parliament.

The four Ombudsmen have a staff of fifty people to assist them, including twenty-three lawyers and twenty-two secretarial and supporting staff. The twenty-three lawyers are highly qualified people. About 40 per cent of them are drawn from the Common Law or Administrative Courts and about 60 per cent from government departments or agencies. The Ombudsmen and their staff contrast very strongly in type and number with the British Parliamentary Commissioner and his staff. Whereas the four Ombudsmen are all legally qualified and their staff includes twenty-three lawyers, the present Parliamentary Commissioner, Sir Idwal Pugh, had been a career civil servant and did not have a legal training. His predecessors, Sir Edward Compton and Sir Alan Marre, had a similar background. Furthermore, the Parliamentary Commissioner's staff does not include one lawyer. All the members of his staff are civil servants on secondment from government departments and serve for only a limited period of time in the Parliamentary Commissioner's office.

The second great contrast is that the Parliamentary Commissioner's staff is much larger than the Swedish Ombudsmen's staff in relation to case-load. The Parliamentary Commissioner is assisted by a staff of fifty-seven working on the Parliamentary Commissioner side. Since he is also Health Service Commissioner some of his staff work solely on Health Service cases and are not included in this total.[1] The Swedish Ombudsmen have a staff of fifty. In 1975 the British Parliamentary Commissioner completed investigation of 244 cases.[2] In the same year the Swedish Ombudsmen completed investigation of 2,293 cases.[3]

This contrast prompts a number of comments. First, we may note the small number of cases, 244, investigated by the Parliamentary Commissioner in relation to the population of the United Kingdom which is more than 55 million. The Swedish Ombudsmen made 2,293 investigations in a country with a population of around 8 million. This illustrates the extent to which the Parliamentary Commissioner's scope for investigation is limited, and access to him is curtailed for members of the public. Second, the Parliamentary Commissioner has a larger staff than the Swedish

[1] See below, p. 177. [2] See below, p. 163.
[3] See Table I, p. 7.

Ombudsmen to investigate a case-load which, in 1975, was one-ninth of the case-load dealt with by the Swedish Ombudsmen.

The explanation of this contrast lies chiefly in the fact that the Parliamentary Commissioner's staff operate somewhat on the model of the staff of the British Comptroller and Auditor-General, and it is significant that the first British Parliamentary Commissioner, Sir Edmund Compton, had previously held the office of Comptroller and Auditor-General. In many cases the Parliamentary Commissioner's staff themselves go to the government departments against which a complaint has been made, and interview the civil servants concerned. The Swedish Ombudsmen and his staff, as we have seen, work mainly by correspondence. Although they are making increasing use of face-to-face inquiries, such inquiries are only made in a minority of cases. Mr. Lundvik would like to make more use of interviews but is limited from so doing by the small size of his staff in relation to the case-load.

This problem of the volume of complaints in relation to the size of the staff is one of the major problems for the Swedish Ombudsmen. Their annual reports give an indication of the increase in the volume of complaints in recent years. In 1969 the Ombudsmen commented that the number of complaints they had received that year, 2,708, represented a 25 per cent increase over the number they had received in 1968 which itself was 10 per cent higher than the 1967 figure. They considered that 'the increase mainly seems to depend on the wave of social consciousness that has swept through the Swedish community particularly during the last year. In an "active society" pressure groups as well as socially committed individuals are inclined to try all means of influencing the social processes. It is not astonishing that they should also try lodging complaints with the Ombudsmen. It is symptomatic that political youth leagues have written to the Ombudsmen during 1969 much more often than in any previous year.'[1] By 1975 the annual figure of complaints dealt with by the Ombudsmen had risen again to 3,202.

This increase would of itself cause problems of overloading but it is particularly worrying to Mr. Lundvik since, in his conception, the Ombudsmen in Sweden ought to have time to seek out deficiencies in the administrative system and make recommendations for their improvement. Thus he feels he was able to produce some

[1] The Swedish Parliamentary Ombudsmen, Annual Report for 1969. Summary in English, p. 521.

improvement in tax administration where a number of cases of a similar character had shown up serious deficiencies and inequities. Where, as in this example, a succession of cases of complaint tends to show a pattern of defects in administration, the Ombudsman needs to have time to follow up these cases by making inspections and himself initiating investigations. If, however, the volume of complaints is very large, he must give all his time to taking up cases of complaint and is not able to attack the general problems.

Mr. Lundvik wonders if there could be some method of screening so that he would not have to look at the 'fool' complaints and could give more time to major cases and general problems. Yet a 'fool' complaint may sometimes reveal a serious abuse. He gave me a rather bizarre example. An Ombudsman once received a letter from a patient in a mental hospital who complained that he was being paid five öre for painting. Five öre is worth about ½p. The Ombudsman was inclined to dismiss the complaint but he decided to ask for an investigation by the hospital authorities. It eventually transpired that the patient was being paid five öre by a homosexual male nurse for painting him on his genitals. Therefore what seemed, at first sight, to be a 'fool' complaint did lead to discovery of a real abuse when investigated.

We saw, at the beginning of this chapter, that the Justitieombudsman was set up, in 1809, to work alongside the King's Chancellor of Justice and the Chancellor of Justice is still in being. He investigates complaints and carries out inspections on similar lines to the four Ombudsmen. The problems which this parallel jurisdiction creates are met in the following way. If a complainant writes to both the Chancellor of Justice and an Ombudsman, the staff of the two offices get on the telephone and establish who received the complaint first. Whoever first received the complaint takes on the case.

The Chancellor of Justice has other functions in addition to his function of investigating complaints. He is the Government's legal adviser and also has special responsibility for supervision of the Press Code. When the Government takes the initiative in commissioning an investigation, it will often entrust the task to the Chancellor of Justice. But this does not mean that all the most serious cases are investigated by the Chancellor of Justice rather than by an Ombudsman. For example, in 1971 an Ombudsman carried out an investigation into the failure of the Swedish police to protect the person of the Yugoslav Ambassador. The Ambassador had been murdered by members of an organization of Yuguslav exiles. In his report the Ombudsman concluded that it was not sufficient for the police to place guards outside embassies in order to carry out their duty of protecting foreign legations. They must also 'actively prevent attacks by observation of exile organizations whose members have shown tendencies to aggression'.[1]

In Sweden a citizen can complain to an Ombudsman about almost any aspect of government service, either central or local. But where would he complain against an Ombudsman if he were dissatisfied with the way in which his complaint was handled? His correct avenue of complaint would be to the Select Committee of Parliament on Constitutional Law. The ultimate sanction which Parliament could then invoke against an Ombudsman, if it were dissatisfied with his conduct, would be to terminate his appointment. Needless to say such an eventuality is most unlikely, but this is the constitutional position.

The Select Committee does not take the continuing interest in the work of the Ombudsman which the British Select Committee on the Parliamentary Commissioner does in relation to the Parliamentary Commissioner. Neither do Members of Parliament have any role in screening complaints to the Ombudsmen. It is unlikely that they would be given such a role since many people in Sweden would feel that this would bring party politics into the functioning of the Ombudsmen.

We have seen that the Ombudsmen in Sweden have a very wide jurisdiction covering almost every area of government. They cannot be denied access to any relevant documents and can undertake inspections whenever they think necessary. They can also command the services of whatever specialists are needed in making their investigations. Every authority is required by law to co-operate with the Ombudsmen. Therefore, if an Ombudsman requiries a specialist assessor or investigator for any case, someone with the highest qualifications will be seconded to him from the relevant department of authority. If he needs a heart specialist, for example, to advise him in a medical case, or a skilled engineer, these advisers will be provided for him.

The Ombudsmen therefore have a very high standing and are very effective in securing redress for complaints. But how widely

[1] The Swedish Parliamentary Ombudsmen, Annual Report for 1971. Summary in English, p. 548.

are they used and how widely are they known? The number of complaints which they investigate each year is some indication of the extent to which they are used. The over-all figures, however, might disguise a bias in the system towards the better educated and more well-to-do sections of the population. Professor W. B. Gwyn has argued in an article that: 'The benefits of an ombudsman reached only on the initiative of a complainant are bound to be enjoyed disproportionately by the affluent and well-educated' as compared to the poor and ignorant.[1]

It may be that this is an accurate observation in respect of the British Parliamentary Commissioner since the procedure for complaining to him via an M.P. is complicated. An unpublished survey made by Professor K. A. Friedmann in 1969 showed that less than 8 per cent of a sample of people interviewed in Britain knew how to get the Parliamentary Commissioner to investigate a complaint. Far more people of above-average socio-economic status knew about the Parliamentary Commissioner than did those of lower status.[2]

Mr. Lundvik, and the Deputy Ombudsmen whom I interviewed, were emphatic in thinking that a similar observation could not be made about the Swedish Ombudsmen. While it is true that retired Swedish professors, living abroad, have written to the Ombudsmen to complain about their tax assessments, complaints from such people are very much in the minority. The majority of letters to the Ombudsmen are written by people who do not seem to be well-to-do. The Ombudsmen mentioned in their Annual Report for 1971 that many of the letters they receive are handwritten 'and few are compiled with the assistance of a lawyer'.[3]

A high proportion of the complaints they receive are from prisoners. In 1975 as many as 216 complaints related to prison administration.[4] In 1971 there were no less than 350 such complaints.[5] Very few prisoners have a high socio-economic status. The Ombudsmen pointed out in their Annual Report: 'In 1971 the number of prisoners' complaints concerning their treatment in prison has again been very large. Many complaints regarding the

[1] W. B. Gwyn, 'The British P.C.A.: "Ombudsman or Ombudsmouse?" ', *Journal of Politics*, 35 (1973), 69.

[2] K. A. Friedmann: 'Complaining: The Case of the British and their Ombudsman', unpublished paper (1971), quoted by W. B. Gwyn, loc. cit. 53.

[3] Annual Report for 1971. Summary in English, p. 541.

[4] Annual Report for 1975, p. 612.

[5] Annual Report for 1971, p. 542.

prisons are now coming from the committees which the prisoners in the big prisons have elected to represent them. The complaints from these committees often concern questions that are of fundamental interest for all prisoners.'[1]

Mr. Lundvik told me that when he visits a prison and goes into a cell it does not usually produce a reaction from the prisoner if he says he is the 'Justitieombudsman'. But if he says 'I am the J.O.', the prisoner will immediately sit up and start to air his grievances. The letters 'J.O.' are known throughout Sweden and people who want to complain to an Ombudsman merely have to address their envelope to 'J.O. Stockholm' and their complaint will be delivered in the right place.

[1] p. 543.

II

THE DANISH OMBUDSMAN

DENMARK has had an Ombudsman since 1955. When a new Constitution was being planned for the country after the Second World War, the Committee on the Constitution proposed that Parliament should elect one or two persons from outside Parliament whose function it would be to supervise the administrative system and the armed forces. The object of the reform would be 'the establishment of increased guarantees for the lawful conduct of the government's civil and military administration'.[1] The Committee gave its opinion that such increased guarantees could be achieved through 'an "ombudsmand" (Parliamentary Commissioner) institution similar to the Swedish prototype'.[2]

The Constitution of June 1953 included a provision on these lines. In 1954 the Act setting up the Ombudsman was passed, and in 1955 Professor Stephan Hurwitz was elected Ombudsman, an office which he held continuously until his retirement in 1971 when Mr. Nordskov Nielsen was elected in his place.

The influence exerted by Professor Hurwitz in shaping the institution of Ombudsman in Denmark has been profound. He was already a public figure before his election since he was known as a Professor of Law who had played an important part during the war in the resistance to the German occupation. Once elected he did a great deal to publicize his office both in Denmark and outside his own country. Indeed, he played a part in assisting the spread of the Ombudsman idea. The establishment of the Ombudsman in New Zealand, and of the Parliamentary Commissioner in Britain, owes a good deal to his willingness to make himself available to people in those countries who were interested in establishing an Ombudsman. For example, he visited Britain on two occasions to

[1] Quoted by S. Hurwitz in *The Ombudsman* (Det Danske Selskab, Copenhagen, 1968), p. 5, from the draft proposed by the Constitution Committee established in 1946.

[2] Ibid., p. 6.

speak to meetings organized by 'Justice', the group of lawyers who were chiefly responsible for getting the idea of a Parliamentary Commissioner adopted in Britain. He was also consulted by Sir John Whyatt who was Director of Research for the Justice Committee which published an unofficial report advocating the reform.[1]

Since the office of Ombudsman in Denmark owes much to the Swedish prototype, it is not surprising to find that the Danish Ombudsman, like his Swedish counterparts, has a very wide jurisdiction. He can investigate complaints against almost any aspect of central administration. He is not, for example, excluded, as the British Parliamentary Commissioner is, from investigating complaints against the nationalized industries, nor is he excluded from considering personnel questions in the public service or the armed forces. Broadly speaking, his jurisdiction can be said to be the same as that of the Swedish Ombudsmen except that he may not investigate complaints against judges. He can, however, investigate complaints against Ministers but only in their capacity as heads of departments, not as members of the Cabinet. This inclusion of Ministers within his jurisdiction follows from the principle as it does in the United Kingdom, that Ministers are directly responsible to Parliament for their departments. Denmark does not have the Swedish system under which the central departments are administered by boards and are not under the direct control of Ministers.

As regards local government, since 1962 the Danish Ombudsman has been competent to investigate complaints against many activities of local authorities. He is not allowed to investigate certain local functions in which there is no provision for appeal to central government, for example slaughterhouses, personnel questions in local government, and the buying and selling of land by local authorities. He is, however, competent to investigate complaints against the use of planning powers by local authorities and against other major local government functions.

He is also limited by a rule which provides that he may not investigate complaints against a decision taken by the full council of a local authority. He can only investigate decisions by officials or by council committees. This is not a serious limitation, however, since he has power, on his own initiative, to investigate a decision by a full council although he may not investigate the decisions in pursuance of a complaint.

[1] See Stacey, *The British Ombudsman*, esp. pp. 18, 21, and 32.

While the Danish Ombudsman has a jurisdiction almost as wide as that of the Swedish Ombudsmen, except that it does not include the courts, he is a somewhat less powerful critic of the administrative services for two reasons in particular. The first reason is that he may not investigate a complaint about a decision until the citizen concerned has exhausted the remedies available to him in appeal to higher authorities. This rule, which was introduced by legislation in 1959, results in the Ombudsman having to decline to investigate a high proportion of the complaints which are sent to him. Thus in 1975 the Danish Ombudsman received 1,889 complaints. He had to decline to investigate 578 of these on the ground that the avenues of appeal had not been exhausted.[1]

The Swedish Ombudsmen are not so limited. They can decline to investigate a complaint if there is another means of redress open to the complainant, but they do so in only a small minority of cases. In 1975, for example, out of 3,202 complaint cases dealt with by the Swedish Ombudsmen, they referred only 95 to other state agencies.[2] Although a case can be made out for the Danish rule requiring the exhaustion of avenues for appeal, it clearly has the effect of reducing the Ombudsman's annual case-load, and it is likely that it has some discouraging effect on complainants. It must be pointed out, however, that whenever the Danish Ombudsman declines to investigate a case, on the ground that all avenues of appeal have not been exhausted, he always indicates the avenue of appeal to the complainant and tells him that he should write to him again if he is dissatisfied after the appeal. The Ombudsman does not, therefore, wash his hands of the complaint but, in effect, declares his continuing interest in seeing that the complainant is fairly treated, even if he is not permitted to begin an investigation straightaway. Also, the rule about the exhaustion of remedies does not apply to complaints about the behaviour of officials, nor to cases which the Ombudsman takes up on his own initiative.

The other main respect in which the Danish Ombudsman is not so powerful a critic of the Executive as the Swedish Ombudsmen is in his inability to require that all the documents in the case be shown to him. Whereas the Swedish Ombudsmen can see all the documents, the Danish Ombudsman need only be shown the correspondence in the case, he need not be shown the department's internal memorandums.

[1] See Table II, p. 21. [2] See Table I, p. 7.

TABLE II

Reasons for rejection of cases by the Danish Ombudsman in 1975

Avenues of appeal not exhausted	578
Complaints outside his jurisdiction, concerned with legislation, private legal matters, etc.	93
Complaints outside his jurisdiction, directed against judges	74
Complaints on local government matters outside his jurisdiction	58
Complaints out of time	46
Complaints withdrawn	80
Inquiries, not real complaints	87
Miscellaneous, including anonymous and obviously groundless complaints	82
Total	1,098

Source: Folketingets Ombudsmand. English version of part of Annual Report for 1975, p. 3.

The Whyatt Committee suggested that the British Parliamentary Commissioner should be limited in a similar way. But when a Cabinet Subcommittee in the Wilson Government planned the Parliamentary Commissioner Act it resolved not to be so cautious.[1] The Act gives the British Parliamentary Commissioner power to see all the papers in a case, including the internal memorandums. In practice, some departments do send all the papers in the case to the Danish Ombudsman. Mr. Nielsen told me that the Taxation Appeal Board, for example, sends him all the internal papers, as does the Ministry of Foreign Affairs. The Ministry of Justice, by contrast, never sends him all the internal papers. He clearly finds it much more satisfactory in assessing a case to have all the internal papers, and the power to require them to be shown to him would strengthen his position.

There is another respect in which the Danish Ombudsman can be said to enjoy less power as an investigator than his Swedish counterparts. Whereas, as we have seen, the Swedish Ombudsmen have wide powers to criticize unreasonable decisions by administrative authorities, the Danish Ombudsman is rather more circumscribed. The Whyatt Committee thought that where administrative decisions involve an exercise of discretion the Danish Ombudsman does not

[1] See Stacey, op. cit., p. 55.

criticize the decision. It recommended that the British Parliamentary Commissioner should, like the Danish Ombudsman, be excluded from considering discretionary decisions except where maladministration was involved.

It has been pointed out that the Whyatt Committee's interpretation does not square with Professor Hurwitz's statement, in a pamphlet which he published in 1962, that there are types of discretionary administrative decisions which the Danish Ombudsman is able to criticize.[1] In a later pamphlet Professor Hurwitz stated the position in a somewhat different way. He said that 'the Ombudsman only criticises discretionary decisions when he can cite the knowledge of experts in support, and when as far as can be ascertained, there exists reliable documentary evidence of an arbitrary or unreasonable decision'.[2] Mr. Nordskov Nielsen clarified the situation for me, in discussion, by indicating that when he, as Ombudsman, is considering a discretionary decision, he is empowered to say whether the decision is illegal or unreasonable. If he considers that the decision is open to question on the grounds of legality, he will normally say that the case is doubtful and recommend that the complainant go to the courts and be given legal aid. He also has the power to say that a decision is unreasonable, but he uses this power with caution, bearing in mind that administrators have special knowledge which he does not himself normally possess. However, his scope in relation to administrative procedures is much wider. He has greater freedom to suggest that there have been faults in administrative behaviour and to recommend changes in procedure. The role of the Danish Ombudsman seems therefore to be nearer, in practice, to that of the British Parliamentary Commissioner, with his limitation to report on 'injustice in consequence of maladministration', than to that of the Swedish Ombudsmen with their wide power to criticize unreasonable decisions by administrators.

The methods used by the Danish Ombudsman in investigating complaints broadly resemble those used by the Swedish Ombudsmen. In the great majority of cases in which a fault in administrative behaviour is alleged, the Ombudsman and his staff do not interview

[1] Stephan Hurwitz, *The Ombudsman. Denmark's Parliamentary Commissioner for Civil and Military Administration* (Det Danske Selskab, Copenhagen, 1962) quoted in Stacey, pp. 24–5.

[2] *The Ombudsman*, p. 9.

the complainant, or the public servants concerned, but reach their decision on the basis of documents. There is, however, a well-defined system for considering the documents. When, on the basis of the original letter of complaint, the case seems to be a simple one in which it is unlikely that the department has been to blame, the Ombudsman merely writes to the department concerned asking for the documents. He may then be able to reach a decision at once, or he may have to write again to the department asking for further elucidation.

If the case is a complicated one, or if it appears that the department may have been at fault, the Ombudsman's office asks the department to take a stand on the case explaining why it reached the decision it did. When the department's statement is received, the Ombudsman may ask for further information, or he may decide to send the department's statement to the complainant asking him to comment on it. The Ombudsman's office may then ask for a supplementary statement from the department in the light of the complainant's comments.

Although the procedure is almost entirely by correspondence and examination of documents in this largest group of cases, there is a type of case in which a face-to-face meeting between the Ombudsman and representatives of the department is usual. This is when a case concerns a decision taken by a Ministry consequent upon law or regulations. Such cases do not arise frequently and are felt to be of such importance that a personal discussion between the Ombudsman and representatives of the Ministry is necessary.

The Ombudsman has power to investigate on his own initiative and uses this power quite widely. In 1975, for example, he initiated an investigation of 120 cases. The stimulus for such initiatives comes from much the same sources as in Sweden, for example from articles in the press and in legal periodicals.

The Ombudsman also has power, as in Sweden, to carry out inspections of state institutions. He has in recent years varied his programme of inspections. In 1973, for instance, Mr. Nielsen inspected four mental hospitals and three institutions for child and youth welfare. In 1974 he inspected three army camps, two local prisons, and two institutions for young people, and in 1975 thirteen local prisons and three hospitals for the mentally retarded.

The law in Denmark provides that the Ombudsman must have had a legal training but neither law nor custom provides that he must have had experience as a judge. Since the Danish Ombudsman cannot investigate complaints against judges, it is clearly not so important that he should have had this kind of experience. Professor Hurwitz had been a Professor of Law before being elected Ombudsman. Mr. Nielsen had been an administrative civil servant, although, like most senior civil servants in Denmark, he was trained as a lawyer. He had been the director of the Prison Administration before being elected Ombudsman in succession to Professor Hurwitz. The Ombudsman is elected by Parliament after every general election. Professor Hurwitz was re-elected several times, serving in all as Ombudsman for fifteen years. It seems likely that his successors will have a similarly long tenure while they continue willing and able to serve.

The Ombudsman's staff is, as might be expected, considerably smaller than the staff of the Swedish Ombudsmen. In April 1977 it consisted of two divisional heads, ten legally qualified investigators, of whom nine were full-time and one part-time, and eight secretarial staff, one of whom was part-time. The Swedish Ombudsmen in 1976 had twenty-three legally qualified staff and twenty-two secretarial and supporting staff. The population of Denmark now approaches 5 million to Sweden's nearly 8 million. We would not expect the Danish Ombudsman, however, to have a staff five-eighths as large as that of the Swedish Ombudsmen since his role is more circumscribed and his case-load lighter. In 1975 the Swedish Ombudsmen completed investigation of 2,293 cases while in the year 1975 (beginning of June) to 1976 (end of May) the Danish Ombudsman completed investigation of 797 cases. The Danish Ombudsman therefore investigated far less than half the number of cases in a comparable period. Nevertheless, the Danish Ombudsman's case-load is heavier than that of the British Parliamentary Commissioner, who investigated 244 cases in 1975 and was assisted by a staff of fifty-seven full-time people.[1]

The Ombudsman's case-load has been discussed here solely in terms of cases investigated, but a good deal of the time of the staff is also taken up, as with the British Parliamentary Commissioner's staff, in deciding whether the Ombudsman is competent to take up a case. The largest single category of cases which the Danish Ombudsman has to decline is provided by the cases in which the avenues of appeal have not been exhausted.[2] He rejected 578 cases

[1] See above, pp. 12–13. [2] See Table II, at p. 21.

on this account in 1975. Another numerically important category was provided by complaints against judges of which he had to decline 74 in the same year. Mr. Nielsen told me that judges had not been included in the Ombudsman's jurisdiction in Denmark because of the feeling that the independence of the judiciary needed to be maintained. Yet, as the figures of complaints in 1975 indicate, there is considerable dissatisfaction with the judiciary in Denmark. Indeed, Mr. Nielsen told me that, in his opinion, Danish citizens in general receive more consideration from administrative authorities than they do from the courts.

Although he is not able to investigate complaints against judges, the Danish Ombudsman can investigate complaints against administrative tribunals. In the twelve months from 1 June 1975 to 1 June 1976, for example, he investigated 89 complaints against the Social Appeal Board and in 23 cases found cause for criticism or recommendation.[1] In the same period he investigated 21 complaints against the police and in 5 cases criticized police conduct or procedures.[2]

He investigated 4 complaints against state prisons in this period and in 2 cases criticized the prison authorities.[3] The Danish State Railways come within his jurisdiction. In the period 1975–6 he investigated 10 complaints against them and in 5 cases found the complaints justified.[4] Out of 40 complaints in all against local authorities, he found that 16 were justified in some degree.[5] Out of the total number of 797 complaints against central and local services in this period, there were 233 cases in which he criticized the administrative authority or recommended a change in procedure.[6]

The press take a continuing interest in the work of the Ombudsman. Every Friday journalists call at the Ombudsman's office in Copenhagen and are allowed to look at the documents on interesting cases decided in the week. Since 1970 Denmark has had a law requiring publicity in administration. The law gives the press and public access to official documents, somewhat on the lines of Swedish practice. The law does not, however, apply to the Ombudsman as it does in Sweden. The Ombudsman does not give the names of complainants, or of officials complained against, either in his annual report or in his special reports. These special reports are

[1] Folketingets Ombudsmand. English version of part of Annual Report for 1975, p. 6.
[2] Ibid., p. 7. [3] Ibid., p. 8. [4] Ibid.
[5] Ibid., p. 9. [6] Ibid.

made to the Select Committee of the Folketing on the Ombudsman when the case has a special interest, or when the Ombudsman recommends a change in legislation. On average, the Ombudsman makes about eight of these special reports every year.

Since the Ombudsman does not mention the names of complainants or officials in his annual or special reports, he expects journalists to withhold names from the stories which they derive from inspecting documents in his office. The journalists respect his wishes and do not normally give the names of people involved, although when a case has become known nationally before going to the Ombudsman, the identity of the persons in the case may be already common knowledge. The Ombudsman, of course, sends a report on every case he has completed to the complainant. It is then a matter for the complainant whether he communicates the Ombudsman's findings to the press.

The Select Committee on the Ombudsman follows up the reports which it receives from the Ombudsman to see if the recommendations are implemented, thus providing a valuable parliamentary backing to his work. From time to time his reports have been the basis for discussion between Ministers and the specialist Committees of Parliament. While, however, the Committee on the Ombudsman takes a close interest in his reports, there is nothing like the frequent contact and continuous relationship which exists between the British Parliamentary Commissioner and the House of Commons Select Committee on the Parliamentary Commissioner. Mr. Nielsen told me that, to his knowledge, Professor Hurwitz had only met the Committee twice during his fifteen-year term as Ombudsman. Mr. Nielsen himself has met the Committee twice during his six years of office from 1971 to 1977. He has, however, had several informal contacts with the chairman of the Committee.

A few, but very few, complaints come to the Ombudsman each year through Members of the Folketing. They average about two a year. As in Sweden, it would be thought rather strange for Members to be a main channel of complaint to the Ombudsman. In Denmark, I was told, Members do not feel themselves to be advocates for all their constituents, irrespective of party affiliation, as British M.P.s do. Members of the Folketing are, relatively, not so active on behalf of individual constituents. For example, although parliamentary question time has existed in the Folketing since 1953, it only happens once a week, on a Wednesday. Only general questions can be raised, not specific grievances of constituents, and only between 3 and 12 questions are dealt with in the allotted hour.

Mr. Nielsen did not think that the Ombudsman is more accessible in Denmark to people of higher socio-economic status than to the less well to do or less well educated. An English translation of a collection of 75 cases decided by the Danish Ombudsman provides a number of instances of quite ordinary people gaining redress through his activities.[1] For example, a former ship's stoker complained to the Ombudsman in 1963 that he had been denied compensation out of money provided by the West German Government for Danes who had been victims of Nazi persecution. He had been sentenced in 1941 to sixteen years' imprisonment for alleged participation in sabotaging ships. The Appeal Board had turned down his claim on the ground that the acts of sabotage concerned had been carried out against Spanish trawlers in 1938. The Ombudsman doubted the correctness of the Appeal Board's decision since the charges against the stoker had been suspended and the Nazi authorities had caused them to be revived after the occupation of Denmark. Since the Appeal Board refused to reconsider its decision, the Ombudsman recommended that the complainant should take his case to court and be granted legal aid. The High Court found for the complainant and awarded him compensation of 6,500 kroner.[2]

On several occasions the Danish Ombudsman has procured redress for prisoners. For example, in 1966 he investigated a complaint by a prisoner that he was not allowed to keep birds in his cell. The prison governor claimed that the birds had caused an epidemic through fowl mites and were a threat to health, and also that some prisoners had constructed such large cages in their cells that there was hardly room in the cells for the prisoners themselves. The Ombudsman took advice from a specialist in poultry diseases who informed him that good ordinary hygiene would protect humans from fowl mites. The Ombudsman then asked the prison governor to reconsider his decision in the light of the report. This he did and prisoners were once more allowed to keep birds in their cells.[3]

In 1955 a woman complained to the Ombudsman that drivers on

[1] Mogens Lerhard (ed.), *The Danish Ombudsman 1955–1969*, trans. Reginald Spink (Schultz, Copenhagen, 1972).

[2] Ibid., pp. 70–1.

[3] Ibid., pp. 88–9.

the State Railway's bus routes were failing to enforce the no-smoking rule in the compartments of buses reserved for non-smokers. She also stated that on one occasion the driver had behaved discourteously to her when she asked him to stop two passengers from smoking. On receiving details of the complaint from the Ombudsman, the State Railways Board instructed drivers 'to ensure observance of the no-smoking rule'. The driver who had shown discourtesy to the complainant was also severely reprimanded and apologized to her. The Ombudsman found this a satisfactory conclusion to the case.[1]

In 1968 the Ombudsman inquired into delays by the Disablement Insurance Tribunal in dealing with appeals. He had received a growing number of complaints about these delays and decided to institute his own inquiry. His conclusion was that the backlog of cases was steadily increasing and that the delays in handling cases were unreasonable. He drew the attention of the Folketing's Ombudsman Committee to the matter, and in the following financial year funds were allocated to establish a third section of the Appeal Tribunal.[2]

These cases involving a former ship's stoker, a prisoner, a woman on a bus, and people appealing to the Disablement Insurance Tribunal are all cases in which the Danish Ombudsman secured redress for quite ordinary people. The case-books also give examples of redress being provided for university professors, business men, civil servants, and lawyers. But they do not indicate a predominance of the higher socio-economic groups among those who benefit from the Ombudsman's activities.

The Ombudsman's office is quite easy for the general public to find in Copenhagen. It is in the complex of buildings in the centre of the city known as the Christiansborg Slot. This is the old royal palace which now houses the Parliament building and a number of government offices. An average of two or three people come each day to the Ombudsman's office to lodge their complaints in person or to seek advice.

There has not been a steady increase in recent years in the number of complaints to the Danish Ombudsman as there has been to the Swedish Ombudsmen. In the years towards the end of Professor Hurwitz's term of office the annual volume of cases had reached a plateau. Each year from 1965 to 1969 there were around 1,100

[1] Ibid., pp. 11–12. [2] Ibid., pp. 105–6.

complaints.[1] After his resignation and the appointment of a new Ombudsman there was an increase in the volume of complaints. In 1971 there were 1,275 complaints and in the following year the volume of complaints rose sharply to 1,741. The totals for 1973 and 1974 were somewhat lower but in 1975 there was another big increase, the volume of complaints for that year rising to 1,889.

TABLE III
The Danish Ombudsman, 1965 to 1975.

Cases rejected as a percentage of cases received*

Year	Cases received	On own initiative	Cases rejected	Cases rejected %
1965	1,146	18	778	67·9
1966	1,106	11	762	68·9
1967	1,095	14	766	70·0
1968	1,158	17	834	72·0
1969	1,130	16	771	68·2
1970	964	11	680	70·5
1971	1,275	47	835	65·5
1972	1,741	100	1,048	60·2
1973	1,461	68	858	58·7
1974	1,687	71	964	57·1
1975	1,889	120	1,098	58·1

* The years 1955 to 1964 are not given since the figures of cases rejected for those years were calculated on a different basis.

Sources: Mogens Lerhard (ed.), *The Danish Ombudsman 1955–1969*, trans. Reginald Spink (Schultz, Copenhagen, 1972), p. 7. Folketingets Ombudsmand. Statistics 1971–5.

In every year a high proportion of the complaints sent to the Ombudsman are rejected because he is not competent to investigate them. In 1968 Professor Hurwitz declined to investigate 72 per cent of the complaints which were made to him. The lowest percentage of complaints which he declined in the six years from 1965 to 1970 was 67·9, in 1965. Mr. Nielsen has consistently declined to investigate a lower proportion of cases. In 1975 he declined 58·1 per cent of the complaints which he received.[2] The main reason for complaints not being taken up is that all avenues of appeal have not yet been exhausted. When Professor Hurwitz was Ombudsman, he found some element of justification in around 10 per cent of the cases he investigated. The highest proportion in the years 1965 to

[1] See Table III. [2] Ibid.

1970 was 11·6 per cent, in 1968. The lowest, in 1969, was 8 per cent. Mr. Nielsen has found cause for criticism or recommendation in a much higher proportion of cases. During four full years in which he has been in office since 1971, the proportion of such cases to all the cases he investigated has never been less than 21·7 per cent. In 1975 it was 29·2 per cent.[1] Since the change of Ombudsman in 1971 there has therefore been an increase in the number of complaints received, a reduction in the proportion of complaints not accepted for investigation, and a considerable increase in the

TABLE IV

The Danish Ombudsman, 1965 to 1975.

Cases in which the Ombudsman found cause for cirticism or recommendation

Year of report	Report period	Cases investigated and concluded	Criticism or recommendat'n	Criticism or recommendat'n %
1965	1.6.65–30.5.66	364	39	10·7
1966	1.6.66–30.5.67	343	36	10·5
1967	1.6.67–30.5.68	338	37	10·9
1968	1.6.68–30.5.69	319	37	11·6
1969	1.6.69–30.5.70	361	29	8·0
1970	1.6.70–1.6.71	289	25	8·6
1971	1.6.71–1.6.72	396	65	16·4
1972	1.6.72–1.6.73	646	140	21·7
1973	1.6.73–1.6.74	626	198	31·6
1974	1.6.74–1.6.75	726	196	27·0
1975	1.6.75–1.6.76	797	233	29·2

Sources: Mogens Lerhard (ed.), *The Danish Ombudsman 1955–1969*, trans. Reginald Spink (Schultz, Copenhagen, 1972), pp. 7 and 8. Folketingets Ombudsmand. Statistics 1971–5.

[1] See Table IV.

proportion of cases investigated in which the Ombudsman has found cause for criticism or recommendation.

By Swedish standards, the office of Ombudsman in Denmark is still young and is still developing. It is possible, however, to give an interim verdict on the institution of the Ombudsman in Denmark, namely that the reform, although in some respects a cautious one, has been markedly successful within the limits set for it. It has been a cautious reform in that all avenues of complaint have to be exhausted before complaints about decisions can be investigated. It is also cautious in not requiring that all documents in the case must be shown to the Ombudsman. The Ombudsman's practice has also been cautious in the restraint he has shown in questioning the reasonableness of administrative decisions. Nevertheless, within these limits the Ombudsman is doing a valuable job. He is striving to see, in Mr. Neilsen's own words to me, that administrative procedures, at all levels of government, are 'humane and considerate' towards the citizen. The few cases quoted here are typical instances of the way the Danish Ombudsman goes about this task.

III

THE NORWEGIAN OMBUDSMAN FOR ADMINISTRATION

NORWAY has had an Ombudsman for Administration since 1962, but she has had an Ombudsman for the Armed Forces since 1952. Therefore, if we were to proceed on a chronological basis we would begin with that office. But it is instructive to look first at the Ombudsman for Administration since there are close similarities between his position and that of the Danish Ombudsman.

The legislative draftsmen who fashioned the *Act of 1962 concerning the Storting's Ombudsman for Administration* took the Danish Ombudsman as their model. Yet there are interesting differences between the two institutions and they have worked somewhat differently in practice. The jurisdiction of the Norwegian Ombudsman is very similar to that of the Danish Ombudsman without his military responsibilities. He is concerned with all central administration except the judges, the Auditor of Public Accounts, and the armed forces. This means that, like the Danish Ombudsman, he is concerned with all aspects of the work of the Foreign Office, the security services, the police, and nationalized industries such as the State Railways. He can investigate decisions by Ministers and complaints against administrative tribunals. For example, he can look into complaints against the Prices Board, the Central Commission to which mental patients may appeal, and the Social Security Court.

The Norwegian Ombudsman for Administration was not initially given power to investigate complaints against local authorities but, in 1969, was given the right to investigate complaints against certain local government services. He is not concerned with decisions about local taxation, the sale of locally owned property, or with the appointment of the most senior officials in local government. He is concerned with such services as town planning and education, including the administration of schools.

As with the Danish Ombudsman, his work is governed by a rule requiring exhaustion of remedies by the complainant. The rule is only strictly maintained in relation to decisions by administrative authorities. If the complaint is not directed against a decision but against the behaviour of an authority, the Ombudsman has more latitude. If the complaint, for example, alleges delay in handling of a case by an authority, the Ombudsman will take it up at once without asking for exhaustion of remedies. If the complaint is against the behaviour of an individual civil servant, a policeman or headmaster for example, the complainant will normally be asked by the Ombudsman to go to the superior authority first. Thus, in the case of a complaint against a headmaster, the complainant would be asked to go first to the school board or to the education authority.

As regards discretionary decisions, the Ombudsman has a limited function but the limits under which he can operate are not quite the same as those which apply to the Danish Ombudsman. The Norwegian Ombudsman for Administration can criticize discretionary decisions if they are 'manifestly unreasonable'. Mr. Tore Sinding-Larsen, the Chief of Office and First Legal Assistant to the Ombudsman, told me that the Ombudsman very seldom criticizes such decisions. He does, however, more frequently use his power to consider whether discretionary decisions are founded on 'proper fact'. In other words, he can look into the question whether an administrative authority has considered all the facts and whether its version of the facts is accurate. He can also consider whether or not a decision has been made in conformity with the law and within the limits which the law prescribes.

As regards access to the documents in a case, the practice is similar to that in Denmark. The Norwegian Ombudsman for Administration can call for all the documents except the internal memorandums on a case. Some departments do send him all the documents, including the internal memorandums. The Department of Communications, which is concerned with Posts, Telegraphs, Roads, Railways, and Internal Shipping, nearly always sends all the documents to the Ombudsman. At the other extreme, the Department of Justice only sends the legal minimum of papers. It is interesting that in both Denmark and Norway it is the Department of Justice which is least co-operative with the Ombudsman in this matter. Or, to put it another way, it is the department which stands most strictly on its legal position.

The procedure in the Ombudsman's office for investigating complaints is similar to, but not identical with, the Danish procedure. Once it is established that the Ombudsman is competent to investigate a complaint, the office has to decide whether there is a prima facie case against the authority concerned. If it thinks there is a prima facie case, the department or agency concerned is asked to comment on the case and send the relevant documents to the Ombudsman. In the great majority of cases the department's comments are then sent to the complainant who has a chance to reply to these comments. The department's comments are only withheld from the complainant if they are highly confidential or could be wounding to him. For example, a medical authority's comments on a mental patient might not be communicated in entirety to the patient if it was thought that this might be hurtful to him.

The department is then sent the complainant's further comments and asked for its views. When these have been received, the Ombudsman makes his report. The Ombudsman sees each case at an early stage and again at the final stage after all the documents have been assembled, when he arrives at his decision. His staff are concerned with the intermediate stages, sending for the documents and evaluating them, sending for further comments, etc. It is rare for public servants in the departments concerned to be interviewed by the Ombudsman's staff, but questions of detail are quite often taken up over the telephone. For example, one of the Ombudsman's counsellors may telephone the department to ask whether there is provision for appeal in a case, or to ascertain how long a delay about which a complaint has been made is likely to continue. The Ombudsman's staff also interview quite a high proportion of complainants since between 400 and 500 members of the public come to the Ombudsman's office every year to make their complaints in person. The Ombudsman's office is quite easy to find in Oslo. It is over a shop in an office building in a busy shopping area of the city centre.

The law provides that complaints to the Ombudsman must be submitted in writing. If anyone has difficulty in putting his complaint in writing he is advised to call at the Ombudsman's office where he is given assistance in drawing up the complaint. This facility is, of course, of little value to people living in the regions of Norway which are remote from the capital. Consequently, an experimental scheme was begun in 1973, and was still continuing in

1976, under which people in the most northerly counties can obtain the assistance of a lawyer, free of charge, in drawing up their complaints.

As in Denmark and Sweden, the Ombudsman has power to initiate his own investigations. He normally decides to initiate an investigation as a result of a press report or broadcast. The Norwegian Ombudsman for Administration uses this power less than the Danish Ombudsman does. He initiates about 20 investigations a year whereas the Danish Ombudsman initiated 120 investigations in 1975.[1] His power to inspect state or local institutions is only used to supplement his investigating function in a case. He does not make periodic inspections as the Swedish Ombudsmen do. Even inspection by the Ombudsman as part of an investigation are very rare.

The position as regards publicity for the Ombudsman's reports is very similar to that in Denmark. In 1970 Norway also enacted a Law on Publicity of Administration. The law gives every citizen the right to examine documents in the offices of central or local departments, but with certain exceptions. The internal memorandums can be withheld. So can all documents concerning taxation, defence, foreign policy, etc. The Ombudsman's office is exempt from the Law on Publicity. He is not therefore obliged to give journalists access to documents. However, the Ombudsman decided in November 1971 that members of the Norwegian Press Bureau can call at his office in Oslo once a fortnight to read his opinions in the cases he has decided. The newspapers then publish information about the reports, but, respecting the Ombudsman's wishes, do not give names of the complainants.

The Ombudsman makes an annual report to Parliament. In this report, besides giving an analysis of his activities, he gives summaries of some of the cases he has decided in the year. In these summaries he does not give the names of complainants nor of the civil servants complained against, but he does identify the departments of the central government which have been involved in the complaint. The Ombudsman's annual report is received by the Committee of Justice of the Storting, but there is usually only a rather brief and formal discussion of the Report in the Committee. Very few complaints come to the Ombudsman through Members of the Storting. In some cases, to the Ombudsman's knowledge, an individual has

[1] See above, p. 23.

been advised by a Member of the Storting to complain to him, and sometimes a Member writes to the Ombudsman enclosing a complaint from an individual constituent.

The Ombudsman is elected by Parliament after every general election, for a four-year term. He is capable of re-election and the first Ombudsman, Mr. Andreas Schei, served for twelve years from 1962 to 1974, being re-elected twice. In July 1974 he was replaced by Mr. Erling Sandene, who, at the time of appointment, was a Judge in the Supreme Court. The law provides that the Ombudsman must have the qualifications to be a Justice of the Supreme Court. He must have a law degree classified in the Laudabilis grade, which is the top classification, attained in practice by about 40 per cent of the law students who graduate. Mr. Schei had also been a Justice of the Supreme Court before being appointed Ombudsman, and had previously been a civil servant.

The Ombudsman is assisted by his Chief of Office, First Legal Assistant, and seven Legal Assistants. The Chief of Office allocates cases to the seven lawyers; he reads all the documents but does not handle the cases himself. Six secretarial staff make up a full complement of fourteen staff aiding the Ombudsman. This makes his staff only a little smaller than the staff of the Danish Ombudsman, who is assisted by two heads of division, ten legally qualified investigators, and eight secretaries. Since one of the Danish Ombudsman's investigators is part-time, as is one of his secretaries, it is difficult to make a direct comparison. If we count each part-time member as one-half, the Danish Ombudsman has a staff of nineteen to the staff of fourteen of the Norwegian Ombudsman for Administration.

Norway has a smaller population than Denmark. In 1970 it was estimated that the population of Norway was approaching 4 million while the population of Denmark was just under 5 million. In 1975 the Norwegian Ombudsman for Administration received a volume of complaints not significantly lower than that received by the Danish Ombudsman. In that year the Norwegian Ombudsman received 1,532 complaints as against the 1,889 sent to the Danish Ombudsman. One must remember also that the figure for the Danish Ombudsman includes complaints from members of the armed forces, whereas Norway has a separate Ombudsman for the Armed Forces.

If we look at the way in which the volume of complaints to the Norwegian Ombudsman for Administration has varied over the years we find that, after an initial surge of complaints in 1963, the Ombudsman's first year, a plateau of about 1,000 complaints a year was attained between 1964 and 1968.[1] From 1 January 1969 his jurisdiction was widened to include aspects of local government. In 1969 the volume of complaints then increased dramatically to 1,507. Since 1970 the annual volume has fluctuated between a low in 1971 of 1,305 to the highest figure of 1,948, attained in 1974.

TABLE V
The Norwegian Ombudsman for Administration, 1963 to 1976.

Cases received and cases investigated

Year	Cases received per year	Cases investigated in the year	Cases investigated %
1963	1,275	327	25·6
1964	1,076	388	36·1
1965	980	363	37·0
1966	1,014	315	31·1
1967	1,103	287	26·0
1968	987	306	31·0
1969	1,507	365	24·2
1970	1,428	408	28·6
1971	1,305	354	27·1
1972	1,476	513	36·0
1973	1,468	562	40·0
1974	1,948	701	38·0
1975	1,532	701	46·0
1976	1,379	715	52·0

Source: Statistics for this table were supplied to the author by the office of the Norwegian Ombudsman for Administration.

The proportion of cases which he investigated, compared with complaints received, varied, in the years from 1963 to 1974, from 24·2 per cent in 1969 to 40 per cent in 1973. The years 1975 and 1976 saw a marked increase in the proportion of cases investigated to 46 and 52 per cent respectively. In 1971 the Ombudsman's office published figures of the total number of cases in which the Ombudsman criticized a department or made a recommendation for a changed decision or procedure in the first eight years of the office from 1963 to 1970. The Ombudsman made a criticism or recommendation in 547 cases in this period, out of a total of 2,351 com-

[1] See Table V.

plaints which he investigated. This is a proportion of 23·3 per cent. The Ombudsman's office also said that in the same period the administrative authority changed its decision in 450 cases while the complaint was still under review.[1]

These figures indicate that the Ombudsman for Administration has a considerable impact and, as in Sweden and Denmark, those concerned with the Ombudsman's office do not think that this impact is made more in favour of middle-class people than of the less well to do. The Ombudsman in Norway is thought of essentially as being the means of redress against government for those who have little or no financial resources. For example, the Ombudsman's office estimated that, between 1963 and 1970, an average of 20 per cent of complaints made to the Ombudsman each year came from prisoners.[2] The Ombudsmen's services are also, of course, available to more affluent sections of the population. Another numerically important category of complaints throughout this period was from civil servants, raising with the Ombudsman grievances over such things as salaries, promotion, and appointment.

Although Norway has a small population, it is a large country in terms of area. It is also an immensely long country in relation to its width. From its southernmost point near Kristiansand to Vardø, which is far within the Arctic Circle and near to the northern most point of Norway's frontier with the Soviet Union, it is more than a thousand miles as the crow flies. It is therefore important that the Ombudsman should be accessible to complainants from the remoter parts of Norway. In his Annual Report for 1976 the Ombudsman for Administration published a table showing the proportion of complaints he had received in that year from each of the twenty counties in Norway. The table showed that the highest proportion of complaints came from Oslo. From this county, which has 12·6 per cent of the total population of Norway, 17·9 per cent of all complaints originated. But each of the three most northerly counties, Nordland, Troms, and Finnmark, provided a proportion of complaints well above its proportion of the total population. Thus Nordland, with 6·3 per cent of the population, accounted for 10·8 per cent of complaints to the Ombudsman for Administration. People from Troms, which has 3·6 per cent of the population, sent in 5 per cent of all complaints and from Finnmark, with 2 per cent

[1] A Brief Survey of the Ombudsman Institution in Norway (Feb. 1971), p. 5.
[2] Ibid.

of the population, there came no less than 4·5 per cent of all complaints.

It is apparent that he is not predominantly the Ombudsman for townspeople or for those who live in the remote rural areas. He is the Ombudsman for the ordinary person throughout Norway.

IV

THE NORWEGIAN OMBUDSMAN FOR THE ARMED FORCES

NORWAY set up an Ombudsman for the Armed Forces in 1952. There were two main reasons for the reform. The first was that it was thought desirable to give the serviceman greater legal security by establishing a military Ombudsman to whom he could appeal, somewhat on the lines of the Swedish Militieombudsman. The second reason was the desire to complement the system of representative committees of servicemen which at that time was being considerably developed and improved.

Provisions for servicemen to elect their own respresentatives who can discuss questions with their superior officers go back in Norway to defence regulations introduced as long ago as 1912. During the Second World War further developments took place, on similar lines, in the Norwegian forces stationed in Britain and Sweden. As is well known, after the invasion and conquest of Norway in 1940 by Nazi Germany, Norwegian units were organized and trained in Britain. But from 1943 onwards there were also Norwegian units in Sweden. They were officially known as 'police reserves' but they were, in fact, military formations preparing to fight for the liberation of their country if called upon to do so.[1]

In both Britain and Sweden Norwegian military units began to group their elected representatives in committees who, together with their commanding officers, played an important part in airing the views of the men and influencing decisions about welfare and other matters. After the war there was a general feeling that this had proved a valuable development and should be introduced as a general and permanent reform. An official committee which reported on the question in 1948 concluded, in a summary of its report, that it 'would constitute a definitely democratic step, and would serve to

[1] See J. Andenaes, O. Riste, and M. Skodvin, *Norway and the Second World War* (Johan Grundt Tanum Forlag, Oslo, 1966), p. 110.

create confidence, co-operation and solidarity among all categories of the defence forces'.[1]

The Military Committee of the Storting approved the report and in 1951 proposed a full-scale reform which not only extended the system of representative committees and gave them permanent form, but also established a military Ombudsman with a Board to assist him. This reform was adopted by the Storting and came into effect in its entirety in 1952. In order to understand the role of the military Ombudsman it is necessary to look first, therefore, at the way in which the representative committees operate.

The system is applied in the Naval and Air Forces as well as in the Army and the latter will be taken as a model. Each platoon elects one representative. There are four platoons in a company and these four representatives, together with the company commander, at first formed the company committee. This was the system when it was introduced in 1951, but since February 1972 some other officers, in addition to the company commander, have been included in each representative committee. The regulations nevertheless provide that the representatives of the conscripted men must always constitute a majority in any representative committee. Each company then elects one representative and, with four companies in a battalion, the four company representatives, together with the battalion commander, and not more than two other officers, constitute the battalion committee.

Between 1951 and 1972 the representative committees were purely advisory, but since February 1972 they have had decision-making powers in some spheres, for example in welfare arrangements and in sport, education, and leisure activities. The committees take up general questions, they do not consider the grievances of individual servicemen. A soldier can ask his platoon representative to take up a grievance for him with the company commander or battalion commander. Or he can complain directly to the military Ombudsman.

The Ombudsman therefore has a dual role in relation to the armed forces. He investigates complaints made to him directly by individual servicemen. He also stands at the head of the system of representative committees. He is, so to speak, its guardian and guarantor. He can be approached by any representative committee, and he and members of his Board periodically visit units of the armed forces to see that the system is working properly.

[1] *Norway's Military Ombudsman and His Board* (Oslo, 1963), p. 1.

Besides the Ombudsman there are six other members of the Board. They are elected by the Storting and, are chosen by the parties represented in the Storting on a broadly proportional basis. In 1977 the Conservative, Agrarian, Christian, and Socialist Left Parties each had one representative on the Board, the Labour Party had two representatives. Members of the Storting are not eligible to be chosen as Board members, but Board members are normally active in politics. In 1977 two of the Board members were newspaper editors by profession, two were secretaries of trade unions (one was a national union secretary and the other the regional secretary of a trade union), one was a manager of a factory, and one a social worker.

The Ombudsman for the Armed Forces is chairman of the Board which meets three or four times a year. He decides what matters to lay before the Board. They will generally be matters of principle which have arisen in the course of his work or major cases which he has investigated. The Board 'is designed primarily as an advisory organ for the Ombudsman'.[1] But it is an advisory body whose members share, to some extent, the functions of the Ombudsman. Like the Ombudsman, Board members visit military units and discuss with officers and elected representatives the problems they are facing.

We have seen that the system of elected representatives has recently been overhauled and extended. In addition to the changes which have been made at unit level, there has been an important innovation at the centre with the introduction of an Annual Congress of elected representatives of the armed forces. Most units send representatives to this Annual Congress which is also attended by representatives of the Ministry of Defence and by the chief commander of the armed forces. The Congress elects a committee which follows up all the problems raised during the sessions of Congress.

The military Ombudsman played a big part in introducing the changes in the system of elected representatives, both in the units and at the centre. His continuing role as head of the representative system is also very important, but before considering it further it is necessary to look at his other main role: investigating complaints from servicemen. The conscripted soldier, sailor, or airman can complain direct to the Ombudsman who will investigate his com-

[1] *Norway's Military Ombudsman*, p. 9.

plaint whether or not he has already complained to his superior officer. In relation to other ranks, therefore, the Ombudsman is not bound by the rule of exhaustion of remedies. Some of his cases, of course, come to him direct from conscripted men, some after the conscripted man has failed to get satisfaction from his superior officer.

In relation to officers, the rule of exhaustion of remedies, in practice, does apply. Officers can complain to the Ombudsman, but they are expected first to go through the normal service channels before complaining to him. Complaints from conscripted men are much more numerous than from officers, therefore we can say that, in the majority of cases, the Ombudsman is not bound by the rule of exhaustion of remedies and, in this respect, his position is stronger than that of the civil Ombudsman. His position is also stronger in that he can ask to see all the documents in the case, and all must be shown to him except those which relate to matters of security.

The Ombudsman and his Head of Office deal with most cases by correspondence, supplemented by telephone calls. In a complicated case the Ombudsman may ask the unit commander, or the doctor if a case is on a medical matter, to come and see him at his office in Oslo. In some cases the Ombudsman himself goes to the Ministry of Defence to try and sort things out. In a number of cases the Ombudsman will ask a complainant to come and see him at his office. He will do this particularly if there is a material disagreement between the accounts of the complainant and the commander. When a complainant is stationed in the north of Norway and this is not feasible, the Ombudsman's office will try to reach him on the telephone so that they can ask him directly about the points on which the Ombudsman wants clarification. Sometimes the telephone will also be used, rather than writing a letter, if the case is straightforward but there is a need for speed. For example, if a serviceman is trying to achieve earlier demobilization in order to go to a university at the beginning of the academic year, the Ombudsman may decide to deal with the matter by telephone in order to try and obtain a concession in the serviceman's favour in time for it to have full value for him.

In many cases when the Ombudsman intercedes for a serviceman, the unit concerned follows the Ombudsman's recommendations. If the unit commander does not do so, the Ombudsman may decide to take the case to the superior headquarters. If he again fails, he may then go to the Ministry of Defence. If the Ministry of Defence fails to give satisfaction, the Ombudsman can report this fact to the Storting. It is a tribute to the effectiveness of the military Ombudsman, as well as to the good relations he maintains with the Ministry of Defence, that he has never had to do this in the twenty-five years since the system was introduced in 1951.

The military Ombudsman has power to inspect military institutions, as part of his investigating activity. If, for example, he receives a complaint from someone in a military prison, he may decide to inspect the prison. In recent years he has only on a few occasions exercised his power to inspect in the course of an investigation.

For many years the military Ombudsman has received between 300 and 350 complaints each year from servicemen. In 1976 he received 355 complaints. The largest group of complaints is concerned with call-up or appeals for exemption from, or postponement of, military service. Merchant seamen, for example, can claim exemption from military service and university students can claim postponement of their service. He also receives numerous complaints from servicemen concerned about transfers and re-postings, and about demobilization. In the 1950s there used to be a lot of complaints about food and living quarters. Nowadays there are not many under either of these headings. There are some, but not many, complaints about leave, and a few complaints which concern disciplinary questions. Quite a number of complaints are about medical and welfare matters. For example, a serviceman who breaks a leg is sent home to recover but is not then accorded any pay or allowances. He then writes to the Ombudsman complaining that it is not reasonable that his family should be expected to maintain him, and the Ombudsman takes up his case.

The military Ombudsman makes an annual report to the Storting. In this report he describes the principal cases he has investigated during the year, but does not give the names of the individuals or military units concerned. His report is first considered by the Defence Committee of the Storting and is then debated in the Storting. Until 1972 it was unusual for the Ombudsman to give evidence to the Storting Committee. Since 1972 the Ombudsman and his Board have had several meetings with the Defence Committee of the Storting or with members of the Committee.

The military Ombudsman, like other members of his Board, is

elected by the Storting for a four-year term. In fact, the Ombudsman is often re-elected. The first military Ombudsman, Arthur Ruud, held office from 1952 to 1964. His successor, Edgar Andreassen, is still in office. There is no requirement that the military Ombudsman shall have legal training. Arthur Ruud, was, in fact, a trade-unionist. By custom, the Ombudsman's Head of Office is a lawyer if the Ombudsman does not have a legal background. Edgar Andreassen was Arthur Ruud's Head of Office from 1952 to 1964. Andreassen is a lawyer. When he became military Ombudsman in 1964 the post of Head of Office to the Ombudsman was taken on by Jack Helle who does not have a law degree. Helle had been a wartime soldier in the Norwegian Army in Britain, rising from the rank of Corporal to Sergeant-Major and then to Lieutenant while serving in several branches of the Artillery in Scotland.

The military Ombudsman's staff is very small. He and his Head of Office are assisted by two secretaries, making a staff of four in all. But the staff is large enough to cope with the duties of the office despite the fact that the military Ombudsman doubles with another office as well. He is also the Ombudsman for Conscientious Objectors. In this role he is not concerned with granting men the right to be registered as conscientious objectors. This is a matter for the Ministry of Justice. Those who are accorded the right by the Ministry work in social institutions such as hospitals, institutions for handicapped children, or approved schools, instead of doing military service. During this period they can complain to the Ombudsman for Conscientious Objectors in much the same way as servicemen can. For a long time conscientious objectors did not formally have their own system of elected representatives, but regulations providing for such a system have recently been approved by the Storting.

There are two main issues which are of interest to the student of comparative Ombudsmen in relation to the Norwegian Ombudsman for the Armed Forces. The first is whether there is a case for having a separate Ombudsman for military affairs, as in Norway. The second is whether it is as important to have a right of complaint by servicemen to an Ombudsman in countries like Britain which have a professional rather than a conscript army.

Sweden, as we have seen, used to have a separate military Ombudsman but in 1968 decided to combine the offices of military and civil Ombudsmen, and since 1968 one of the Ombudsmen in

Sweden has investigated complaints from servicemen as well as being concerned with complaints against certain sectors of civil administration. The Danish Ombudsman has from his inception in 1955 been concerned with complaints from servicemen as well as with complaints against the civil administrative authorities.

When Norway decided to set up an Ombudsman for Administration in 1962, consideration was given to the idea that the Ombudsman for the Armed Forces might be merged with the new office. But the idea was rejected largely on the grounds that it was important that the Ombudsman for the Armed Forces should have a separate identity because of his role as head of the system of elected representatives. As that system has since been extended and developed, the argument for maintaining his separate existence has been correspondingly strengthened. It is undeniable that his two roles of investigator and guarantor of the representative system do not conflict but rather enrich each other. The military Ombudsman is more effective in each role because of the knowledge and understanding which he gains when wearing his other hat. The problem of overlapping jurisdiction between the civil and military Ombudsmen does, of course, arise but is resolved without friction. It arises most often when one of the Ombudsmen receives a complaint from a civilian employee of the Ministry of Defence. The conflict of jurisdiction is then normally decided by telephone quite easily between the offices of the two Ombudsmen.

Only one country besides Norway now has a military Ombudsman. This is the Federal Republic of Germany.[1] But the situation is different in Germany in that there is no civil Ombudsman at federal level. The two offices also differ greatly in their origins.

In the German case the office of *Wehrbeauftragter des Bundestages* (Defence Commissioner of the Federal Parliament) is just one of a series of institutional and legal measures designed to ensure the democratic reliability of the armed forces or Bundeswehr, which were set up in 1955. Another measure is civilian control of the Bundeswehr through the Defence Minister who, unlike his (often military) predecessors in the Weimar Republic, is head of the armed forces in peacetime. Thirdly, two committees of the Bundestag, those of Defence and of the Budget, have important res-

[1] This section was contributed by Dr. David Childs, Reader in Politics, University of Nottingham. All the figures are taken from the annual reports of the Wehrbeauftragter published in Bonn. (M.S.).

ponsibilities regarding civilian control of the armed forces. The legal safeguards relate to the rights of servicemen defined in the Soldatengesetz of 19 March 1956. Briefly, the aim was to create an army of 'citizens in uniform' with far greater rights, including the right to join a trade union, than German soldiers had ever enjoyed before. Further legal safeguards are enshrined in the military criminal code. All serious offences, such as desertion, disobedience, or mistreatment of subordinates, committed by military personnel, are dealt with by civilian courts. There are no military courts in the Federal Republic. Finally, West Germany's military Ombudsman is part of a system which claims to have developed a democratic military ideology known as 'Innere Führung', a very difficult and elusive doctrine to define.

Unlike the Norwegian military Ombudsman, the Wehrbeauftragter was surrounded by controversy from the start. Many right-wing politicians and old-style military men feared that the Defence Commissioner would be used by Social Democrats and others to undermine military discipline. This controversy explains why it took eighteen months to appoint the first incumbent, and why the first two holders of the office were military men. Both were forced to resign. The first after a personal scandal, and the second, Vice-Admiral Heye, for causing a political scandal. Herr Heye alleged that the armed forces were once again becoming a 'state within the state' and exposed a number of cases of abuses of power. That was in 1964. Since then there have been three other Defence Commissioners who appear to have been less controversial. One wonders whether this is due to greater acceptance of the office or because the more recent incumbents have been more circumspect in their activities.

Under the law of 26 June 1957 establishing the office, the Wehrbeauftragter is elected by the Federal Parliament and appointed by its President. The appointment is for five years and may be renewed for a further term. The Bundestag can direct its President to relieve the Defence Commissioner of his duties. Under article 16 of the law he is under the administrative control of the President of the Federal Parliament. He is responsible to the Bundestag, and is required to submit an annual report to that body. The Bundestag and its Defence Committee can at any time demand the attendance of the Defence Commissioner. Clearly, the Wehrbeauftragter is regarded as the servant of Parliament. To emphasize this his office is in the Parliament building in Bonn. But he also has independent premises in the government quarter of the capital. To help him he has a staff of over 60, 11 of them lawyers.

Article 2 of the 1957 law sets out the main tasks of the Defence Commissioner. He must investigate specific matters on the instructions of the Bundestag or its Defence Committee. Further, acting on information received from M.P.s, members of the forces, or other sources, he must investigate 'circumstances which lead him to believe that there has been a breach of the soldiers basic rights or an infringement of the principles of "Innere Führung". He shall inform the *Bundestag* of the outcome of his investigations either in a special report or within the scope of his annual report.' Naturally, 'He may at any time visit any troops, headquarters, administrative agencies and establishments of the armed forces without prior notice.' He also enjoys the right of attending any judicial proceedings, whether in the criminal courts or in the disciplinary tribunals—even in closed session—in matters pertaining to his field of responsibility. Federal, regional (*Länder*), and local authorities are required to assist him.

As citizens in uniform, under article 7, every serviceman has the right to address requests or complaints to the Defence Commissioner direct. 'No person shall be reprimanded or discriminated against on the grounds of his having applied to the Commissioner.' Anonymous complaints, will not, however, be dealt with.

Looking through the published figures one gains the impression that West German servicemen have been prepared to make use of the Wehrbeauftragter. In 1961 there were nearly 4,000 requests for his assistance. The number rose to nearly 6,000 in 1963. In the mid-sixties there was a falling-off of complaints. However, the last years of the decade saw big increases. In 1970 there were 7,142 references to the Wehrbeauftragter. Of these 550 were on matters beyond the competence of the Defence Commissioner. A further 16 were dismissed because they were anonymous petitions. By way of comparison, in 1975 there were 6,439 cases but again some of these were not within the competence of the Commissioner. The total number of cases investigated was therefore reduced to 4,906. In both years the great majority of complaints were made by the soldiers themselves. Most of the rest originated either from the families of soldiers or among former servicemen. Members of the Federal Parliament played only an insignificant role in raising matters with the Defence Commissioner. In 1970 they brought 46 cases to his attention, but only one case in 1975.

What did West German soldiers complain about? In 1975, 62·5 per cent of the complaints were connected with pay, promotion, leave, and living conditions. There were, however, a not insignificant number of cases concerned with 'basic rights' such as freedom of opinion, human dignity, constitutional rights, and so on.

As one would expect, conscripts made the great number of complaints. In 1975 West Germany's 218,000 national servicemen made 2,676 complaints. Nevertheless, an almost equally large number of complaints came from the professional soldiers and those on short-term engagements.

One intriguing question is how successful was the Defence Commissioner in satisfying his clientele. It is impossible to be exact about this. In 1975 the Wehrbeauftragter claimed success in 1,826 cases, partial success in a further 467, and admitted failure in 3,084. The results in the final 1,529 processed, some of these from the previous year, were unclear.

Apart from the Wehrbeauftragter, the institutional arrangements in the West German armed forces resemble those of Norway in another way. This is in the provision for elected representatives of soldiers and officers. It must be pointed out, however, that the German system is not so well developed as the Norwegian.

Under article 35 of the Soldatengesetz N.C.O.s and soldiers in each unit elect, for a minimum period of three months, a representative and two deputies. The representative (Vertrauensmann) contributes to the development of 'responsible co-operation between superiors and subordinates' and the creation of an atmosphere of 'comradely trust' in his unit. He has the right to be heard when making proposals in the fields of welfare, career advancement, off-duty social life, and questions regarding the life of the unit.

There was no obvious connection between the decision to have elected representatives and the later decision to have a Defence Commissioner. Nevertheless, the Vertrauensmann system does stem from the same basic desire to overcome Germany's past and to ensure that servicemen are citizens in uniform.

As we have seen, the Scandinavian Ombudsmen and the Wehrbeauftragter developed out of different conditions. In Scandinavia only Norway has a military Ombudsman. It is perhaps significant that the Norwegian armed forces are the only ones, of the three, involved in prolonged war service, and that, in a sense, the Norwegian armed forces were an army which had been shattered and reborn out of a democratic and patriotic resistance movement. Whether a civilian Ombudsman exists or not it would seem that, given the different conditions prevailing in the armed services, the establishment of a separate military Ombudsman is a desirable step in the advancement of individual rights and democratic consciousness. The existence or non-existence of conscription is not really relevant to the argument. The Scandinavian states have national service, Britain does not. But, as we have seen, in the Bundeswehr many professional soldiers feel the need to consult the Defence Commissioner. Of course the establishment of a military Ombudsman need not necessarily lead to the setting-up of a system of elected representatives as well. However, these representatives have proved their worth in both Norway and, one imagines, West Germany. There is no evidence to indicate they have been anything other than responsible.

V

THE PROVINCIAL OMBUDSMEN IN CANADA

IN North America the most rapid application of the Ombudsman idea has taken place in Canada. Whereas, at the end of 1976, only four states of the United States had appointed Ombudsmen (Hawaii in 1969, Iowa in 1970, Nebraska in 1971, and Alaska in 1975) in Canada eight out of ten provinces had set up an Ombudsman. New Brunswick and Alberta were the first to establish an Ombudsman, both in 1967. Quebec followed in 1968 by setting up a Protecteur du Citoyen (Protector of the Public) and in 1969 Nova Scotia and Manitoba also appointed an Ombudsman. In Saskatchewan an Ombudsman was appointed in 1973. The Ombudsman for Ontario was appointed in May 1975. Finally, in July 1975 Newfoundland appointed an Ombudsman under a law which had been first passed in 1970 but not at that time brought into operation.

Neither the United States nor Canada has an Ombudsman at the federal level although, since 1971, Canada has had a language Ombudsman for federal government. The Commissioner of Official Languages for Canada investigates complaints that the status of an official language (English or French) has not been respected in the federal public service. Canada also has an Ombudsman for federal prisons.

The provincial Ombudsmen in Canada well repay study. In the first place, the provinces have extensive powers in the Canadian federal system. The provision in the British North America Act, 1867, stating that provincial legislatures have power over 'Property and Civil Rights in the Province' (Section 92–13) has been interpreted widely by the Judicial Committee of the Privy Council and the Supreme Court in Canada. As a result we find, for example, the government of the province of Quebec exercising important powers in the following fields: transport, cultural affairs and education, social affairs, justice, industry and commerce, public works, agriculture, lands and forests, labour and manpower, tourism, and fish and game. The Quebec provincial government has ministries in all these fields.

Some of the Canadian provinces have large populations and nearly all administer large geographic areas. Quebec has a population of more than 6 million and a geographic area of nearly 600,000 square miles. Alberta's population is nearly 1,700,000 and Manitoba has nearly a million. New Brunswick and Newfoundland have the smallest population of those provinces with an Ombudsman. New Brunswick has 635,000 people, but it has a geographic area of more than 28,000 square miles. The population of Newfoundland (42,734 square miles) is 522,104. Another interesting feature of the Canadian provincial Ombudsmen is that they all have wide powers, on the New Zealand model, to report on unreasonable action by a government department or agency. All allow the complainant ready access to the Ombudsman, and some have developed interesting new ways for easing access.

Since I was limited by time to making a special study of some and not all of the Canadian Ombudsmen, I decided to give particular attention to Quebec which until 1975 was the most populous of Canadian provinces to have an Ombudsman, and to select also for study one of the prairie provinces with an Ombudsman, and one of the three maritime provinces. In these categories I chose Manitoba and New Brunswick, and I shall deal in turn with these three provinces.

THE QUEBEC PUBLIC PROTECTOR

The official title of the Quebec Ombudsman is 'Le Protecteur du Citoyen' or, in English translation, 'The Public Protector'. As with the British Parliamentary Commissioner, people in Quebec commonly speak of him as 'The Ombudsman'. The initiative for the law of November 1968 which set up the Public Protector was taken by the Union Nationale Prime Minister of Quebec, Mr. Daniel Johnson. In 1967 Sir Guy Powles, the New Zealand Ombudsman, visited Montreal for the World Fair. Mr. Johnson met him and then determined to set up an Ombudsman in Quebec partly on the New Zealand model.

The Public Protector Act of 1968 follows the New Zealand Parliamentary Commissioner Act closely in some respects, although in some ways the office of Public Protector is nearer to the Swedish pattern. It also has unique features of its own. The Public Protector is appointed by the National Assembly of Quebec for a five-year term, on a motion by the Prime Minister. His appointment must be approved by two-thirds of the Members of the National Assembly and a two-thirds majority must be found in the Assembly for a resolution to dismiss him. The Public Protector can be reappointed and the Act obviously envisages that he will often be reappointed because it goes on to say that if, after fifteen years in office, he ceases to perform his duties, he shall be entitled to a pension equal to three-quarters of his salary. (A pension of one-half of the salary is payable after ten years and of one-quarter of the salary after five years.)

The first Public Protector to be appointed was Dr. Louis Marceau. He served until December 1975 when he was appointed a Judge of the Federal Court of Canada. Dr. Marceau had been a Professor of Law at Laval University in Quebec. His successor as Public Protector is Miss Luce Patenaude who took office on 1 September 1976. She had previously been a Professor of Law at Montreal University. The Act also provides for the appointment of an assistant to the Public Protector. The appointment is made by the Lieutenant-Governor of the Province, on the recommendation of the Public Protector. The assistant is also, in effect, deputy to the Public Protector since the Act provides that he shall take the Public Protector's place during his absence or illness. The first assistant to the Public Protector to be appointed was M. Robert Lévêque, Q.C. M. Lévêque, on appointment, was Secretary of the Bar Association for Quebec Province. He had previously been Law Editor of the Law Reports for the province, and previously a practising barrister.

The Act provides that the Public Protector shall appoint the other members of his staff. They comprise nine other assistants, in addition to her deputy and six secretaries. The staff is divided between two offices. In Quebec city the office is headed by the Public Protector and in Montreal by her deputy. It is appropriate that Miss Patenaude herself should head the office in Quebec city because this is the seat of government and, as we shall see, the Public Protector deals directly with Ministers and the permanent heads of departments. On the other hand, Montreal is the commercial capital and is a much larger city. Montreal has a population of 1,466,500, the city of Quebec only 193,984. It made sense therefore for the Public Protector to have an office in Montreal headed by her chief assistant.

The Public Protector can investigate complaints against all departments of the provincial government. Nothing is excluded from her purview. She also has powers, though of a more limited nature, to examine complaints against a number of quasi-judicial bodies in the province. We need first to consider her powers in relation to the provincial departments. These are described in Sections 13 and 26 of the Public Protector Act of 1968. Section 13 states that the Public Protector shall investigate wherever he has reason to believe that a provincial official has 'wronged' the person complaining. The word 'wronged' is defined in Section 26 which states that 'The Public Protector shall notify the head of the department or body concerned whenever he is of the opinion after completing an investigation that a person has been wronged . . . because a functionary, officer or employee

(a) has not complied with the law,
(b) has acted in an unreasonable, unjust, arbitrary or discriminatory manner,
(c) has failed in his duty or has been guilty of misconduct or negligence,
(d) has committed an error of law or fact,
(e) in the exercise of a discretionary power, has acted for an injust purpose, has been actuated by irrelevant motives or has failed to give reasons for his discretionary act when he should have done so.'[1]

It will be apparent that there is some similarity with the key provision in the New Zealand Parliamentary Commissioner (Ombudsman) Act, 1962, which states, at Section 19, that the Commissioner can report upon any decisions, recommendation, act, or omission which, in his opinion, after investigation

(a) appears to have been contrary to law; or
(b) was unreasonable, unjust, oppressive, or improperly discriminatory;
(c) was based wholly or partly on a mistake of law or fact; or
(d) was wrong.

While, however, the Public Protector's power in relation to government departments are similar to the New Zealand Ombudsman's powers, he also has important powers to investigate complaints against quasi-judicial bodies which the New Zealand Ombudsman was not given under the 1962 Act. The Public Protector can

[1] Legislative Assembly of Quebec, Public Protector Act, 1968, Sect. 26.

investigate a complaint that the proceedings of a government body exercising a quasi-judicial function have been affected by 'some gross irregularity and that justice has not been, or will not be done'.[1] Bodies with quasi-judicial powers, against whose proceedings the Public Protector investigated complaints in 1974, included the Workmen's Compensation Commission, the Minimum Wage Commission, the Liquor Permit Control Commission, and the Police Commission.

We may sum up the character of the Public Protector's powers to investigate in this way. In relation to the decisions or other acts of provincial departments he has powers, as wide as those of the New Zealand Ombudsman, to report that an official has acted in an unreasonable, unjust, arbitrary, or discriminatory manner. In relation to quasi-judicial bodies he can report that there have been faulty procedures and that, as a consequence, the complainant has suffered injustice. Here his power is wider than that of the New Zealand Ombudsman who is not empowered to investigate a complaint against an administrative tribunal. The Quebec Protector of the Public is more comparable here to the Swedish Ombudsmen who do have such powers although he is not empowered to investigate complaints against the ordinary courts, as the Swedish Ombudsmen are.

The ease with which the Public Protector can be approached by a member of the public is also, as in Sweden, a marked feature of the Quebec Ombudsman system. Any member of the public can telephone the Public Protector's office in either Quebec or Montreal to state his complaint. The assistant who answers will often, early in the conversation, ask the caller to give his number and then ring him back. The main conversation therefore takes place at public expense and allows the assistant time to take down fairly full details of the complaint. He will then ask the caller to send in documentary evidence to substantiate the complaint. Such evidence is necessary since the Act states that complaints to the Public Protector must be written. But the assistant does not wait for the supporting letter and other documents from the complainant before beginning his investigation. He will normally telephone the government department concerned as soon as possible and ask it to look into the case.

The Public Protector also receives many written complaints without a preliminary telephone call, but the ease with which he

[1] Ibid., Sect. 13.

can be contacted by telephone, and his readiness to begin investigation on receipt of a telephone call, helps to account for the large number of complaints which he investigates each year. In 1974 he completed investigation of 2,369 cases. This is a very high figure in relation to the Quebec population of a little more than 6 million. Indeed, *pro rata* he deals with a higher volume of complaints than the Swedish Ombudsmen. In Sweden, which has a population of 8 million, the three Ombudsmen together in 1974 investigated a total of 2,368 cases. The Swedish Ombudsmen, as we saw, are widely known by members of the ordinary public. The Quebec Public Protector is clearly not so well known. He has only been in existence for eight years. But the ease with which he can be contacted by telephone may have helped to make him the Ombudsman who deals with the highest volume of complaints in relation to the population he serves.

Of course, the crude statistics of cases investigated by an Ombudsman must be subjected to closer examination. Here closer scrutiny brings out a further very interesting feature of the way in which the Public Protector operates. In his annual report he divides the cases he investigates into three categories. Thus in 1974 there were 1,662 cases in which he did not recommend a change of decision by the department or agency concerned. This category he calls *status quo*. The second category is provided by the cases in which he makes a 'formal recommendation'. There were 61 of these in 1974. The third category consists of cases in which there was a 'non-formal recommendation'. These amounted to 646 in 1974.

What is meant by the description in this last category is that only a non-formal recommendation was necessary because on receipt of this recommendation the department or agency concerned provided what was, in the Public Protector's view, adequate redress to the complainant. Therefore only when a department fails to provide adequate redress at this stage does the Public Protector go on to make a formal recommendation. The two categories of 'non-formal' and 'formal' recommendations, therefore, can be grouped together comprising all those cases where the Public Protector finds an element of fault in the administrative process which can be remedied.

This does not mean to say, however, that when the agency does not give redress at the stage of 'non-formal' recommendation, the individual concerned is unlikely to secure redress. What it means is that a case which receives a formal recommendation from the Public

Protector is a case on which it has not been possible to secure redress for the complainant without going to the top level. If redress cannot be secured by one of the Public Protector's assistants, dealing directly with the middle-rank official in the department, then the Public Protector may himself take up the case and he will go to see the Minister or the Deputy Minister (equivalent to the Permanent Secretary of the Department in British parlance) with the file, to try and secure redress. In about 90 per cent of such cases he is then able to secure redress after a formal recommendation. To sum up, therefore, it is accurate to say that in all cases where there is a non-formal recommendation the department has provided some redress. In the great majority of cases on which there is a formal recommendation the Minister, or the authority concerned, also provides redress.

There is one aspect of the Public Protector's power to investigate which remains obscure. Section 17 of the Public Protector Act, 1968, provides that the Public Protector shall not investigate 'when the person applying for an investigation has under any law a right of appeal or an equally adequate recourse'. The Public Protector interprets this to mean that there must be a specific recourse or channel of appeal for the complainant, usually in the form of a quasi-judicial body. In practice, it is therefore not very restrictive for the Public Protector and, as we have seen, he can examine complaints against an administrative tribunal or quasi-judicial body. Therefore although he must decline to investigate if there is a specific channel of complaint to an administrative tribunal, he may be called upon later to examine a complaint against the handling of the case by the tribunal. Dr. Marceau himself was not happy with the lack of clarity in Section 17. In his Annual Report for 1973, in which he made a general report on his office after five years' activity, he suggested that Section 17 should be modified to give him discretion whether to investigate a case when there was 'under any law a right of appeal or an equally adequate recourse'.[1]

In order to appreciate the impact of the Public Protector we can appropriately at this stage consider those areas in which he receives and investigates most complaints. Table VI analyses the complaints he investigated in 1974, ranked by department (only the nine departments or agencies in which the most investigations were carried out are included). The Department of Social Affairs, with

[1] Public Protector, *Fifth Annual Report, 1973* (Quebec, 1974), pp. 70–2.

405 cases, was the leading department in terms of cases investigated. In every year since 1971 this department has had the largest number of complaints investigated by the Ombudsman. The majority of complaints against the Department are from the less well-to-do sections of the population and many of them are about the administration of social aid. For example, in one case quoted by the Public Protector in his Report for 1972, as typical of those he deals with, a mother had complained to him that her monthly social aid allowance had been reduced because one of her daughters had reached the age of eighteen, although the mother's expenses had been in no way reduced. The Public Protector established that the daughter was, in fact, a full-time student and wholly dependent on her mother. The Department had not recognized this situation and, on the Ombudsman's recommendation, reassessed the allowance.[1]

TABLE VI

Quebec Public Protector, 1974.

Complaints fully investigated (ranked by department)*

	Status quo	Formal recommendat'n	Non-formal recommendat'n	Total
Department of Social Affairs	261	21	123	405
Dept. of Transport	234	6	104	344
Workmen's Compensation Commission	168	3	107	278
Dept. of Justice	207	3	40	250
Dept. of Revenue	137	5	66	208
Dept. of Education	102	3	29	134
Pension Board	80	—	45	125
Pension Commission	48	—	17	65
Health Insurance Board	39	—	17	56

* Departments against which less than 50 complaints were investigated in the year are not included in this table.

Source: Public Protector, *Sixth Annual Report, 1974* (Quebec, 1975), Table 5-B, pp. 176–8.

The department in which in 1974 the second largest number of investigations were carried out was the Department of Transport with 344 cases. The complaints received by the Public Protector against this Department fall broadly into three categories: those concerned with 'expropriation' (in British terminology compulsory

[1] *Fourth Annual Report, 1972* (Quebec, 1973), pp. 47–8.

purchase) of property required for road-widening or new roads; those arising out of claims for damages caused by road-building, dynamiting, loss of access, etc., and complaints against the Motor Vehicle Bureau.

In his Report for 1971 Dr. Marceau had commented that, in his opinion, too much was left to negotiation between the official and the individual householder, or property owner, whose property was being expropriated. He argued for 'the establishment of criteria and standards of assessment valid for the whole province, which would allow the gathering of more precise and more complete data and reduce today's relative importance of personal opinion and approximation in the evaluation process'.[1] He continued to find much to criticize in this area in subsequent reports. But in his Report for 1974 he was able to point to some distinct improvements in the procedures for expropriation. In 1973 a new Expropriation Act had been passed. If it was fully implemented he forcsaw that the outcome would 'contrast happily with the situation I have criticised in most of my previous reports'.[2]

The department with the third highest number of investigations in 1974 was a quasi-judicial body, the Workmen's Compensation Commission, against which 278 complaints were investigated. The Public Protector's role in relation to this Commission is of such interest that it is appropriate to consider it later in more detail. For the time being, we will pass to the Department of Justice which with 250 complaints in 1974 had the fourth highest number of investigations. There are three principal categories of complaint against the Department of Justice: complaints from prisoners about their treatment in places of detention, complaints against the police, and complaints about the administration of the Department on such matters as the recovery of, or indemnity for, stolen property which is in police custody, or the pressing of charges, etc. If we take, firstly, complaints against the police, a good example is provided by the case in 1972 in which forty-five demonstrators complained that they had been arrested, finger-printed, and photographed, for violation of only a minor law. The Public Protector found their complaint was justified and the complainants' records, including finger-prints and photographs, were all destroyed.[3] In another case

[1] *Third Annual Report, 1971* (Quebec, 1972), p. 113.
[2] *Sixth Annual Report, 1974* (Quebec, 1975), pp. 115–6.
[3] *Fourth Annual Report, 1972*, p. 30.

a man claimed compensation for having been wrongfully arrested on the ground that he had not complied with a subpoena to appear in court as a witness in a criminal case. The Public Protector established that the subpoena had never been in fact served on him and compensation was paid.

The Public Protector is able to examine all the files relevant to a complaint against any department or commission. This power extends to police files. In the case of police files, however, the Public Protector or one of his principal assistants has to go to police headquarters to examine the files. When he does so he takes a tape-recorder with him and is thereby able to produce his own transcript of the material in the files which is relevant to the case.

Only complaints against the Quebec provincial police force are subject to investigation by the Public Protector. The Royal Canadian Mounted Police are a federal agency and are not therefore within his jurisdiction. The main cities in Quebec province have their own municipal police forces. The Public Protector cannot directly investigate a complaint against one of the municipal police forces. This is a matter for the Police Commission. He can look into an allegation that the Police Commission had not adequately investigated a complaint against one of the municipal police forces, and in 1974 he investigated one such complaint.

Every year the Public Protector receives many complaints from prisoners. The Public Protector Act, 1968, provides, as does the New Zealand Ombudsman Act, that an officer of a prison or mental hospital must forward a letter from a prisoner, or patient, to the Public Protector without opening it and without any delay (Section 21 of the Public Protector Act). He has found much to criticize in prison administration. In a long section of his Report for 1972 he pointed to the unnecessary restrictions on communication with the outside world by means of visits, newspapers, telephone calls, and letters which were imposed on their inmates by many prisons. He called for more general respect for 'the prisoner's person as a social individual' and a speedier implementation of plans to make prisons in Quebec 'rehabilitation centers rather than houses for punishment or restriction'.[1]

The Department of Revenue, with 208 cases, had the fifth highest number of investigations. Complaints here are mainly concerned with income tax and sales tax. The Public Protector in

[1] *Fourth Annual Report, 1972*, p. 22.

1974 obtained redress for the complainant in around a third of the complaints against the Revenue which he investigated. Complaints relate to such matters as delay in securing reimbursement when too much tax has been paid, sales tax being levied when it was not payable under the law, and incorrect taxation of a federal government employee.

In 1974 he investigated 135 complaints against the Department of Education which thus had the sixth highest number of investigations. A good proportion of these complaints concerned the administration of student loans and scholarships. Dr. Marceau had been critical of features of the administration of this system for several years. In his Report for 1970 he had criticized the application of Section 10 of the law which penalized severely any student who made a false declaration when applying for a scholarship. If, for example, a student failed to declare all his summer vacation earnings he could be refused a loan or scholarship for two years from the date of the declaration. This, as the Public Protector commented, was a very severe penalty since it could mean a fine of between $2,000 and $2,500 and might force the student to give up his studies.[1]

The law was not amended, but some of the severity of its impact was mitigated by administrative changes which the Public Protector welcomed in his Report the following year. He commented that the Department had improved its application forms, provided more information for applicants, and was requiring students to submit supporting documents for their applications as soon as possible, thus reducing the risk of inaccurate declarations which could incur the penalties under Section 10. In his Report for 1974 he expressed continuing disquiet about the system. In particular he criticized the procedures in the Department for reviewing special cases when the degree of parental contribution was being assessed. 'For the review is not flexible and open, as one would be led to believe, until now it has been marked by a formalism and rigidity seemingly based not only on a certain pursuit of efficiency, but also on a sort of distrust and a fear of abuse, which is always surprising.'[2]

Another area of complaint to the Department of Education relates to its power to regulate private schools. For example, the principal of a private school complained to the Public Protector in 1972 that the Department of Education had sent him a brief note

[1] *Second Annual Report, 1970* (Quebec, 1971), pp. 63–4.
[2] *Sixth Annual Report, 1974*, p. 42.

advising him that his school would no longer be recognized for grant purposes, after the current year, and that its teaching licence had been withdrawn. The Department had declined to give the headmaster an opportunity to object to the reasons put forward for this decision. The Public Protector, after investigating the case, decided that the complaint was justified. He commented in his Annual Report: 'It is inadmissible that such a far-reaching decision, affecting a person's rights and privileges, be made without allowing the person concerned to oppose, if possible, the accusations made against him. The decision to withdraw was suspended to allow complainant to appear before the advisory committee of the private education branch and it was finally cancelled.'[1]

The Public Protector cannot investigate complaints about the administration of state schools, except when the provincial Department of Education has become involved. Publicly financed schools in the province are administered by autonomous school boards. There can be appeal from a decision of a school board to the Department under certain conditions and, in such a case, the Public Protector can investigate the action of the Department of the appeal. Similarly, the Public Protector cannot investigate complaints about services provided by local authorities, but he can investigate the action of a provincial department or commission to which there is provision for appeal against the decision of a local authority. Thus the Municipal Commission is a provincial body which has responsibility for supervising local government and investigating appeals. Employees of a local authority, for example, have the right of appeal to the Municipal Commission if dismissed. Complaints to the Public Protector about the Municipal Commission are not numerous. He investigated only one such complaint in 1974. The Public Protector can also investigate complaints against the Municipal Affairs Department of the provincial government. He investigated 38 such complaints in 1974, the majority of them being concerned with protection of the environment.

Returning to the table of investigations per department, we see that the Pension Board was the next with 125 cases. This Board comes under the general aegis of the Social Affairs Department and its cases could well be added to those of the Department since it deals especially with matters like family allowance payments which are of particular importance to the less well-to-do sections of the

[1] *Fourth Annual Report, 1972*, p. 69.

population. The Pensions Commission follows the Pension Board with 65 cases in 1974. It is a new Commission which administers a newly established provincial superannuation scheme.

Finally, in 1974 the Public Protector investigated 56 complaints against the Health Insurance Board. The provincial health insurance scheme provides for reimbursement of medical or hospital expenses incurred in Quebec, or while someone is living outside the province, provided they are not away for more than six months. The Public Protector receives a number of complaints about the administration of this provision. Thus in 1972 he investigated a complaint from a man who had been denied reimbursement of medical expenses which he had incurred during a trip to Europe. He had been away for over six months but he had suffered a very severe heart attack while in Europe, had spent nearly three months in hospital, and was only allowed by his doctor to travel back to Canada when he had completed a further four months' convalescence. The Public Protector upheld his claim and commented that it would be unfair to apply the six months' rule 'even in cases such as this which involved all the elements of an Act of God'.[1] The Health Insurance Board then revised its decision in the case.

None of the other provincial departments, commissions, or boards which were investigated by the Public Protector in 1974 had as many as 50 complaints directed against them. They are therefore not included in the table. However, reference should be made to the Civil Service Commission and the Civil Service Department partly because they have in some years been an important target for complaints (for example, in 1972 the Public Protector investigated 109 complaints against the Civil Service Commission) and partly because the exclusion of Civil Service personnel matters from the Parliamentary Commissioner's terms of reference is still a matter of controversy in the United Kingdom. The majority of complaints against the Quebec Civil Service Commission in 1972 were from people who claimed they had not been allowed to sit the entrance examination, or had been wrongly failed in the examination, from civil servants who disputed their classification in the Civil Service in view of their qualifications, and from candidates for promotion who had been refused promotion and felt they were being discriminated against.[2] Many complaints against the Civil

[1] *Fourth Annual Report, 1972*, p. 54.
[2] Ibid., p. 148.

Service Department were from temporary civil servants who were dissatisfied with their conditions of service. In his Report for 1974 the Public Protector commented that the position of temporary civil servants had caused him concern in the past few years but that the situation was improving. Indeed a new Civil Service Department regulation, which was announced after his report had been drafted and was mentioned in a footnote, would apparently meet their case.[1] In his report for the previous year Dr. Marceau had indicated that he was not happy about some provisions in the statute limiting his power to investigate complaints from civil servants. The Public Protector Act states, at Section 16, that 'The Public Protector shall not investigate any act or omission . . . of any functionary, officer or employee . . . in his occupational relations with another functionary, officer or employee'. Dr. Marceau said that he had interpreted this to mean that he could not consider complaints about the organization of work in provincial departments or agencies, about relationships within the administrative hierarchy, and about the sharing of responsibilities in government services. He had investigated many other kinds of complaints from civil servants, but he used his powers in this field with some reticence and he called for clarification of the statute.[2]

It will be apparent from the survey we have made here of departments and commissions investigated by the Public Protector that his annual reports are a mine of information. In fact, if a prize were to be awarded for the most informative Ombudsman's reports, Dr. Marceau's reports would surely gain the Grand Prix. What was also impressive about the reports, as some of the extracts given here show, was that he frequently recommended changes in administrative practice and later was able to comment on the effect these changes had. He also took the opportunity, quite frequently, to criticize the whole tone and character of an aspect of administration.

Perhaps the best example of his role was given by the investigation of complaints against the Workmen's Compensation Commission. Even more important, however, than the volume of complaints which he examined was the long-term scrutiny he was exercising over the work of the Commission. In his first Annual Report (for 1969) he deplored the long delays in consideration and evaluation of claims for compensation. He reiterated this view in 1970 and

[1] *Sixth Annual Report, 1974*, p. 30.
[2] *Fifth Annual Report, 1973*, pp. 68–70.

suggested that delays were partly due to 'too great a centralization of an already deficient administration and to too much tolerance towards employers or physicians who neglect to fill out the reports that the law requires of them'. He was, however, able to report that a major administrative reform had been undertaken in the Commission to improve the 'file-analysis procedure'. He also noted that employers who delayed sending in reports of accidents were now being more severely disciplined.[1]

More fundamental than his criticisms of these administrative procedures, important though they were, were his criticisms of the restrictive interpretation which the Commission was giving to some of the key sections of the Act. For example, he had found that the Commission was ruling that an accident which took place at work was not an accident, within the meaning of the Act, if an employee was doing work which he was not hired to do, or was carrying out the work he was hired to do in an abnormal way so as to increase the danger of accident. The Public Protector pointed out that the Act stated that it applied to an accident 'arising out of *or* in the course of the work, and only denies recourse to the injured man when his fault may be called "gross" '.[2]

In his Report for 1972 he commented that 'the attitude of the Commissioner's administrators has undeniably evolved over the last few years'. In particular, he was able to report that the Commission was giving a less restrictive interpretation to the Act in deciding what constituted an accident at work. He was not altogether satisfied by the modified practice but could point to some improvement of interpretation.[3] In his Report for 1974 he welcomed the announcement that the Act governing the Commission was soon to be amended and that it had been decided to undertake a complete reorganization of the internal structure of the Commission. He commented that tendencies to interpret the term 'accident at work' in a harsh and rigid way had not yet been completely eliminated and that it was important to see that in the reorganized structure this harsh interpretation was eliminated 'definitively and at all levels'.[4]

In this example, as in some of the areas we have examined previously, we can see the Public Protector performing the broader

[1] *Second Annual Report, 1970*, p. 132.
[2] Ibid., p. 134.
[3] *Fourth Annual Report, 1972*, pp. 163–4.
[4] *Sixth Annual Report, 1974*, pp. 149–50.

function which all Ombudsmen can to some extent achieve, namely using the knowledge they gain from examining individual grievances to recommend improved administrative procedures, a more satisfactory interpretation of the law, and, in some cases, changes in the law. The Public Protector is not precluded from recommending changes in the law and every year some laws are amended in response to his recommendations.

To sum up, we may say that, seen from almost any angle, the office of Public Protector in Quebec is a very effective institution. The Public Protector is able to inquire into all aspects of provincial administration, he has wide-ranging powers to report on occasions when a citizen has been 'wronged' by a government department, or when there have been faulty procedures in a quasi-judicial body. He investigates each year a greater volume of complaints than any other Ombudsman and in a high proportion of cases secures redress for the complainant, without formal recommendation, or after formal recommendation. Dr. Marceau's annual reports were most informative and included numerous recommendations for improved administrative procedures and more humane interpretation of the law.

He is accessible to members of the public. The Public Protector's own office is in the Rue Haldimand in the Old City of Quebec, close to the Parliament Building. His chief assistant's office, in Montreal, is in one of the busiest shopping streets in the city. The ease with which members of the public can initiate a complaint by telephone is another valuable feature of the Public Protector's office.

Dr. Mareau's Report for 1974 provided interesting tables of the number of complaints by language of communication and by region. In 1974 the great majority of complaints, 90·6 per cent, came from French-speaking people in the province and the remaining 9·4 per cent from English-speaking people. The distribution of complaints by region shows that in some of the remote regions of the north he is reasonably well known, but in others very little known. For example, from the north-west region, where 2·8 per cent of the population in the province live, there came 2·3 per cent of the 5,304 complaints he received in the year. But from the Outaouais region, also in the far north, there came only 2·4 per cent of the complaints he received, although that region has 4·1 per cent of the population of the province.

More than 73 per cent of all complaints in 1974 came from the two great cities, Montreal and Quebec. Montreal, which has 56·9 per cent of the population, was the source of 38·1 per cent of complaints while Quebec, which has 15·6 per cent of the population, was the source of 35·2 per cent of complaints. This latter was the highest proportion of complaints in relation to population of any region in the province. Dr. Marceau's own explanation to me of the high proportion of complaints from Quebec was that the Public Protector is best known and understood by civil servants and their relatives, a very great number of whom live in the Quebec region.

This leads to the chief defect of the Public Protector in Quebec. He is still too little known. Dr. Marceau was aware of this and gave up some of his time to going on tours of the various regions. He also took part in several radio programmes. But all of this takes time from the main function of the Ombudsman. One way in which the Public Protector could secure greater publicity for his office would be to give greater access to journalists to examine his reports, in the manner of Scandinavian Ombudsmen. But Quebec law does not give the right of access to official documents which is provided by Swedish, Danish, and Norwegian law. The Public Protector has to work within the context of a less open system of government and within this context he clearly operates very effectively.

In the preface to his Report for 1973 Dr. Marceau, in his survey of the operation of his office in its first five years, commented that 'apparently the number of people who have no idea what an ombudsman is remains considerable'. He continued, 'Efforts to make the Service and its possibilities known must doubtless be increased and made more diverse, but it does seem that much more time and effort will be required to give the institution a more appreciable impact on the public.'[1] In his review, however, he was in general reasonably satisfied with the effectiveness of his office, as indeed he was entitled to be. But in his opinion his activities had not resulted in alienating the Civil Service. He commented that 'generally speaking, the Administration reacts in a very positive manner to the Service's (i.e. the Public Protector's) methods of investigation and with the exception of a few sporadic negative reactions, it is increasingly co-operative'.[2]

Between December 1975, when Dr. Marceau was appointed to the Supreme Court of Canada, and September 1976, when Miss

[1] *Fifth Annual Report, 1973*, p. 22.
[2] Ibid., p. 26.

Patenaude took over as Public Protector, M. Robert Lévêque was Acting Public Protector. He was the author of the Annual Report for 1975 and his Report continued in the style which Dr. Marceau had developed. Miss Patenaude, however, made a major change in the style and method of reporting on her activities as Public Protector. Dr. Marceau had always published one annual report each year giving his general conclusions on the operation of his office, examples of complaints investigated, and full statistics of the handling of cases. The full text of the annual report was separately published in French and English.

In her first annual report, published on 31 March 1977, Miss Patenaude announced that she had decided to divide her report into two parts. The first part, which would be published in the spring during the parliamentary session, would discuss the inconsistencies in legislation revealed by her investigations and would make proposals for amendments to legislation. The second part, published in the summer, would give examples of cases investigated and give an account of the over-all activities of the Ombudsman's office.[1] Miss Patenaude also announced that a full English version of the Public Protector's report would no longer be published. She said that this decision had been taken solely on grounds of economy. 'The translation and a second printing would have entailed the expenditure of some $9,000, and when one considers a distribution of approximately 100 copies sold in Quebec, this seemed quite excessive'.[2] But, to comply with the suggestion of the Ombudsman's Committee of the International Bar Association, she had decided 'to issue a comprehensive albeit short summary in the English language'.[3]

The explanation given for this decision was in fact inconsistent with a section of her full report in which Miss Patenaude said that the office of Public Protector was too little known about by the general public.[4] A full and informative annual report is one of the best ways in which an Ombudsman can make his activities better known. Although Miss Patenaude pointed out that only about 100 copies of the English version of the report were sold each year, copies of the report would undoubtedly have been seen by English-

[1] Le Protecteur du Citoyen, *Rapport annuel 1976* (Quebec, 1977), pp. 6–7 and *Summary in the English Language of the Eighth Annual Report of the Quebec Public Protector* (Quebec, 1977), p. 2.

[2] *Summary in the English Language* (1977), p. 2.

[3] Ibid.

[4] *Rapport annuel 1976*, p. 7.

language newspaper editors and broadcasters and would have been one of the chief means by which information about the Public Protector reached the English-speaking public. The summary in English issued in 1977 was only ten pages long, compared with the fifty-one pages of the full report in French. If the information given in English continues to compare so unfavourably with the French texts of the Public Protector's reports, this is likely to restrict even further access by members of the English-speaking population to the Public Protector. As we saw, in 1974 less than 10 per cent of the complaints to the Public Protector came from English-speaking people. But English-speaking Canadians account for about 20 per cent of the population of Quebec province. Even when the full text of the Public Protector's annual report was available in English, he was therefore significantly less used by the English-speaking element in the population than by the French. If only a brief summary of the annual reports is now made in English, the use made of the Public Protector by English-speaking people, compared with the French-speaking, is likely to diminish still further.

There seems little doubt that the decision to cease publishing a full English version of the Public Protector's annual report was connected with the change of government which followed on the provincial election in November 1976. At that election, the Parti Québecois led by M. René Levesque won a majority of seats, formed a government and launched upon a separatist programme of which French linguistic nationalism was one of the main planks.

Another change of policy which Miss Patenaude announced in her report for 1976 was her decision to reduce her staff in the Montreal office and to concentrate in the Quebec office as much as possible of the work on investigation of complaints. The staff remaining in the Montreal office will be largely concerned with receiving complaints, either by telephone, by letter, or by personal interviews.[1] It is too early to judge what the effect of this change on the operation of the office of Public Protector is likely to be. Although it is clear that Miss Patenaude has set a new style, in many respects different from that set by her predecessor, Dr. Marceau, it remains to be seen whether she will be less, or more, effective in exposing administrative and legislative deficiencies, and in securing redress for complainants.

[1] Ibid., p. 6.

THE MANITOBA OMBUDSMAN

Legislation setting up an Ombudsman for the province of Manitoba was passed in 1969. The New Democratic Party (broadly the equivalent in Canada of the British Labour Party) had, when in opposition, criticized the former Government's proposal for an Ombudsman who could only be approached through Members of the Legislative Assembly. When the New Democratic Party was successful at the polls and formed a Government, one of its first acts was to secure the passage of legislation setting up an Ombudsman for Manitoba who could, on the New Zealand pattern, be approached directly by members of the public.

The 1969 Ombudsman Act follows closely on the New Zealand model in other ways, even more closely than the Quebec Public Protector Act of 1968 did. Thus the Manitoba Ombudsman Act states at Section 36(1) that the Ombudsman, after investigation, can report on any decision, recommendation, act, or omission of a provincial department which appears to have been

'(i) contrary to law, or
(ii) unreasonable, or
(iii) unjust, or
(iv) oppressive, or
(v) improperly discriminatory, or
(vi) in accordance with a practice or procedure that is or may be unreasonable, unjust, oppressive, or improperly discriminatory, or
(vii) based wholly or partly on a mistake of law or fact, or
(viii) wrong'.

This wording is almost identical with the wording in Section 19 of the New Zealand Parliamentary Commissioner (Ombudsman) Act, 1962, which we earlier reproduced in discussing the Quebec Public Protector Act.[1] The following section of the Manitoba Ombudsman Act, Section 36(2), then goes on to reproduce the latter part of Section 19 of the New Zealand Act by saying that the Ombudsman may recommend that an omission should be rectified by a department, or a decision cancelled or varied, that the practice of a department should be altered, or that any law on which a departmental decision was based should be reconsidered.

[1] See above, p. 54.

The Ombudsman's jurisdiction extends to all provincial departments and agencies. He can see all the documents relating to an investigation, including all relevant documents from provincial departments. The one significant limitation on the Manitoba Ombudsman which is not placed on the New Zealand Ombudsman is the provision at Section 19(1) of the Manitoba Act that 'Where the Attorney-General certifies in writing to the Ombudsman that the investigation of a matter would be contrary to the public interest under the circumstances, the Ombudsman shall not investigate that matter, or if he has commenced an investigation of that matter, he shall discontinue the investigation.' The next part of the Section goes on to say that where such a certificate has been issued by the Attorney-General, the Ombudsman shall mention that fact, and the circumstances surrounding the issuing of the certificate, in his next annual report.

This provision is reminiscent of the proposal in the 1961 Whyatt Report in Britain that a Minister should be able to veto an investigation by the Parliamentary Commissioner. The proposal was rejected by the committee of the Wilson Cabinet which planned the Parliamentary Commissioner Act, 1967.[1] The Manitoba provision is less sweeping because it confines the power of veto to the Attorney-General, but the provision is nevertheless potentially weakening to the institution of Ombudsman. However, this provision has not been invoked in the history of the Manitoba Ombudsman.

The Ombudsman in Manitoba is appointed by the Lieutenant-Governor in Council on the recommendation of a special committee of the Legislative Assembly. The Ombudsman holds office for six years, and can be reappointed for a second six-year term, but cannot be reappointed after he has served for twelve years. The first Ombudsman to be appointed, in April 1970, was George Maltby and he is still in office. George Maltby, although a Canadian citizen, as required by the Act, was born in Yorkshire. He served for twenty-five years in the Hull City Police, becoming an Inspector in 1953. In 1960 he was appointed Deputy Chief of Police in the City of St. James, which borders on Winnipeg, and before long was promoted to Chief of Police. When the Ombudsman Act was passed in 1969, he applied for the post and was appointed. In March 1976 he was reappointed for a further six years.

It seems at first sight strange to find an ex-policeman holding the

[1] See Stacey, *The British Ombudsman*, pp. 55–6.

office of Ombudsman. In fact, there was a precedent in Canada since the Alberta Ombudsman from 1967 to 1974, George McClellan, was also a former policeman.[1] There can be advantages for an Ombudsman who has to investigate complaints against the police in having had police experience. He is then familiar with police methods and with the sort of covering-up which can go on when the police abuse their powers. Until 1974 the Manitoba Ombudsman investigated complaints against the Royal Canadian Mounted Police who act as provincial police in those provinces such as Manitoba which do not maintain their own provincial police forces. George Maltby made some valuable reports on such investigations. But in 1974 a court in Saskatchewan ruled that the Saskatchewan Ombudsman did not have jurisdiction to investigate complaints against the Royal Canadian Mounted Police acting in provincial matters. The judgement of the Court of Queen's Bench was that the R.C.M.P. was an agent of the Federal Government of Canada and even when R.C.M.P. units were acting on behalf of a provincial government, they were not subject to investigation by a provincial Ombudsman. Since this decision, the Ombudsman of all three prairie provinces, Alberta, Manitoba, and Saskatchewan, have ceased to investigate complaints against the R.C.M.P. In the provinces of Quebec and Ontario, which maintain their own provincial police forces, the Ombudsmen continue to investigate complaints against the provincial police.

The fair-minded attitude which George Maltby showed in police investigations has characterized his investigations into other matters of provincial administration. He is a lively person with a humane attitude, as the texts of his reports show. He has three investigating assistants of whom the most senior are Dick Glover and Max Regiedzinski. Dick Glover comes from a farming family, worked on the railways and, for fifteen years, in the Winnipeg police. He then for a while ran his own road haulage business, but prior to appointment as assistant to the Ombudsman had been working for the provincial government, in the taxation department. His varied experience and farming background are of value to the Ombudsman since many complaints come from farmers. Max Regiedzinski is a Polish–German immigrant who speaks not only Polish and German, but also Ukranian, Russian, and six European languages. His

[1] Before his appointment George McClellan had been Head of the Royal Canadian Mounted Police.

linguistic ability is an asset since Manitoba has several large immigrant groups in relation to the total population. Out of a total population of 988,000 in 1972 there were 123,000 German-speaking Manitobans, 114,000 Ukrainian speakers, 86,000 French speakers, and 43,000 Polish speakers, as well as 414,000 Manitobans of British extraction.[1]

The investigating assistants, and the Ombudsman, are available for consultation by telephone, or at the Ombudsman's office in the centre of Winnipeg. The investigating assistants also travel widely throughout the province to interview complainants, to visit prisons or hospitals when the complaint is from a prisoner or patient, or to examine a site about which there is a dispute. Because of the size of the province this can entail journeys of six hundred miles or more. The Ombudsman himself undertakes such visits when the difficulty of a case indicates that he needs to see for himself.

George Maltby has done a great deal to try and secure publicity for his office, so that his services can be adequately used. About four times a year he puts advertisements in the newspapers saying that anyone who feels he has a complaint against a department or agency of the provincial government may write to him at his Winnipeg office. The advertisement concludes in heavy type *There Is No Charge For The Services Of The Ombudsman.* George Maltby always finds an increase in his post-bag of complaints after the advertisement has been in the newspapers. There are a large number of ethnic newspapers in Manitoba, in the languages of the immigrant groups, and the Ombudsman sees that his advertisement appears regularly in these papers too.

The publication of his annual report is also an occasion for publicizing the activities of the Ombudsman. The press give good coverage to his annual report. The Ombudsman sends copies of his report not only to the Members of the Legislative Assembly, the departments and agencies of the provincial government, and the press and radio stations, but also to local authorities, schools, trade union branches, prisons, the universities, and the Indian Chiefs. He also visits Indian groups, as well as business organizations, service clubs, high-school students, and so on, as frequently as possible, to discuss the work of the Ombudsman's office.

Originally, George Maltby had a full-time legal adviser in his office. He decided, however, that it was more appropriate to secure

[1] By 1976 the total estimate of population of Manitoba had risen to 1,018,000.

legal advice *ad hoc*, where a case made it advisable, from a lawyer practising in Winnipeg.

The Manitoba Ombudsman, like the Quebec Public Protector, has power to investigate complaints against quasi-judicial bodies. Thus, in a complaint against the Liquor Control Commission, the counsel for an applicant for a licence complained to the Ombudsman that all the members of the Commission had received a confidential report about the application which the counsel was not allowed to see. The Ombudsman investigated the case and reported that, at hearings of the Commission, all documents relative to the application should be shown to the applicant, that evidence should be on oath, and that there should be the right to cross-examine. The Commission accepted these recommendations.

The Ombudsman also made recommendations about a quasi-judicial body in his Report for 1972. He investigated a complaint against the Discipline Committee of the Department of Education which had recommended to the Provincial Minister of Education that a teacher's Certificate should be immediately suspended, and for an indefinite period. The ground for the suspension was that the teacher concerned had shown violence towards other teachers. There was no evidence that he had ever struck a student. He was known to be suffering from emotional stress and he was receiving medical treatment.

The Ombudsman, after investigation, found numerous defects in the procedure followed at the hearing of the Discipline Committee. Three members of the Executive Committee of the Manitoba Teachers' Society who were on the Discipline Committee at the hearing were known to have prejudged the case against the complainant. Hearsay evidence from a School Inspector's report was admitted at the hearing, and an unsatisfactory attempt to clarify the evidence was made by a long-distance telephone call to the Inspector. There was no quorum at the meeting and, in other respects, the Committee was not properly constituted as provided by the relevant section of the Department of Education Act.

The Ombudsman reported all these defects and drew them to the attention of the Minister. He also recommended that the teacher should receive a cheque for one month's salary in lieu of the one month's notice which he had not been accorded by the Discipline Committee. The Minister replied that he did not accept the Ombudsman's recommendations. It is very interesting to see what was the Ombudsman's response. He wrote to the Minister of Education saying that he would report to the Lieutenant-Governor in Council, in accordance with the provisions of Section 37(2) of the Ombudsman Act, that no action was being taken by the Department on his recommendation. Not long after he heard from the Minister that the Ombudsman's recommendation would be accepted, and, after a Review Committee hearing, the teacher was reinstated.[1]

Table VII lists the departments and agencies ranked by the number of complaints received by the Ombudsman in 1974. The Manitoba Public Insurance Corporation with 85 cases was the agency against which most complaints were made. This is a provincially owned corporation providing insurance for motorists. Most of the complaints were about the amount of settlement of a claim, after an accident, or about delays in settling a claim. In well over a quarter of the cases the Ombudsman procured redress for the complainant.

The second highest number of complaints, 81, were levelled at the Department of Health and Social Development. A rather high proportion of these were complaints about the confinement of patients in mental hospitals or a psychiatric institute. The remainder were mainly concerned with poor facilities, or loss of privileges, in correctional institutions, with medical treatment, or with social assistance, or were complaints from employees of institutions in the health sector. In less than 10 per cent of cases was redress achieved by the Ombudsman. But one of the concerns of this Department is the restriction of civil liberties in the case of people compulsorily confined in mental hospitals and correctional institutions. In these areas the proportion of cases found justified is often low, but the right to complain is extremely valuable.

The Department of the Attorney General was third, with 42 cases. There was a great variety here in the subject-matter of complaints. Some were concerned with detention in the cells or remand in custody, some with the summoning of witnesses and other aspects of court administration. In more than one-fifth of the cases redress was secured in 1974.

The Department of Highways, with 35 cases, had the fourth highest number of complaints. All the complaints were in one of two categories. They were either complaints about damage caused by highway construction or maintenance, or were grievances about

[1] Province of Manitoba, *Report of the Ombudsman for the period January 1st 1972 to December 31st 1972*, pp. 82–95.

the administration of driving-licences. The Ombudsman secured redress in one-seventh of the cases which he received.

TABLE VII
Manitoba Ombudsman, 1974.

Complaints dealt with (ranked by department)*

	Not justified	Declined, with-drawn or informa-tion supplied	Pending	Referred to pro-vincial authority	Recom-mendat'n by Ombuds-man	Rectified	Total
Manitoba Public Insurance Corporat'n	21	30	8	—	1	25	85
Dept. of Health and Social Development	25	37	4	5	2	8	81
Dept. of the Attorney General	10	14	3	5	1	9	42
Dept. of Highways	8	19	2	1	—	5	35
Dept. of Mines, Resources and Environmental Management	3	15	7	—	—	6	31
Workers' Compensa-tion Board	2	19	5	—	—	4	30
Dept. of Agriculture	3	5	9	1	—	—	18
Dept. of Consumer, Corporate and Internal Services	9	2	—	1	1	2	15
Dept. of Public Works	—	6	3	—	—	4	13
Dept. of Colleges and Universities Affairs	2	6	1	—	—	4	13
Manitoba Telephone System	1	1	2	—	—	8	12
Manitoba Hydro	2	5	—	—	—	4	11
Dept. of Urban Affairs	3	3	2	1	—	2	11

* Departments concerned with fewer than 10 complaints in the year are not included in this table.

Source: Province of Manitoba, *Report of the Ombudsmen for the period January 1st 1974 to December 31st 1974.*

The Department of Mines, Resources and Environmental Management, with 31 cases, was fifth. A number of these complaints concerned compensation for flooding, or compensation for damage to crops caused by protected wildlife. Some were concerned with pollution and some with fishing-licences. In just under a fifth of complaints the Ombudsman secured redress.

Thirty complaints were levelled against the Workers' Compensation Board. In 11 cases the complaint was that compensation was denied by the Board and in 10 cases that insufficient compensation was paid. The Ombudsman secured redress for two complainants who alleged that their compensation was insufficient and for one who had been refused compensation.

The Department of Agriculture was the target of 18 complaints. These concerned crop insurance, licences, the milk quota system, and a variety of other subjects. In no case was redress secured for a complainant in 1974, but 9 out of 18 cases were still in course of investigation.

There were 15 complaints in the year against the Department of Consumer, Corporate and Internal Services. In 3 out of the 15 cases redress was secured or a recommendation made by the Ombudsman. The Department of Public Works was the target of 13 complaints. Seven of these were concerned with compensation for the acquisition of land and in 3 such cases redress was secured for the complainant.

There were 13 complaints against the Department of Colleges and Universities Affairs. Ten of these concerned the provincial student aid programme and in 4 such cases redress was secured. Against the provincially owned Manitoba Telephone System there were 12 complaints in 1974. These complaints were mainly from subscribers and concerned such matters as disconnection of telephones, disputes over bills, etc. In 8 out of 12 cases redress was secured by the Ombudsman.

The Manitoba Hydro, which supplies electricity in the province, was the target of 11 complaints in the year. Eight of these were consumers' complaints and 3 were complaints of damage or nuisance caused by power-supply installations. In 4 cases the Ombudsman secured redress. Finally, there were 11 complaints against the Department of Urban Affairs. The majority of these concerned the Manitoba Housing and Renewal Corporation. In 2 of the complaints redress was secured for the complainant and in 2 others investigation was continuing.

The departments and agencies who were concerned with fewer than 10 complaints in 1974 are not listed in the table. Those who were concerned with between 6 and 9 complaints were the Department of Finance (9 complaints of which 2 were rectified), the Department of Labour (7 complaints with none rectified in the year), the Department of Tourism, Recreation and Cultural Affairs (7 complaints of which 5 were pending), the Civil Service Commission (7 complaints of which 2 were pending) and the Department of Education (6 complaints of which 1 was rectified and 1 was pending).

When we survey the main areas in which the Manitoba Ombudsman received complaints in 1974 we see therefore that a high proportion of them were concerned with the problem of ordinary people: complaints about social assistance, about the rights of the mentally ill, about the Workers' Compensation Board, or consumers' complaints about publicly owned utilities. A large number of complaints, as we have seen, are also concerned with the provincial car insurance corporation but in Canada many car owners are among the less-affluent sections of the community.

THE NEW BRUNSWICK OMBUDSMAN

New Brunswick is one of the oldest of Canada's provinces. It was granted the status of a province by George III in 1784 and named after one of his ancestral domains in Germany. It has a population of 635,000 and an area of 28,354 square miles. About 40 per cent of the population are French-speaking. All legislation and the Ombudsman's annual reports are printed in English and French.

The law establishing an Ombudsman in New Brunswick was passed in 1967. The moving force behind the reform had been the Liberal Prime Minister of New Brunswick, Louis J. Robichaud. His administration had promoted a great deal of centralization in government. Under his leadership the county councils had been abolished and education, justice, health, and welfare functions transferred to the provincial government. Only the elected city and village authorities remained in being. To counterbalance this centralization of power, which had been carried through in the name of efficiency, M. Robichaud favoured the appointment of an Ombudsman to recommend redress of individual grievances.

The Ombudsman Act of 1967, like the Quebec and Manitoba Acts which it preceded, incorporates the principal features of the New Zealand Parliamentary Commissioner (Ombudsman) Act of 1962. The New Brunswick Ombudsman can report that a grievance exists against a department or agency of the provincial government because that department or agency is administering a law of New Brunswick 'unreasonably, unjustly, oppressively or in a discriminatory manner', or 'wrongly', or is 'using a discretionary power for an improper purpose'. These are some of the phrases used in Section 21 of the New Brunswick Ombudsman Act and they follow closely the terminology used in the New Zealand Act. If the department or agency does not respond to the Ombudsman's report and cancels or rectifies a decision, as the case may be, the Ombudsman can send a copy of his report and recommendation to the Lieutenant-Governor in Council and subsequently to the Legislative Assembly.

The New Brunswick Act also follows the New Zealand Act in providing that any person in custody, whether in a prison, private sanatorium, or mental hospital, must have his letter to the Ombudsman immediately forwarded to the Ombudsman unopened. The Act provides that the Ombudsman shall not investigate where there is an adequate right of remedy or appeal. This is interpreted to mean that he does not investigate where there is a clear right of appeal to an administrative tribunal. As regards appeal to the courts, he does not investigate if there is specific provision for appeal to a court, provided for in a statute. He is not prevented from investigating on the ground that there is a general appeal to a court by prerogative writ, such as certiorari.

The New Brunswick Ombudsman cannot investigate a complaint against an administrative tribunal. Here he is more limited than the Quebec and Manitoba Ombudsmen are for, as we have seen, they can investigate complaints about defective procedure in administrative tribunals. The New Brunswick Act provides that the Ombudsman shall have a salary and pension equivalent to that of a judge of the Supreme Court of New Brunswick. He is appointed to office by the Lieutenant-Governor in Council, on the recommendation of the Legislative Assembly. He holds office for ten years and is then eligible for reappointment.

The office of Ombudsman in New Brunswick has not, however, enjoyed the continuity for which these provisions would seem to be designed. In fact, since 1967 there have been four Ombudsmen. The first three died in office. The first Ombudsman, who held office from 1967 until his death in 1971, was the Reverend Ross Flemington. When appointed, Flemington was President of Mount Allison University in New Brunswick. He was a theologian and educationist by training. In the First World War he had been a pilot in the Royal Flying Corps, but in the Second World War he saw service first as chaplain to a Canadian regiment and was then appointed Principal Protestant Chaplain Overseas, holding the rank of Colonel. Returning to education in 1945, he became well known on the national and the provincial plane. He was Director of Education for External Aid for Canada from 1962 to 1965. In 1966 he was appointed chairman of a Provincial Commission to inquire into the need for a medical school in New Brunswick. He was appointed Ombudsman because he was known as a man of great integrity and independence of outlook.

By all accounts he was successful as an Ombudsman. He was not legally trained and received legal advice from a lawyer practising in the provincial capital, Fredericton. The lawyer who advised him, Mr. Eric Appleby, told me that in Mr. Flemington's case it was not a disadvantage that he did not have legal training. In fact, in some instances he was willing to intercede for a complainant on grounds of humanity where a lawyer might have hesitated to do so. He made himself very accessible to the public, working from an office right beside the legislative building in Fredericton. The simplest of addresses sufficed to reach him. For example, one letter which Flemington received was addressed to

The Ambushman,
Fredericton.

Unfortunately, he was not able to help the author of the letter. This was an old man who was afraid that his relatives were planning to take away his land. By no stretching of the rules could Flemington have investigated his complaint, but what is interesting is that the letter reached him with no delay.

On Flemington's death in 1971 he was succeeded by Mr. Charles Léger, who, unlike Flemington, was a lawyer. He was a Queen's Counsel and had been president of the Barristers' Society of New Brunswick. However, he became ill in 1973 and died in September of that year. His successor was not appointed until February 1974.

During Léger's illness, and in the intervening period following his death, the role of Ombudsman was to some extent carried on by the Secretary to the Ombudsman, Mrs. Magella St-Pierre, and by members of the law firm of Appleby, Olmstead, and Quinn in Fredericton. They replied to complainants, took up the less difficult cases with departments, but held over the more difficult cases until a new Ombudsman should be appointed.

The new Ombudsman, appointed early in February 1974, was George McAllister, also a Queen's Counsel. He was to hold office only until August 1975 when he died after a short illness. His period of office was, however, memorable for a big expansion in the number of cases dealt with by the Ombudsman, for a considerable increase in the size of his staff, and for the distinctive style of operation which he adopted during these eighteen months. In the calendar year from 1 January to 31 December 1974 the Ombudsman received 627 complaints. This was a very big increase over the 280 complaints received by Mr. Léger in 1972, his last year when he was in full health. Indeed the annual average of complaints between 1967 and 1972 was approximately 285.[1]

The reasons for this great increase, suggested to me in 1975 by the Acting Ombudsman for New Brunswick, Mr. Charles Ferris, were threefold. First, Mr. McAllister, because of his strong personality and distinctive methods of operating, attracted more attention to the office. Second, he made considerable use of mass advertising to publicize the services of the Ombudsman. Third, a Canadian Broadcasting Corporation programme called 'Ombudsman' attracted attention on a nation-wide basis. A purist might object that the word 'Ombudsman' was misused for this programme since its pattern was for the spokesmen of a government department to be confronted with a grievance or problem that was first aired in the studio with a complainant. But whether or not the word is technically appropriate it seems to have inspired interest in the concept and services of the Ombudsman.[2]

In order to cope with the increased volume of complaints, Mr. McAllister pressed for and secured a big increase in staff. Previously the Ombudsman had enjoyed the full-time services of only the Secretary to the office, Mrs. Magella St-Pierre, and the part-time services of a legal adviser as required. Between May and December 1974 Mr. McAllister secured three additional full-time appointments to his office. Mrs. Magella St-Pierre was promoted to the post of Administrative Assistant, and a Secretary was appointed in her place with the support of a full-time typist. In December 1974 Mr. Charles Ferris, one of the lawyers in the firm of Appleby, Olmstead, and Quinn, was appointed as full-time Legal Adviser to

[1] Province of New Brunswick, *Eighth Report of the Ombudsman* (Fredericton, 1975), p. 6.

[2] See also below, p. 91.

the Ombudsman. These new appointments were not only necessary to secure adequate handling of complaints, but they made possible invaluable continuity after Mr. McAllister's death. Charles Ferris was then able to take over as Acting Ombudsman.

The other major change which Mr. McAllister made was in his style of investigation. In particular, he invoked a provision in the 1967 statute which empowered him to hold formal hearings, on judicial lines, for some of the more important grievances. This was quite unprecedented in New Brunswick. Mr. Flemington had worked informally, often by directly visiting the Minister or Deputy Minister concerned, to discuss the complaint with him. Mr. Léger had never held hearings.

Another important change which Mr. McAllister helped to bring about concerned the implementation of reforms. Each year the Ombudsman makes recommendations for legislative and administrative reforms as a result of cases he has investigated during the year. Many of these were implemented but there was no formal machinery to see that the Ombudsman's recommendations for reform were taken up. After the Ombudsman's Report for 1974 was presented to Parliament in February 1975 the Prime Minister of the province referred the recommendations in the report to the Law Reform Division of the Department of Justice. This Division was instructed to refer recommendations which it considered viable to a Committee of the Executive Council for consideration for legislative implementation.

Table VIII gives the departments and agencies against which the Ombudsman in New Brunswick received the largest numbers of complaints in 1974. The Department of Highways had the largest number, 55. Some of these were concerned with expropriations (compulsory purchase of land or property) as in Quebec. A good number were complaints that highway construction had caused damage to houses. For example, an elderly couple complained that their well had been damaged by seepage of gas and oil during construction of a highway. Mr. McAllister found that the complaint was justified. The Department drilled a new well and installed a new pump at their house.[1]

Next was the Workmen's Compensation Board with 42 complaints. A number of these cases concerned the termination of compensation payments. For example, in one case in which Mr.

[1] *Eighth Report of the Ombudsman*, pp. 66–7.

McAllister procured a review, the decision by the Board to end compensation payments was revised and a 50 per cent partial disability payment was awarded to the complainant, subject to periodic review. Close behind in the number of complaints in 1974 was the Department of the Provincial Secretary with 40 cases. This Department has a variety of functions including licensing car drivers and motor taxation.

TABLE VIII
New Brunswick Ombudsman, 1974.

Complaints dealt with (ranked by department)*

Complaint:	Not justified	No jurisdiction or discontinued or information given† etc.	Under investigation	Referred to provincial authority	Recommendat'n by Ombudsman	Rectified	Total
Dept. of Highways	9	12	15	—	1	18	55
Workmen's Compensation Board	11	14	10	—	—	7	42
Dept of the Provincial Secretary (includes driving-licences, car tax, etc.)	10	19	2	4	—	5	40
Dept. of Social Services	11	10	5	2	—	9	37
Dept. of Justice	7	15	8	1	1	3	35
Dept. of Municipal Affairs	4	12	2	—	—	3	21
Dept. of Health	11	3	3	—	—	2	19
Dept. of Education	3	6	3	3	—	2	17
New Brunswick Electric Power Commission	3	1	3	—	—	6	13
Treasury Board	6	3	2	—	—	1	12

* Departments concerned with fewer than 10 complaints in the year not included in this table.

† In total, complaints were judged to be outside jurisdiction in 52 cases; were discontinued in 10 cases; information was given in 29 cases; one was judged premature, and 3 were withdrawn (M.S.).

Source: Compiled by the author from statistics in Province of New Brunswick, *Eighth Report of the Ombudsman* (New Brunswick, 1975).

The Department of Social Services, with 37 cases, was also the target of a large number of complaints, although it did not rank so high in the list of such departments as in Quebec. Of the 8 cases in which the New Brunswick Ombudsman procured redress for the complainant, 6 were concerned with some aspect of welfare, 1 with a disability allowance, and 1 with assistance towards the purchase of a hearing-aid.

Complaints against the Department of Justice, which numbered 35 in 1974, included complaints against prisons and complaints about the administration of justice. Many of the complaints against the Department of Municipal Affairs, which numbered 21 in 1974, were about local property taxes. These were, at that time, outside the jurisdiction of the Ombudsman. He also received complaints about the administration of elections, about denial of the right to choose a lawyer in a case in which the Department was involved (here the Ombudsman secured redress for the complainant), and a complaint about non-enforcement of the law which the Ombudsman found unjustified.

Complaints against the Health Department, of which there were 19 in 1974, in part concerned environmental health (there were 2 complaints about sewerage and 1 about a refuse dump, for example), in part Medicare, and in part the compulsory hospitalization of mental patients (there were 2 such complaints). Complaints against the Department of Education, numbering 17, were very varied. Some were complaints from staff about dismissal, a pension grievance, or a licence to teach, some were parents' complaints, others from students in higher education.

In respect of both the Department of Health and the Department of Education, the Ombudsman found that only a small proportion of the complaints were justified and secured redress for the complainant; about one-ninth of complaints against Health and one-eighth against Education. But Mr. McAllister secured redress for complainants in nearly half of the 13 cases which concerned the New Brunswick Electric Power Commission. The complaints which he received against this Commission were from consumers, employees, and from property owners affected by electricity works. Finally, the 12 complaints against the Treasury Board were mostly complaints from civil servants about their pay and conditions. He found only one of these complaints justified.

The great variation in New Brunswick in the proportion of complaints he found justified is of interest, but not necessarily significant. There are certain departments such as the Department of Highways against which all three Canadian provincial Ombudsmen we have studied normally gain redress for a good proportion of complainants. This is because in the nature of the work in which they are engaged there are many occasions when these departments cause minor, and sometimes considerable, damage to householders or are lacking in proper standards of fairness in providing compensation. There are other departments where the proportion of complaints found justified is normally low but where the avenue of complaint to the Ombudsman is an invaluable safeguard. Good examples here are the Departments of Justice and Health. The number of complaints against mental hospitals and prisons which are found justified is often low, but the safeguard against abuse which is provided by access to the Ombudsman is very important.

Charles Ferris was appointed Acting Ombudsman in August 1975. He continued in this capacity for almost a year until 9 June 1976, when a new Ombudsman was appointed. He is Mr. Joseph E. Bérubé, aged forty-five, much younger than any of his predecessors. Before his appointment he was Judge of the Family Court for Madawaska, Victoria, and Restigouche Counties in the Province of New Brunswick. He entered upon a larger jurisdiction as Ombudsman than his predecessors, since in June 1976 an Act to Amend the Ombudsman Act was passed by the New Brunswick Legislature. The new Act provided that the Ombudsman may investigate complaints against local authorities and may also himself initiate investigations into the administration of local authorities.[1]

OMBUDSMEN IN THE OTHER PROVINCES

In this chapter we have given special emphasis to the provincial Ombudsmen in Quebec, Manitoba, and New Brunswick. The other five provincial Ombudsmen in 1977—for Ontario, Alberta, Saskatchewan, Nova Scotia, and Newfoundland—are also of great interest and to complete this chapter it is appropriate to make some brief comparisons between them and to highlight some of their principal characteristics.

The Ombudsman for Ontario was only appointed in 1975, but there is a case for considering him first because Ontario, with a population of 7,703,106, is comparable in size to Quebec with its population of 6,027,764. The first Ombudsman for Ontario, appointed in May 1975, was Arthur Maloney. He was fifty-five years old when appointed and was, at that time, one of Canada's

[1] *An Act to Amend the Ombudsman Act* (New Brunswick, 1976), Sect. 3.

leading criminal lawyers. He had been a Federal Member of Parliament during the Diefenbaker years and sat as a Conservative. His appointment as Ombudsman was, however, endorsed by the three main parties in Ontario, the Conservative, Liberal, and New Democratic Parties. He had become very well known as a champion of civil liberties and was widely considered an appropriate choice as Ombudsman. In May 1975 he had just completed a report to the Metropolitan Toronto Board of Commissioners of Police on the operation of the Complaint Bureau of the Toronto police force.[1]

The Ontario Ombudsman Act, 1975, follows in many respects on the lines of the Canadian Ombudsman statutes we have already examined. He is empowered to report that a decision, recommendation, act, or omission of an Ontario department or agency has been contrary to law, unreasonable, unjust, oppressive, or improperly discriminatory, or wrong. Like the other Canadian Ombudsman we have studied, therefore, he is established on the New Zealand pattern and many other provisions in the Ontario statute are derived from the New Zealand model. For example, we find again, as in New Brunswick and Manitoba, the admirable provision that any letter written to the Ombudsman by 'an inmate of any institution or a patient in a provincial psychiatric facility shall be immediately forwarded unopened to the Ombudsman by the person in charge of the institution or facility' (Section 17–(2)).

There are some differences of detail. For example, if the Ontario Ombudsman finds that his recommendation is not acted upon by the department or agency concerned within a reasonable time, he is empowered by the Act to send his recommendation to the Premier and may also report on the matter to the Legislative Assembly. In some other provinces, for example Quebec, Manitoba, and New Brunswick, the Ombudsman is empowered in such circumstances to send his recommendation to the Lieutenant-Governor. We saw that this power was used by the Manitoba Ombudsman in 1972.[2]

The style of operation of the Ontario Ombudsman is similar to that of the Quebec Public Protector. His staff have tried to make themselves as readily available to the public as the Quebec Ombudsman's staff have done. The Ontario Ombudsman can receive

[1] Arthur Maloney, Q.C., *Report to the Metropolitan Toronto Board of Commissioners of Police. The Metropolitan Toronto Review of Citizen–Police Complaint Procedure* (Toronto, 1975).

[2] See above, p. 75.

complaints against a similar range of provincial departments and agencies as in the other provinces. He investigates complaints against industries which are publicly owned, for example against the Electric Power Commission for Ontario.

The Ontario Ombudsman is empowered to recommend ways in which, in his view, his powers need to be enlarged. Arthur Maloney emphasized the value of this power in his speech to the International Ombudsmen Conference at Edmonton, Alberta, in September 1976. He said that he intended to use this power to recommend extension of his jurisdiction to include local authorities and the 'actions or omissions by authorities that do not fall within the definition of "governmental organisation" contained in the Ontario Act, yet nevertheless are substantially funded from the public purse'.[1]

The Alberta Ombudsman was set up by the Alberta Ombudsman Act, 1967. Alberta is the largest of the three prairie provinces. It has 1,772,000 people to Manitoba's 1,018,000. It is a little larger in terms of area, having 255,285 square miles to Manitoba's 251,000 square miles. As in Manitoba, agriculture is the main industry but Alberta has a larger urban population. Alberta has three cities with a population of over 400,000. Calgary, Edmonton, and Lethbridge, while Manitoba only has Winnipeg with a population of more than 400,000.

The first Ombudsman for Alberta to be appointed, on 1 September 1967, was George McClellan who until his appointment had been Head of the Royal Canadian Mounted Police. George McClellan served as Ombudsman for nearly seven years. In May 1974 he was succeeded by Dr. Randall Ivany who prior to his appointment was an Anglican clergyman. He had been Dean of Edmonton and Rector of All Saints Cathedral. He was originally an electrical engineer, then was ordained and was for seventeen years an Anglican priest before being appointed Ombudsman. In 1976 he was elected chairman of the International Ombudsman Steering Committee which organizes international conferences of Ombudsmen and co-ordinates information among Ombudsmen on a worldwide basis.

The Albertan Ombudsman has a staff of eighteen including six investigators and a full-time legal adviser. The staff are divided

[1] A. Maloney, Speech on 'The Powers of the Ombudsman and their Judicious use' (cyclostyled text of proceedings of the International Ombudsman Conference, Sept. 1976), p. 16.

between two offices, the principal Ombudsman's office being in Edmonton with a secondary office in Calgary. The Ombudsman's staff are active in interviewing both complainants and the public servants concerned in complaints. When the Ombudsman has decided to investigate a complaint, the investigator will normally go to the provincial department to examine the file and interview the civil servants concerned. Investigators also generally interview the complainant at least once.

The Manitoban Ombudsman makes use of his statutory power to investigate or inspect on his own initiative. Dr. Ivany told me that in the last three years he has made seven such investigations or inspections. These are often decided upon as a result of reports in the media, but sometimes they are indicated by the recurring pattern of complaints in a certain area of administration. Thus in 1974 he made a special investigation of the Teachers' Retirement Fund following a series of complaints from retired teachers. Similarly, in 1976 he conducted a personal inquiry into the treatment of people detained in the Calgary Remand and Detention Centre. Having advised the Minister responsible that he would be visiting the Centre, but not giving a precise day or time for his inspection, he arrived there one evening at midnight and with the help of two of his investigators inspected the whole premises, thereby uncovering several examples of harsh or inhuman treatment of people in detention. Subsequently, he held a formal hearing into the administration of the Remand Centre, taking evidence on oath, and published a special report on the whole investigation.

In May 1977 a Select Committee of the Alberta Legislative Assembly, set up to review legislation on the Ombudsman Act, recommended that the Ombudsman should make such inspections of prisons and detention centres on a regular basis. It thereby indicated its approval of the Ombudsman's use of his power to inspect, although in some other respects the Select Committee did not recommend extention of the Ombudsman's powers. For example, it advised against extending his jurisdiction to cover complaints against local authorities.[1]

The third prairie province to appoint an Ombudsman was Saskatchewan whose population, at 920,000, is a little smaller than that of Manitoba. The Saskatchewan Ombudsman Act became law

[1] *Report of the Select Committee of the Legislative Assembly to Review Legislation on the Ombudsman Act* (Alberta, May 1977), pp. 15 and 31.

in 1972. The first Ombudsman to be appointed, in May 1973, was Mr. E. C. Boychuk, a Queen's Counsel, who had previously been a provincial judge. He resigned in January 1976 when he was appointed Chief Judge of the Magistrates' Court for the province. No successor was chosen until April 1977 when Mr. David A. Tickell was appointed Ombudsman. Mr. Tickell was, immediately prior to his appointment, Crown Solicitor in the Saskatchewan Attorney-General's Department. Previously he had been a solicitor in Ontario, working partly in private practice and partly for the Government of Ontario. From January 1976 to April 1977 the Chief Assistant to the Ombudsman, Mr. W. K. Barker, was Acting Ombudsman for Saskatchewan.

The two maritime provinces to have Ombudsmen, in addition to New Brunswick, are Nova Scotia and Newfoundland. The Nova Scotia Ombudsman is much the longer established. The Ombudsman Act came into operation in 1969 and Dr. Harry Smith, the first Ombudsman to be appointed, is still in office. Prior to his appointment Dr. Smith was President of King's University in Nova Scotia and prior to that had been a Professor of French. The powers of the Nova Scotian Ombudsman are similar to those of the Ombudsman in the other provinces, except that he has always had power to investigate complaints against local authorities. Dr. Smith, like several of his other Canadian colleagues, has been active in making the facilities of his office known to the general public. For example, in 1974 he put an advertisement in all the Nova Scotia newspapers in which he asked readers: 'Do you have a complaint against the administration of the laws of Nova Scotia (provincial and municipal)?' He then repeated the notice three weeks later in the same newspapers.[1]

Nova Scotia has a population of 813,000 and Newfoundland 522,104. Newfoundland originally passed legislation setting up an Ombudsman in 1970, but the law was not put into effect until 1975. Ambrose Peddle, who was appointed Ombudsman, was a business man who had formerly represented a Newfoundland constituency in the Federal Parliament as a Conservative. His powers are similar to those of the other provincial Ombudsman.

Only two provinces in Canada have yet to appoint an Ombudsman. These are British Columbia which has a population of 2,184,621 and Prince Edward Island whose population is only 111,641.

[1] *Fourth Annual Report of the Ombudsman for Nova Scotia* (Halifax, 1974), p. 7.

Legislation is currently in passage in British Columbia to establish an Ombudsman. It seems probable, therefore, that by the end of 1977 all except for the 100,000 or so Canadians who live in Prince Edward Island, and the inhabitants of the remote territories like the North West Territory and the Yukon, will be able to complain to an Ombudsman about the actions or omissions of provincial departments and agencies.

The Canadian provincial Ombudsmen have basically similar powers. All their statutes are modelled on the New Zealand Ombudsman statute and the detailed differences between the statutes are less important than the similarities. The main difference is in the power to investigate complaints against local authorities which is possessed by the Nova Scotia and New Brunswick Ombudsmen but not, at present, by any of the other provincial Ombudsmen.

The people who have served, or are serving, as Ombudsmen have had a variety of former occupations. Eight had a legal background. But among these eight lawyers there are some interesting subdivisions. Two were formerly university teachers of law: Dr. Marceau and Miss Patenaude (Quebec). Two were former judges: Mr. Boychuk (Saskatchewan) and Mr. Bérubé (New Brunswick). Two had been lawyers in private practice: Charles Léger and George McAllister (New Brunswick). One had been a lawyer in private practice, but had also been a parliamentarian: Arthur Maloney (Ontario). One had been a lawyer in provincial government service: David Tickell (Saskatchewan). One was a business man but had also been a parliamentarian: Ambrose Peddle (Newfoundland). Two had been clergymen: Mr. Flemington (New Brunswick) and Dr. Ivany (Alberta). Two were formerly senior police officers: George McClelland (Alberta) and George Maltby (Manitoba). One had been the head of a university and a Professor of French: Dr. Harry Smith (Nova Scotia).

Only one of the Ombudsmen, therefore, was serving as a provincial government official when he was appointed Ombudsman. Their staffs have a similarly varied background. Some have served in provincial departments, but they by no means predominate. Many, but by no means all, the provincial Ombudsmen are legally qualified. Those who are not legally qualified have legal advisers, either on their staffs or in private practice.

All the provincial Ombudsmen are aware of the need to secure publicity for their activities and for the service they can provide. All have a reasonably high case-load in relation to the populations they serve. In the paper which he prepared for the International Ombudsmen Conference at Edmonton in 1976, Karl Friedmann compared the number of complaints received annually by the Ombudsmen in Alberta, New Brunswick, Quebec, Manitoba, Nova Scotia, and Saskatchewan. Until 1974 the Quebec Public Protector had much the highest case-load in terms of complaints received. For example, in 1973 he received 87·5 complaints per 100,000 population. The next highest case-loads were experienced by the Saskatchewan and Alberta Ombudsmen who received 59·7 and 46·1 complaints respectively per 100,000 population.[1] But in 1974 the flow of complaints, outside Quebec province, increased markedly. In 1974 the Nova Scotia Ombudsman received 114·5 complaints per 100,000 population, the New Brunswick Ombudsman 94·7, the Saskatchewan Ombudsman 88·5, the Manitoba Ombudsman 63·4, and the Alberta Ombudsman 54·4. The Quebec Ombudsman in 1974 received 86·5 complaints per 100,000 population.

Dr. Friedmann attributed this increased volume of complaints partly to the efforts made by Ombudsmen to publicize their activities. We saw, for example, that it was in 1974 that Dr. Smith ran a systematic advertising campaign in Nova Scotia. But more important, in Dr. Friedmann's view, was the effect of the Canadian Broadcasting Commission's programme 'Ombudsman'.[2] This programme was networked throughout Canada, except in Quebec. It was one of the three most popular TV shows put out by the Canadian Broadcasting Commission with an audience rating of almost one and a half million viewers. Since the volume of complaints remained stable in Quebec, where the programme was not seen, and rose in the provinces where the programme was shown, in some cases dramatically, he suggested that it had a significant effect in increasing public interest in the Ombudsman idea. There is no doubt that the provincial Ombudsmen in Canada are becoming widely known and that they are readily accessible to the public.

[1] Karl A. Friedmann, 'Canadian Ombudsmen' (Cyclostyled paper prepared for the International Ombudsman Conference, Edmonton, Alberta, Sept. 1976), Table 8.

[2] Ibid., pp. 21–2 and see above, p. 81.

VI

THE FRENCH MÉDIATEUR

THE office of Médiateur in France was set up by the law of 2 January 1973. It was to many British observers a surprising development, particularly to critics of the Ombudsman idea who argued that a well-developed system of administrative justice provided more effective redress for the citizen against public authorities than could be provided by an Ombudsman. Since France, with its Conseil d'État and subordinate tribunaux administratifs, had the most admired system of administrative courts in the world, it was surprising to find that the French Parliament had decided to set up an Ombudsman to complement the work of the Conseil d'État. One possible hypothesis was that the Médiateur was merely a piece of window-dressing and did not have an effective role. But experience has shown that this is far from being the case.

Another interesting feature of the office of Médiateur is that he is only the second Ombudsman concerned with civil affairs to be established in an advanced European country with a large population. The Parliamentary Commissioner in the United Kingdom was the first and the authors of the law of January 1973 in France consciously drew upon British, as well as Scandinavian, experience in planning the office of Médiateur. They decided that, as in Britain, the Ombudsman would not be accessible directly to the aggrieved citizen. The law of 1973 provides that the Médiateur must be approached through a Member of either House of Parliament, the National Assembly or the Senate. Here, of course, is a difference from the United Kingdom where the Parliamentary Commissioner can only be approached through a Member of the House of Commons. The Whyatt Report of 1961 had proposed that Members of the House of Lords should also be a channel of complaint to the Parliamentary Commissioner, but this suggestion had been turned down by the Wilson Government because of the non-elective character of the House of Lords. Since the Senate in France is indirectly elected, by electoral colleges consisting of local councillors and parliamentarians, there is a stronger case for making Senators a channel of complaint to the Médiateur.

In most other respects the Médiateur is very different from the Parliamentary Commissioner. He is not limited to investigating maladministration and his jurisdiction is much wider. His role in investigations is also considerably different from that of the Parliamentary Commissioner, drawing upon different methods and principles of inspection and investigation in French administration.

The law setting up the Médiateur was initiated by the Government of M. Messmer, who was then Premier, during the presidency of Georges Pompidou. The law was a response to a considerable campaign extending over more than nine years for improved machinery for the protection of individual liberty and protection against administrative abuse. M. Antoine Pinay, who was the first Médiateur to be appointed, had himself introduced a Private Member's bill on the liberties of the subject in 1964 which was not enacted. Other initiatives which were not followed up included a proposal in 1972 by M. Poniatowski for a High Commissariat for Defence of the Rights of Man, and in the same year a Socialist deputy, M. Chandernagor, proposed a Parliamentary Delegate for Liberty (Délégué parlementaire à la liberté). Also in 1972 the Senate decided to send a commission of Senators to interview Ombudsmen in Scandinavia. A number of infringements of liberty in France at this time by public authorities fuelled the fire of the campaign. There was, for example, considerable public concern about the use of police powers and the forcible repatriation of a foreign journalist. All these factors helped to induce the Pompidou–Messmer Government to initiate the reform.

The law provides that the Médiateur is appointed by decree of the Council of Ministers for a six-year term. He cannot be re-appointed. The provision for nomination by the Government of the day was criticized by the opposition during passage of the law. They argued that the Médiateur should be nominated by Parliament. But although appointed by the Government, he can only be removed from office for incapacity or impediment as defined by the Conseil d'État. The words used in the law are 'en cas d'empêchement constaté dans des conditions définies par décret en Conseil d'Etat'.[1] He is therefore guaranteed a degree of independence of

[1] Loi numéro 73–6 du 3 janvier 1973 instituant un médiateur, Art. 2 (hereafter referred to as 'law of 1973'.)

the Government. The law also provides that the Government cannot give him instructions. 'Dans la limite de ses attributions, il ne reçoit d'instruction d'aucune autorité'. This also is an important guarantee of his independence.

The Médiateur's jurisdiction is very wide since the law provides that he can investigate complaints about 'le fonctionnement des administrations de l'Etat, des collectivités publiques territoriales, des établissements publics et de tout autre organisme investi d'une mission de service public'.[1] This means that he is concerned with all departments of the central government, all local authority functions, and the nationalized industries where they are monopolies. Thus the railways and the electricity and gas authorities are within his jurisdiction, but Air France and the Renault car works are not, although they are publicly owned, because they compete with private concerns.

The Médiateur cannot consider complaints from serving civil servants, or other state employees against public authorities in their role as employers.[2] This restriction is strictly comparable to the provision in the Parliamentary Commissioner Act, 1967, under which the Parliamentary Commissioner may not consider complaints in personnel matters from civil servants. The French civil servant has two main avenues of complaint in personnel matters. First, he can take his case to the Conseil d'État or to a tribunal administratif, and many civil servants (including teachers) use these channels. Second, they also make considerable use of their trade unions to take up a case with the Ministry. The Médiateur similarly cannot consider a complaint by a serviceman against the service authorities but, as in Britain, he can consider a complaint from a member of the public against one of the armed services, for example when a householder complains that a wall of his house has been damaged by an army tank.

In other respects, however, there are few limitations on the Médiateur's sphere of investigation comparable to those placed on the Parliamentary Commissioner. Where there are limitations they tend to be less extensive than in Britain. Thus the Médiateur cannot consider complaints in cases which have already been to the courts

[1] Ibid., Art. 1.

[2] Since December 1976 retired civil servants have been able to complain to the Médiateur in Civil Service personnel matters. See loi numéro 76–1211 du 24 décembre 1976 complétant la loi numéro 73–6 du 3 janvier 1973 instituant un médiateur, Art. 2 (hereafter referred to as 'law of December 1976'.)

or to administrative tribunals, neither can he consider a complaint about a decision of a court or tribunal.[1] But he can consider complaints which could go to the courts or to administrative tribunals. Here he has more freedom than the Parliamentary Commissioner who is instructed by the 1967 Act not to investigate a complaint which could go to a court or a tribunal, unless he is satisfied that it would not have been reasonable, in the circumstances, for a complainant to go to a court or administrative tribunal.

In some respects, however, the Médiateur is more restricted than the Parliamentary Commissioner. Originally he could only examine complaints made by individuals; he could not consider complaints from corporate bodies or associations which the Parliamentary Commissioner is empowered to do. The law establishing a Médiateur provides that he can investigate complaints from 'toute personne physique'.[2] In French law, 'une personne physique', an individual, is sharply distinguished from 'une personne morale', which is a group of people. The Parliamentary Commissioner, by contrast, can examine a complaint from an individual or from 'any body of persons whether incorporated or not' so long as they are not a local authority or other public authority. Thus he can examine complaints from private firms, trade unions, or other organized groups, but he cannot examine complaints from local authorities, nationalized industries, or any kind of government department or agency.[3] However, the law of December 1976, modifying the law of 1973, provides that a corporate body ('une personne morale') can complain to the Médiateur, if that complaint is presented by an individual ('une personne physique') who is himself directly concerned in the matter about which the complaint is made (see law of December 1976, Art. 1).

The Médiateur is also more limited than the Parliamentary Commissioner in that he can only consider a complaint after it has been taken to the relevant government authority. Article 7 provides: 'La réclamation doit être précédeé des démarches nécessaires auprès des administrations intéressées.' The Parliamentary Commissioner is not so limited.

On the question of discovery of documents, the Médiateur has

[1] The law of December 1976 provides that although the Médiateur cannot intervene in a judicial process or call into question a judicial decision, he can make recommendations to the judicial body concerned. See law of December 1976, Art. 4.

[2] Law of 1973, Art. 6.

[3] Parliamentary Commissioner Act, 1967, Sect. 6–(1).

powers almost as wide as those of the Parliamentary Commissioner. He can require the production of all departmental files and documents except for secret documents which concern national defence, the safety of the state, or foreign affairs. The Parliamentary Commissioner must be shown all documents but a Minister can instruct him not to reveal the contents of a document where, in the Minister's opinion, disclosure of the document 'would be prejudicial to the safety of the State or otherwise contrary to the public interest'.[1] Since the Parliamentary Commissioner is also excluded, by provisions in Schedule 3 of the Act, from investigating actions taken in matters relating to foreign affairs or concerned with the security of the state, it would seem there is little difference in practice between the Médiateur's and the Parliamentary Commissioner's powers to examine government documents.

There is, however, a big difference in the terms of reference of the Médiateur and the Parliamentary Commissioner in relation to investigations. The Parliamentary Commissioner investigates complaints made to M.P.s by members of the public who claim 'to have sustained injustice in consequence of maladministration', as a result of an action, or failure to act, by a government department. The Médiateur investigates a complaint that a public authority has not acted in accordance with its mission of public service ('n'a pas fonctionné conformément à la mission de service public qu'il doit assurer').[2] This is a much wider frame of reference than is given to the Parliamentary Commissioner. It is interpreted to mean that the Médiateur can consider not only whether a public authority has acted in a systematically obstructive or hasty manner but also whether it has acted without due equity or humanity. The Médiateur, M. Paquet, himself told me that he is concerned to establish whether there has been 'manque d'équité' or 'manque d'humanité' on the part of the public authority concerned.

It is this wide frame of reference which enables the role of the Médiateur to be clearly distinguished from that of the Conseil d'État, or the tribunaux administratifs. The Conseil d'État and the tribunaux administratifs are concerned with the legality of action taken by public authorities. This is interpreted widely by the Conseil d'État which can rule not only that there has been 'excès de pouvoir' (use of power beyond legal authority) but also 'détourne-

[1] Ibid., Sect. 11–(3).
[2] Law of 1973, Art. 6.

ment de pouvoir' (abuse of power) by a government department or agency. Nevertheless, the Médiateur can go further than the Conseil d'État, and can complement its role, by saying that although a public authority has not acted illegally, it has not acted fairly or with proper humanity. A specific example, even though a very minor one, can illustrate this difference. The Médiateur described in his Annual Report for 1973 a case in which a citizen complained to him that he was being required to pay charges for the supply of water for a house in which he was not living. The authority had replied that the charges must be paid because the complainant had not informed them that he had vacated the house. The complainant had no case in law, but the Médiateur argued that it was not reasonable to require payment of the charges since the authority did not dispute the fact that the house had been standing empty during the period in question.[1]

This wide frame of reference is appropriately matched by power to recommend improvements in administration and legislation. The law of 1973 states, at Article 9, that when the Médiateur finds a complaint is justified, he can not only recommend redress for the individual complainant but also suggest ways in which the administration of the service concerned can be improved. He can also propose changes in legislation where he finds that the law is working inequitably. This power was not mentioned specifically in the 1973 Act and, to ensure greater certainty, the law of December 1976 provides that the Médiateur can propose changes in laws and regulations where he finds they are resulting in injustice.[2]

If, having made his recommendations following an investigation, the Médiateur does not receive a satisfactory reply from the public authority concerned, he can publicize his recommendations in a special report which he sends to the President of the Republic and to Parliament (Articles 9 and 14 of the 1973 Act). He also has another sanction if the authority concerned is not willing to act on his recommendations. He can, under Article 10, invoke a disciplinary procedure against the official concerned or take judicial action against him. The words used in Article 10 say that he can 'engager contre tout agent responsable une procédure disciplinaire ou, le cas échéant saisir d'une plainte la juridiction répressive'.

[1] *Rapport annuel du Médiateur* (Paris, 1973), p. 214.

[2] Law of December 1976, Art. 3.

The Médiateur therefore has powers comparable almost to those of the Swedish Ombudsmen in being able to invoke disiplinary procedures against recalcitrant civil servants. But up until March 1976 he had not had to resort to these procedures on any occasion. Neither had he, on any occasion, had to use his power to issue a special report to the President of the Republic and to Parliament, in addition to his annual report.[1]

The Médiateur's staff in Paris is headed by his Délégué Général. The first Délégué Général was M. Jacques Legrand who held office from 1973 until November 1975. M. Legrand obtained a Doctorate in Law before entering the Civil Service. After a period with the Préfecture of the Seine, and with other préfectures, in both Metropolitan France and Algeria, he served as Directeur of a cabinet du ministre before becoming Directeur Général du Travail et de l'emploi. In the two years in which he served as Délégué Général to the Médiateur he was influential in developing the office of Médiateur and played a major part in drafting his annual reports. In November 1975 he left to become Directeur Général of the Groupe des Industries Métallurgiques de la Région Parisienne. His place as Délégué Général to the Médiateur was then filled by M. Jean Ravail who had been an inspecteur général de l'administration for the preceding six years. He entered the Civil Service in 1947 after studying at the École Nationale d'Administration. His career had included a period as chef de cabinet for the Minister of State in charge of constitutional reform. This was in 1953. He subsequently served in the Secretariats for the Armed Forces, for Public Health and Population, and in the Prime Minister's Secretariat, and for two years (from 1959 to 1961) was Director of Studies at the Institut des Hautes Études de Défense Nationale. The other staff of the Médiateur in his Paris office consist of the Secrétaire Général, and the assistant Secrétaire Général, twelve executive and clerical staff.[2]

The Médiateur therefore has a much smaller full-time staff than the Parliamentary Commissioner. But the law of 1973 provides, at Article 12 that Ministers and all other public authorities must facilitate the task of the Médiateur. They must also instruct the relevant corps de contrôle to undertake investigations on behalf of the Médiateur. The Vice-President of the Conseil d'État and the

[1] *Rapport annuel du Médiateur* (Paris, 1976), p. 179.
[2] *Rapport annuel du Médiateur* (Paris, 1975), pp. 177–8.

President of the Cour des Comptes must also, by law, advise the Médiateur at his request.

This means that the extensive apparatus of inspectorates within the French administrative system, such as the inspecteurs des finances and the inspecteurs des préfectures, is at the disposal of the Médiateur. He has also been able to recruit a part-time specialist staff to his office from among the ranks of senior officials, both retired and still in service. Thus in 1975 he had two chargés de mission, one who was an honorary councillor in the Cour de Cassation (France's equivalent of the Court of Appeal) and was concerned with questions of justice, the other, an honourary inspector-general of social security, with social security questions. In addition, he had as technical advisers (counseillers techniques) an inspecteur général civil from the Ministry of Finance, (for social security questions), a sous-préfet who is chargé de mission at the Ministry for Foreign Affairs (for foreign affairs, repatriated persons, agriculture, and industry), a maître des requêtes at the Conseil d'État (for 'l'équipement' and the quality of life), and a retired director of taxes (for tax questions).[1] The Médiateur has one regional office. This is at Grenoble where the staff consists of a chargé de mission and a technical counsellor (both part-time) and three secretaries, one of whom is part-time.

Two men have so far held the office of Médiateur and both were formerly parliamentarians. Antoine Pinay, the first Médiateur to be appointed, had been Minister of Finance from 1958 to 1960 in the governments formed by De Gaulle after the 1958 crisis. Pinay was born in 1891 and was therefore eighty-two when appointed Médiateur in 1973. Two things, however, told strongly in his favour. In the Fourth Republic he had won a great reputation and esteem as Prime Minister when he 'saved the franc' and put French finances on a sound footing after a period of severe inflation. Second, he had campaigned for better safeguards for the individual against the administration.

Pinay resigned in 1974 and was succeeded by Aimé Paquet who, like Pinay, had been a leading member of the group of Republican Independents in the National Assembly. Paquet had in fact been

[1] *Rapport annuel du Médiateur* (1975), p. 178. Note the French concept of 'l'équipement' has no exact, or close, equivalent in English. In practice, many of the services which are grouped under the heading of 'l'équipement' in France would in Britain be the concern of the Department of the Environment.

President of the group, which stands on the right of centre in politics, since 1969. He was a Deputy for Isère from 1951 to 1974, serving as a junior Minister in the 1960s. He is a farmer and was mayor of the little town near Grenoble where he lives, Saint-Vincent de Mercuze, from 1947 to 1974. He was born in 1913 and was therefore sixty-one on taking office as Médiateur. Both Pinay and Paquet are members of the coalition of Gaullists and Independent Republicans which has held power since 1958.

France is not altogether exceptional in appointing parliamentarians to serve as Ombudsmen. The *Land* of Rhineland-Pfalz in the Federal Republic of Germany appointed, in 1974, as its first Ombudsman, Dr. Johannes Baptist Rösler who was at that time President of the Land Assembly and head of its Petitions Committee. But this is a special case since in Rhineland-Pfalz the office of Ombudsman is associated with the Petitions Committee.

The reasoning behind the decision to choose parliamentarians for the office of Médiateur, at least in the first stages of the office, seems to have been based on the following considerations. A civil servant would not be appropriate because the Médiateur's function would be to investigate the actions of civil servants and he would be able to call on the aid of senior civil servants, members of the corps de contrôle, as well as having civil servants on his staff. It was not essential to have a lawyer; since a high proportion of senior civil servants have law degrees he would not be lacking in legal advice. Therefore it was argued that it would be appropriate for him to be a parliamentarian, particularly since access to him would only be through Deputies or Senators.

Table IX analyses the cases submitted to the Médiateur by Deputies and Senators, and the cases investigated by him, in the first three years of the office of Médiateur, 1973, 1974, and 1975. The final column permits comparison with the Parliamentary Commissioner's performance. When we compare the records of the Médiateur and the Parliamentary Commissioner in 1975, we find that the Médiateur received more than three times the number of complaints from Deputies and Senators that the Parliamentary Commissioner received from M.P.s. The Médiateur received 3,150 complaints from parliamentarians (2,746 from Deputies and 404 from Senators) while the Parliamentary Commissioner received only 928 complaints from M.P.s.

We also see that there was a big rise in the number of complaints submitted to the Médiateur between 1974 and 1975, from 1,659 to 3,150 cases, while between 1973 and 1974 there had been a small decline, from 1,773 to 1,659 cases. Both these changes require explanation. The decline between 1973 and 1974 is partly explained by a long postal strike in 1974 which considerably interfered with the flow of complaints from citizens to their Deputies and Senators. The big increase in the number of complaints received between 1974 and 1975 is largely to be explained by a systematic campaign to secure greater publicity for the office of Médiateur begun by M. Paquet in 1974 and continued in 1975. This campaign took four principal forms. First, the Médiateur's office produced a brochure summarizing the contents of his Annual Report for 1974. The brochure, which appeared under the title *La Mission du Médiateur.*

TABLE IX
The French Médiateur, 1973–1975

	French Médiateur			U.K. Parliamentary Commissioner in 1975	
	1973	1974	1975		
Cases submitted by Deputies	1,597	1,489	2,746	928	Complaints received through M.P.s
Cases submitted by Senators	176	182	404		Peers not a channel
Total of cases submitted by parliamentarians	1,773	1,659	3,150	928	
Outside jurisdiction (irrecevables)	564	507	915	576	Outside jurisdiction
Investigations abandoned	53	19	52	19	Investigations discontinued
Investigations completed	469	876	1,074	244	Investigations completed
Redress secured (Réclamations satisfaites)	70	162	245	90	Cases where maladministration leading to injustice was found
Redress partially secured (Réclamations partiellement satisfaites)	112	170	165		

Source: Médiateur's Annual Reports for 1973, 1974, and 1975. H.C. 141 of 1975–6. Second Report of the Parliamentary Commissioner for Administration, Annual Report for 1975.

Ses activités en 1974, was attractively designed. On the first page, under photographs of the first two Médiateurs to hold office, MM. Pinay and Paquet, the origin, history, and scope of the office were succinctly set out. There followed a section on the functioning of the office which opened with the following words (freely translated): 'To humanize relations between the public and an Administration which has become more and more opaque and complicated: to secure respect for the rule, when decisions have tended to stray away from it, or simply to soften the effects of a regulation in the name of equity; to uncover and eliminate cases of "maladministration" which are as damaging to the public image of the Administration as they are frustrating for the victims of "maladministration": such are the tasks of the Médiateur and of his services.' The rest of the brochure continued in a similar way explaining in straightforward but effective terms the role and activities of the Médiateur. This brochure was given a wide circulation.

Second, the Médiateur established and has maintained links with the national and regional press and with radio and television. He took part in several radio and television programmes in order to get his office known as widely as possible. Third, he commissioned an opinion poll to try to find out how widely known he was, and how he could best increase public knowledge of his work. Fourth, he made a series of visits to regional centres, going to Lyons, Rennes, Marseilles, Metz, Bordeaux, Strasburg, Clermont-Ferrand, Dijon, Montpellier, and Poitiers. There he met préfets, parliamentarians, presidents of chambers of commerce, industry, and agriculture, bodies concerned with regional development, representatives of trade unions and voluntary associations, and the press. He was concerned in all these meetings to give information about the scope and working of his office, and to acquire information about the impact he was or was not making in different sectors.[1] The results of these initiatives have clearly been quite striking. But the Médiateur is fully aware that he needs to apply continuing effort to secure more publicity and, in his own phrase, to reduce the gap between the public perception of the Médiateur and the potentialities of his office.

The restriction of public access to him by requiring citizens to go through Deputies or Senators must anyway reduce the number of complaints examined. The 1,074 cases which he investigated in 1975 must be compared not only with the 244 cases which the Parliamentary Commissioner investigated in 1975 but also with the 2,293 cases which were investigated by the Swedish Ombudsmen in 1975. All Ombudsmen have a problem in making themselves sufficiently known to the public. For the two Ombudsmen whose system does not permit direct access to them by members of the public, the French Médiateur and the British Parliamentary Commissioner, this problem is particularly acute. How then do we

[1] *Rapport annuel du Médiateur* (1975), pp. 185–6.

explain the greater use being made of the French Médiateur by the public than is made of the Parliamentary Commissioner by citizens in the United Kingdom although the population of the United Kingdom is somewhat larger than that of France? The population of the United Kingdom, at the 1971 census, was 55,514,603. The estimated population of France in 1973 was 51,921,400.

One possible explanation lies in the much wider jurisdiction enjoyed by the Médiateur. Since all spheres of administration, both central and local, except foreign affairs and the security of the state, come within the jurisdiction of the Médiateur, it is far less difficult for the citizen, or for the Deputy or Senator, to work out whether a grievance is or is not a question which the Médiateur will be able to investigate. Again, since his frame of reference is so much wider than that of the Parliamentary Commissioner, in that he can report on the failure of a public authority to act with humanity or equity, it is easier to predict whether a case will come within his remit than it is to predict whether or not a complaint to the Parliamentary Commissioner will reveal 'injustice in consequence of maladministration'. Another obvious contrast is provided by the active measures being taken by the Médiateur to win publicity for his office and the relative shunning of publicity which characterized the tenure of the office as Parliamentary Commissioner of Sir Edmund Compton and to a lesser extent of Sir Alan Marre.[1] A further possible explanation is the greater tendency in some parts of France, compared with Britain, for the ordinary citizen to contact his Deputy and use him to pursue a grievance. In Britain nowadays it is assumed that M.P.s will be active constituency members and will spend a great deal of time and energy in taking up constituents' cases. In fact this is a relatively recent development and Earl Attlee deplored the tendency as a diversion of an M.P.s energies from what he saw as the main task of the M.P.: to concern himself with national issues and problems. In France the practice is much more deep-rooted. J. E. C. Bodley, writing in 1899, commented on the tendency of Frenchmen to lobby their Deputies and to expect them to achieve almost anything from the administration, even, on occasion, attempting to enlist their aid to persuade university professors to allow their sons to pass university examinations.[2] This tradition

[1] See below, pp. 142–50.

[2] J. E. C. Bodley, *France* (Macmillan, 2nd edn. 1899), p. 363.

continues unabated in certain parts of France. There is a marked difference, as Table X shows, between south-eastern France and the north-east and north-west in the volume of cases submitted to the Médiateur. In the Provincc–Cote-d'Azur region (which incorporates 6 départements) there were 349 cases submitted to the Médiateur in 1975. In the same year in the Rhone–Alpes region (which includes 8 départements) no less than 801 cases were sent to him by Deputies and Senators. On the other hand, from Alsace (which includes 2 départements) only 34 cases were sent to him in 1975. Similarly, only 31 cases came from Basse–Normandie (3 départements) and only 33 cases from Haute–Normandie (2 départements). Since it is known that in Provence and in the south-east there is a lively tradition of 'pressuring' Deputies by the public, it seems reasonable to conclude that the much higher volume of complaints reaching the Médiateur from those regions largely results from the more vigorous and continuing ties between the citizen and his Deputy than in the less 'radical' regions of Alsace and Normandy. M. Paquet himself explained the contrast to me in terms of the activist tradition and temperament in the south-east compared with the phlegmatic temperament in Alsace. Certainly, it is most unlikely that the explanation for the great difference in the volume of complaints from these regions is to be found in a less efficient standard of administration in the south-east. It seems much more likely that it lies in differing temperaments and political attitudes. In the table, Paris and the Paris region have been included for comparison. Although the concentration of population there is high, the volume of complaints from Paris and the Paris region (486 in 1975) is not particularly high. The figures for the selected regions are also given for the two-year period 1973 to 1974. They provide a strong contrast in the earlier years, as in 1975, between the south-east regions on the one hand and the north-west and north-east on the other.

M. Paquet told me that relations between the Médiateur and parliamentarians have always been very good. As Table IX shows, a much smaller proportion of cases are submitted to him by Senators than by Deputies, but he told me that the cases sent by Senators are often well supported. In his letter forwarding a complaint, a Senator will often show a better knowledge of the work of the Médiateur than is shown by the average Deputy. He may well, for example, refer to cases which the Médiateur has described in one of his annual reports. This greater knowledge is thought in the Médiateur's office to reflect the by and large greater ability and calibre of Senators. It may also be connected with the lower pressure of parliamentary work in the Senate.

TABLE X

Complaints to the Médiateur submitted by Deputies and Senators in selected regions

	1973 and 1974 (two-year period)	1975
Provence–Cote-d'Azur (6 départements)	411	349
Rhone–Alpes (8 départements)	497	801
Alsace (2 départements)	61	34
Basse–Normandie (3 départements)	43	31
Haute–Normandie (2 départements)	39	33
Ville de Paris	274	208
Région parisienne (7 départements)	406	278

Source: Médiateur's Annual Reports for 1974 and 1975.

Relations between the Médiateur and senior civil servants, including members of the Conseil d'État, were in the early stages of the office decidedly cool. Civil servants in the departments were fearful of what the Médiateur might attempt to do and members of the Conseil d'État saw him as a rival. But before long, relations with both civil servants and the Conseil d'État improved a great deal. Civil servants saw some of the benefits which the Médiateur could bring in proposing improvements in the service, and the Conseil d'État began to provide, and continues to provide, help and advice to the Médiateur.

We have noted the ways in which the law of 1973 provides that all public authorities must assist the Médiateur and put their own investigating staff at his disposal. It is appropriate at this point to discuss the way in which the Médiateur goes about investigating a complaint. The Médiateur has himself described the procedures followed in his office for dealing with complaints in his Annual Report for 1974.[1] The following account derives largely from his

[1] *Rapport annuel du Médiateur* (Paris, 1974), pp. 16–18.

1974 Report, although it is supplemented with material from my own interview with M. Paquet and his Délégué Général, M. Legrand. When a complaint arrives at the Médiateur's office a dossier is opened in the name of the complainant and the parliamentarian forwarding the complaint. The dossier is then immediately transferred to the Médiateur's section d'instruction. This consists of four assistants to the Médiateur, all of whom are lawyers. Each of three of these assistants is allotted one of the three main sectors of government: social affairs, the environment, taxes and pensions. The fourth assistant deals with complaints against all other public services.

The assistant in charge of the dossier in the section d'instruction makes a preliminary study of the case, in order to decide whether it comes within the jurisdiction of the Médiateur. Sometimes, but not always, the complaint has already been studied, at the request of the parliamentarian forwarding the complaint, by members of the staff of the National Assembly or the Senate and any such study is available to the assistant.

If after this preliminary study it appears that the complaint does not fall within the competence of the Médiateur, the parliamentarian concerned is informed of this decision. If the complaint nevertheless appears to raise a considerable problem of general interest, the dossier is sent to the relevant Ministry so that it can study the question. Similarly, the dossier might be sent to one of the Users' Committees (Comités d'Usagers) which were set up in 1974 alongside each of the seventeen Ministries or State Secretariats. Each one of these Committees, consisting of representatives of those using the service concerned, is presided over by a parliamentarian and has the function of making known the views of interested parties and proposing improved procedures which would humanize the relationship between the citizen and the Administration. The Médiateur reported in 1975 that he had actively co-operated with these Users' Committees not only by sending them dossiers of cases where he did not have competence but in which the Committee might be able to propose reforms, but also by informing them of improved procedures which he had recommended as a result of investigations he had completed. The Committees had taken up a number of the reforms he had suggested and urged them upon the Government.[1]

[1] *Rapport annuel du Médiateur* (1975), pp. 186–7.

If the assistant finds that the complaint does come within the competence of the Médiateur, he informs the parliamentarian that the complaint is being investigated. At this stage, he satisfies himself that the dossier is complete. If some of the necessary information is lacking he will ask the parliamentarian whether he can obtain further material from the complainant, or the Médiateur's staff may themselves contact the complainant by telephone, or may, for example, ask an inspector or judge to visit the complainant and try to secure the necessary additional information.

When the dossier is complete the assistant draws up a detailed memorandum setting out the facts and highlighting the issues on which the complainant contests the Ministry's decision. The assistant then sends this memorandum to the Médiateur's 'correspondant' in the Ministry concerned. Each Ministry has designated a 'correspondant' to the Médiateur. The 'correspondant' is a member either of the Minister's 'cabinet' (this is a small, high-powered personal staff advising the Minister: there is no exact parallel in the British system although there has been increased use of personal advisers by Ministers in Britain in recent years) or of the corps de contrôle of the Ministry. The inspection générale des affaires sociales, which is one of the authorities against which a great many of the complaints to the Médiateur are directed, has set up a more elaborate organization to correspond with the Médiateur. They have established a cell (cellule), drawn from members of the Inspectorate and from an independent secretariat, to correspond with the Médiateur and commission the inquiries which his cases necessitate. Two other Ministries which are main clients of the Médiateur, the Ministère de l'Équipement and the Ministère de l'Économie et des Finances, have set up similar machinery.[1]

Several Ministries have additonal 'correspondants' who liaise with the Médiateur's technical adviser when the Médiateur has found, as a result of his investigations, that complainants have not been able to secure redress because the rules currently in operation ('la réglementation en vigueur') do not permit it. These 'correspondants' work out with the Médiateur's technical adviser what changes in the rules could be adopted in order to enable redress in similar cases in the future.[2]

After a delay which, in the Médiateur's own words, may be from

[1] *Rapport annuel du Médiateur* (1974), p. 15.
[2] Ibid., p. 16.

some weeks to two months, according to the complexity of the dossier and the diligence of the authority concerned in dealing with it (sometimes, he notes, the delay is even longer despite pressure from the Médiateur), the Médiateur receives an answer to the questions he has posed. The reply will normally consist of a critique ('une analyse critique') of the complaint and a statement of the departmental position. It should also provide the necessary background information to enable the Médiateur to see how far the complaint is a valid one. It may also include possible courses of action, in the Ministry, for improving administration of the service if this has been shown to be defective, or for modifying the regulations.

The Médiateur notes here that there is no formal requirement for a particular kind of reply from the Ministry. It may take the form, according to the decision of the 'correspondant', of a technical memorandum, a note signed by him, or a letter signed by the Minister. What the Médiateur does consider essential is that the note should reply, precisely and completely, to the arguments put forward by the complainant.

If it does not do this to the Médiateur's satisfaction, the 'correspondant' is telephoned or interviewed to try and secure further information. If necessary, any of the following additional courses of action may be taken by the Médiateur. He may make inquiries from other government departments. He may ask the Conseil d'État, or the Cour des Comptes, to study the question and advise him. He may ask a corps de contrôle to undertake an inquiry. Only when the Médiateur is able, in view of all the information and advice collected, to come to a clear opinion on the validity ('le bien-fonde') of the complaint is the 'instruction' considered complete.

If the Administration's arguments appear well founded, the Médiateur writes to the parliamentarian concerned saying that the complaint is rejected, but he also provides all the necessary information to explain the nature of the problem; information which is often unknown to the complainant. If, on the other hand, the complainant seems to have had right on his side and to have been a victim of malfunctioning of the service, the Médiateur tells us that it is rare for the Administration not to join with him in devising means through which redress can be provided for the complainant. If the Administration, however, is reluctant to recognize the rights of the complainant, and if the Médiateur cannot persuade it to do so, then he can make a recommendation. He rarely has to do so and when he has made a recommendation it has always, up until now, produced a satisfactory result. He has not had to resort to the further sanctions provided by law of making a special report to Parliament, and the President of the Republic, or invoking disciplinary action against the civil servant concerned.[1]

The Médiateur noted in his 1973 and 1974 Reports that, in the majority of cases, the complainant is objecting to a regulation or is asking for the retrospective application of a new and more favourable regulation which was not in force at the time of the decision he was complaining about. In neither case can the Médiateur secure redress for the complainant. But where he considers that there is an anomaly in a regulation he can, and does, attempt to secure, with the co-operation of the authority concerned, an improvement in the regulation.

The procedure so far described is the normal procedure for a complaint against a Ministry or other national authority. When the complaint is against a local authority, the Médiateur normally uses a different procedure which he calls the preliminary inquiries ('pré-enquêtes') procedure. The inspecteur général de l'administration, chargé de mission with the Médiateur, is entrusted with these preliminary inquiries. The inspecteur général often asks the Préfet for the département or region concerned to study the dossier and bring together, if appropriate, the complainant and the representative of the local authority against which he is complaining, or, if this is not appropriate, to establish exactly what is the position of both sides.

The Médiateur has found that this system in general has good results. The Préfets usually produce their reports for the Médiateur more quickly than 'correspondants' in the Ministries do. They also give their reasoned opinion about the case and may, and sometimes do, ask for advice from the regional tribunal administratif. (The tribunaux administratifs, at regional level, form the base of the pyramid of French administrative justice of which the Conseil d'État is the summit.) The Médiateur pointed out in his Report for 1974 that since the members of the tribunaux administratifs are experienced administrators, as well as experienced lawyers, they can often give good advice on questions of administration as well as being able to advise on the law.[2]

[1] See above, p. 97.

[2] *Rapport annuel du Médiateur* (1974), p. 19.

The preliminary inquiry may not, however, produce a resolution of the complaint at local level. If it does not, the Médiateur continues with the normal procedure which we have already described. The findings of the preliminary inquiry are placed in the dossier and a memorandum on the complaint is sent to the 'correspondant' in the central Ministry which has final responsibility for the local service against which the complaint was lodged.[1]

The Médiateur has himself, on occasion, undertaken one of these local inquiries. For example, in his Annual Report for 1975 he described how he had himself visited the locality where a complainant had alleged that the public inquiries into objections to a new road development had been held at Easter and during the summer holidays, in order to minimize the opportunity to register objections. The Médiateur found that the first inquiry had been held near Easter, but a number of objections had been made then. The second inquiry had been held in September and not in the summer holidays as the complainant had maintained.[2]

The Médiateur also instigates a preliminary inquiry in cases where a complaint is made to him against the administration of justice at local level. He has the assistance of a retired judge who scrutinizes such complaints and, where appropriate, asks for the advice of the Procureur Général of the court for the locality in which the complainant is living. The retired judge, or the Procureur, then assembles all the material necessary for the case and, in most instances, also interviews the complainant. He then reports to the Médiateur.

The burden of complaint in most of these cases is either that the outcome of a judicial procedure has not been satisfactory, or that proceedings are being so long drawn out and complicated that the complainant is not being fairly treated. The Médiateur is not able to investigate the majority of such cases because the law of 1973 at Article 11 prevents him from intervening in a case which has gone to court or from questioning the validity of a judicial decision. When he informs a complainant that he cannot investigate, the Médiateur does, however, advise him of his legal rights in the matter, pointing out, for example, if he has another course of appeal in law.

[1] Central Ministries in France have a much closer control over local authorities than the equivalent British Ministries do. Indeed, in law and practice, the central Ministries exercise a continuous surveillance (tutelle) over local authorities.

[2] *Rapport annuel du Médiateur* (1975), p. 183.

When the complaint is about the preparation of a case before the judicial process has begun, the Médiateur is not excluded by Article 11 of the law from investigating. The Médiateur pointed out in his Report for 1974 that he can intervene, either during the preparatory phase or on the completion of the preparatory phase, before the case goes to court, to see that the administration of justice is properly carried on and the interests of the parties are safeguarded.[1] If the complaint is that an individual has been denied legal aid, the Médiateur can ask the Procureur Général to study the possibility of an appeal against this decision. The Procureur Général can also intervene to speed up the preliminary procedures in a case, and here also the Médiateur can prompt his intervention.

What impact is the Médiateur having on the French administrative system? The Médiateur has been himself particularly concerned to provide answers to this question in his reports. For example, in a chapter of his Report for 1975, entitled 'Les résultats acquis', he discusses under three headings: A. the redress of grievances he has been able to secure for individual complainants, B. the improvements he has been able to bring about in the functioning of services, and C. the improvements he has suggested in regulations and legislation.[2]

Under the first heading he points out that the most frequent kind of complaint with which he deals does not arise from a major malfunctioning of the service or from a defect in departmental regulations. Nevertheless, in many of these straightforward cases he is able to unblock a delay in the consideration of the case ('déblocage d'un dossier en souffrance'), or to bring about the correction of an error in administration, or induce a more flexible attitude towards the complainant's claims.

On the question of delay, he commented in 1975 that there were still numerous delays in the treatment of cases in the social security services, but that administrative delays were a more general phenomenon, and he cited public works and fiscal administration as two areas which were prone to excessive delays. On the correction of administrative errors, and in encouraging departments to modify the rigour of their attitude to complainant's claims, the Médiateur normally finds that the department is prepared to correct a mistake or to consider adopting a more flexible approach. In only a minority

[1] *Rapport annuel du Médiateur* (1974), p. 21.
[2] *Rapport annuel du Médiateur* (1975), pp. 13–23.

of cases, as we have seen, does the Médiateur have to proceed to a formal recommendation. In 1975 he made 17 such recommendations. Of these 17, he noted in his Report for 1975 that 6 had secured favourable action by the department. Ten cases had not yet been resolved, in that either a reply had not yet been received from the department, or the differences of opinion between the Médiateur and the department had not yet produced either agreement or a complete divergence of view. In one case the Médiateur had changed his mind and accepted the department's view after further submissions by the department.

The great majority of cases in which the Médiateur finds for the complainant are dealt with less formally. Table IX shows that in 245 cases redress was secured for the complainant in 1945, and in 165 cases redress was partially secured. If we therefore subtract the 6 cases in which redress was secured after formal recommendation, in that year, we are left with 404 cases in which the Médiateur secured complete or partial redress without resorting to a formal recommendation.

The degree of complexity and the speed with which these 404 cases were dealt will of course have varied very greatly. One of the occasions in which very rapid redress was secured by the Médiateur for a complainant was described in his Report for 1975. A complaint that a young man had been called up for military service, although he had family dependents and was therefore exempt from service, was followed by a telephone call from the Médiateur's staff to the military authorities. As a result, when the young man arrived at the military depot to begin his military service he was informed that there had been a mistake and he could return home.[1]

Under his heading B, the improvements which he has been able to bring about in the functioning of services, the Médiateur listed in his Report for 1975 a number of recommendations he had made which had been acted upon. These included a recommendation that the organization of sittings of the Commission for suspending driving-licences should be improved, so that people summoned to attend should not be kept waiting for long periods. He recommended to the Secretary of State for Posts and Telecommunications improvements in the procedure for connecting new subscribers. He had received complaints about the date from which new subscribers were being required to pay for the costs of connection and also

[1] *Rapport annuel du Médiateur* (1975), p. 179.

about the phrase used, 'taxe de raccordement', which implied, in many cases misleadingly, that new wiring had to be undertaken in order to connect a new subscriber. The Ministry agreed to change the operative date for charges and to give a new title for the charges for connections: 'frais forfaitaires d'accès au réseau'.[1] In a recommendation to the Ministry for the Economy and Finances, he said that it should improve liaison between bureaux within the Ministry in view of his finding that two different bureaux had handled an identical case in a quite different way. The Minister replied that he would take the necessary measures to improve liaison.[2]

Finally, under his section C, improvements he has suggested in regulations and legislation, the Médiateur reviewed the proposals for reform which he and his predecessor had made since the office of Médiateur had been established. During this period (from April 1973 to December 1975) the Médiateur had made 90 proposals for modification of laws or regulations. Of these, 22 had been fully acted on by new legislation or by issuing new regulations. In 7 cases the Médiateur's proposals had been partly acted on, 15 proposals had been deferred, and 46 were still in the course of examination. He then went on to subdivide the 22 cases in which his recommendations had been acted upon. In 12 cases there had been changes in legislation: 7 in the field of Social Affairs, concerned with old-age pensions, maternity rights, handicapped children, orphans, etc.; 2 in the field of Economy and Finances; 1 in Équipement; 1 in Justice, concerned with delays in divorce proceedings; and 1 in Information, on television transmissions and reception. Five of his recommendations were implemented by decrees: 3 in the field of Social Affairs and 2 in Justice. One was implemented by an arrêté issued by the Ministry of the Economy and Finances. This modified, for customs purposes, the conditions under which vehicles registered abroad could be used in France. Three of the Médiateur's recommendations were implemented by the issue of departmental circulars or instructions: 1 in Social Affairs, 1 in Economy and Finances, and 1 was concerned with pensions for relatives of war victims. Of his 7 recommendations which were partly acted upon, 3 were in the field of Social Affairs, 3 in Economy and Finances, and 1 in Équipement.[3]

He notes that where one of his recommendations has only been partially implemented, he retains the right to point out that the

[1] Ibid., p. 17. [2] Ibid. [3] Ibid., pp. 18–23.

modified provision is unsatisfactory, if it does not work out well, and to press for further reform with the department concerned. He also draws attention to the fact that he is now sending copies of his recommendations to the relevant committees of the National Assembly and Senate.[1] Both Houses of the French Parliament have a range of 'departmental' committees whose function it is to scrutinize the activities of a government department or group of departments.

The Médiateur has not limited himself to proposing only detailed changes in legislation. On one subject in his 1975 Report he made proposals for a new law of far-reaching importance. This was a law on the right to information. Both M. Pinay and M. Paquet have emphasized in their reports how frequently they find that the administration is at fault in not providing sufficient information, and sometimes in refusing altogether to provide the information desired by citizens. He instanced, in particular, the difficulties experienced by complainants in obtaining information from official medical records about themselves or their relatives.[2] The Médiateur therefore lent his weight to proposals put forward by the Commission on Co-ordination of Administrative Documentation (Commission de coordination de la documentation administrative). This Commission, which was set up in the Prime Minister's office in November 1971, reported in 1974 in favour of legislation to provide a right of access for the public to government information.[3] But the Médiateur, in his 1975 Report, argued that the proposed new law should go much further than was suggested in the Commission's report. The Commission had proposed that the right of public access should be limited to documents which were general in content, that is documents laying down general lines of policy or instructions. The Médiateur proposed that the law should also give interested persons the right to documents which concerned their particular cases ('aux documents particuliers constituant le dossier de leur affaire').[4]

He summarized the four lines of reform which he considered necessary. In the first place, legislation should recognize, as a matter of general principle, the right of every citizen ('tout administré') to

[1] Ibid., p. 23. [2] Ibid., p. 89.

[3] *La Coordination documentaire. L'Accès du public aux documents administratifs* (La Documentation française, Paris, 1974).

[4] *Rapport annuel du Médiateur* (1975), p. 90.

information from the Government. Second, the system for communicating documents to the citizen should be organized in as liberal a way as possible. Third, in principle, the Administration should be required to give reasons for any decision. Exceptions permitted to the general duty to give reasons should be clearly specified. Fourth, all training programmes for public servants should emphasize the obligation on the part of officials to provide information to the public. The whole experience of his office since 1973, and the instances of poor communication between government departments and the citizen which it revealed, led him to urge upon the public authorities the need to begin reforms such as these as soon as possible.[1]

How should we assess the operation of the office of Médiateur in its first three years? The Médiateur has had no spectacular cases like the Sachsenhausen case which first caused the Parliamentary Commissioner in Britain to be noticed, and helped to convince many British critics of the reform that it had some value. In no comparable case have senior French Ministers denied redress to complainants and then been persuaded to change their decision as did British Ministers in the Sachsenhausen case, after the Parliamentary Commissioner's investigation and the strong support in Parliament and the press for the Commissioner's findings.

The Médiateur himself commented in his 1974 Report, with some surprise, that few of the complaints made to him were to do with individual liberties or with grave abuses in administration.[2] As he pointed out, Article 13 of the Act of 1973 weakens his position, to some extent, in matters of civil liberty because it allows the Administration to refuse access by the Médiateur to secret documents which concern national defence, the safety of the state, and foreign affairs. In fact, people who have complaints against the police, except in such areas as traffic control, go to the courts and not to the Médiateur. Similarly, prisoners mostly prefer to complain to the President of the Republic. The Médiateur has also noted that the complaints which go to him, in all sections of government, are with rare exceptions concerned with the 'small change' of dissatisfaction with government; with complaints about the denial of pension rights or about losses incurred through public works or the operation of planning procedures.

[1] Ibid., p. 92.
[2] *Rapport annuel du Médiateur* (1974), p. 10.

Two points can be made on this observation. First, although no cases concerned with fundamental human rights had reached the Médiateur by 1974, such cases can come to him. Indeed, early in 1976 *The Times* reported that he had secured redress in a minor, although highly emotionally charged, case concerned with human rights affecting a Breton family. The father of the family, M. Le Goarnic, had complained that the secretary of the Mairie in Boulogne-sur-Seine had refused to register the names of his six children, Adraboran, Maiwenn, Gwendal, Diwezha, Sklerijen, and Brann. The secretary contended that these Breton names were not covered by the relevant law, passed during the French Revolution, which stipulated that first names must be taken from one of the recognized calendars.

For a time M. Le Goarnic received no family allowances for his children and even after the Court of Appeal in Rennes ruled in 1962 that he should receive the allowances, no arrears were paid. M. Le Goarnic tried all national and international avenues of appeal in order to get redress, including appeal to the International Court at The Hague which declared itself incompetent in the matter. The case was then submitted to the Médiateur who in January 1976 informed M. and Mme. Le Goarnic that the Minister of Justice had entrusted the public prosecutor at Rennes with the task of 'obtaining a regularization of the official registration of their children'.[1]

The second point which can be made is that all Ombudsmen deal predominantly with the 'small change' of administrative failures. The Parliamentary Commissioner has had his Sachsenhausen but his quarterly reports are full of less exciting cases to do with pension rights, planning procedures, and complaints about unfair treatment of individual firms in the regulation of industry or the operation of grants to certain industrial sectors. All these questions, it should be remembered, are not 'the small change of administrative failure' to the complainant concerned whose sense of grievance and, in many cases, hardship is very real.

What is much more significant about the Médiateur's record is not that he has had no spectacular case but that he has dealt with so many cases and brought either full or partial satisfaction to the complainant in so many cases, compared with the Parliamentary Commissioner. We saw in Table IX that in 1975 the Médiateur

[1] Report in *The Times*, 10 January, 1976.

completed the investigation of 1,074 cases compared with the Parliamentary Commissioner's 244. In that year he secured redress wholly for 245 complainants and partially for 165. This makes a total of 410 cases in which he secured redress which must be compared with the 90 cases in which the Parliamentary Commissioner found elements of maladministration leading to injustice.

The number of complaints investigated is still smaller than it would be in a system which permitted direct access, as our earlier comparison with Sweden and Quebec province has shown. Nevertheless, when the two countries which only permit access to the Ombudsman through parliamentarians, the United Kingdom and France, are compared, the French Médiateur is seen to have by far the greater case-load. This is, as we have seen, partly to be explained by the much greater publicity sought, and achieved, by the Médiateur; his desire to maximize publicity and knowledge of his office is a strong point of the French system. Another factor which promotes more use of the Médiateur compared to the Parliamentary Commissioner is his much wider frame of reference for investigation. His ability to report on a lack of humanity or equity in administration is less inhibiting than the Parliamentary Commissioner's instruction to report on injustice incurred in consequence of maladministration. Finally, the much wider coverage of government agencies is a further explanation of the larger number of cases reaching him and a third advantage which the French Ombudsman system shows over the British.

Table XI compares the complaints received by the Médiateur, ranked by department, for the two years 1973 and 1974, compared with the complaints received by the Parliamentary Commissioner in the same years.[1] In each case, only those complaints which reached the Ombudsman through the recognized channel of a Deputy or Senator, in France, or through an M.P., in the United Kingdom, are included. The figures are for the total number of complaints so received. The Médiateur does not give a breakdown of the complaints received by department indicating the number of complaints in which he did not recommend a change of decision, the number of complaints in which a change of decision was obtained without formal recommendation, and the number of cases in which a formal recommendation was necessary, as in fact is done each

[1] The table gives statistics for 1973 and 1974 as these are the only years for which the Médiateur so far has provided statistics of complaints received by department.

year by the Quebec Public Protector. The Parliamentary Commissioner provides rather more statistical information than the Médiateur does, but he does not provide a complete analysis, by department, of the number of cases in which he found maladministration. Table XI does not therefore permit as useful a comparison as would be possible if the Médiateur and the Parliamentary Commissioner provided as much statistical information as, for example, the Quebec Public Protector does.

TABLE XI

Complaints to the Médiateur and the Parliamentary Commissioner in 1973 and 1974 (ranked by department)*

France		U.K.	
Department	Complaints received by the Médiateur (through Deputies and Senators)	Department	Complaints received by the Parliamentary Commissioner (through M.P.s)
Economy and Finance	794	Health and Social Security	235
Health–Labour	595	Environment	210
Équipement	388	Inland Revenue	184
Interior	307	Trade and Industry (combined Department to April 1974, separate departments thereafter)	92
Defence	211	Defence	48
Justice	201	Home Office	44
Education	179	Employment	33
Agriculture	119	Education	31
Ex-Servicemen	96	Scottish Office	29
Industry and Research	73	Foreign and Commonwealth Office	20
Post and Telecommunications	71	Agriculture	19
Foreign Affairs	63	Customs and Excise	18
Transport	50	Civil Service Department	13

* Departments against which less than 50 complaints were received by the Médiateur and less than 10 complaints by the Parliamentary Commissioner, in the two-year period, are not included.

Source: Compiled from the Médiateur's Table VII in *Rapport annuel du Médiateur, 1974*, p. 270, and from the *Parliamentary Commissioner's Annual Report for 1973* (*H.C. 106 of 1973–4*), pp. 16 and 17, and from his *Annual Report for 1974* (*H.C. 126 of 1974–5*), pp. 16 and 17.

We can, however, make two comments on Table XI. The first is that in every sector of government, except one, the Médiateur receives a much larger volume of complaints than the Parliamentary

Commissioner receives. The one exception is Trade and Industry where in the two years concerned the Parliamentary Commissioner received 92 complaints whereas the Médiateur received 73 complaints against the Department of Industry and Research. The comparison is here anyway probably misleading since many of the functions of the United Kingdom Department of Trade (subsumed in the table under Department of Trade and Industry) are in France exercised by other departments than the Department of Industry and Research.

The second comment we can make is that complaints to the Médiateur were rather more evenly spread over a greater range of departments than were complaints to the Parliamentary Commissioner. Four sectors predominated in these two years in providing cases for the Parliamentary Commissioner: the Department of Health and Social Security, the Department of the Environment, the Inland Revenue, and the Department of Trade and Industry. In France seven sectors of government were important in providing cases for the Médiateur: Economy and Finance, Health and Labour, Équipement, Interior, Defence, Justice, and Education. The other six departments in the table all were concerned with sizeable numbers of complaints, varying from the 119 complaints in Agriculture to the 50 in Transport. Whereas the six departments in the United Kingdom table with the least number of complaints ranged from Education with 31 complaints to the Civil Service Department with 13. The Médiateur's wide coverage of sectors of government is therefore, as we might expect, reflected in this broader spread of complaints received.

Another valuable feature of the Médiateur is his ability to recommend reforms. As we have seen, he has been active in recommending changes in regulations and in legislation as well as in recommending improved procedures and systems. The Parliamentary Commissioner has, from time to time, suggested improved procedures but the first holder of the office, Sir Edmund Compton, did not consider himself empowered to suggest changes in legislation, and only considered that he was able to recommend that a department should revise a departmental rule. His successors have taken a wider interpretation of their powers to recommend changes in regulations and legislation but they are still less active in recommending such changes than the Médiateur is.[1]

[1] See below, pp. 154–61.

There are four respects, therefore, in which a direct comparison between the Médiateur and the Parliamentary Commissioner shows the Médiateur in a more favourable light and indicates ways in which the Parliamentary Commissioner system could be improved. First, the Médiateur has done much more to secure publicity for his office than the Parliamentary Commissioner has done. Second, the Médiateur has a much wider frame of reference for investigating complaints: this makes him more intelligible to the complainant and means that he has a greater chance of securing some redress for the complainant. Third, he has a wider coverage of government agencies than the Parliamentary Commissioner has. Fourth, he is able to recommend changes in legislation, departmental regulations, and administrative procedures and has used these powers with some vigour.

There are some features of the Médiateur's system, however, which, although they seem to work well, could not easily be adapted to British circumstances. Thus the Médiateur's use of the corps de contrôle and of the Conseil d'État could not be paralleled in Britain since they have no British equivalent. There are also some ways in which the Parliamentary Commissioner has advantages over the Médiateur. He clearly has a more important role in relation to Ministers than the Médiateur has and on a number of occasions he has not hesitated to criticize the role of Ministers, for example in the Sachsenhausen and Duccio painting cases and in the Court Line case.[1] Another advantage of the Parliamentary Commissioner system lies in the greater parliamentary backing he receives through the activities of the Select Committee on the Parliamentary Commissioner.

The Médiateur himself is fully aware of the need to develop his office and make it more effective. For example, in his 1974 Report he expressed the view that the initiative in setting up the office of Médiateur had been justified by the results he was obtaining from his investigations, but that these investigations themselves revealed how much remained to be done in providing better redress for the citizen. The initiative had been justified but it was far from having borne all its fruits.[2]

The other necessary development which he has recently emphasized is the need to make his services known to a much wider

[1] See below, pp. 152 et seq.

[2] *Rapport annuel du Médiateur* (1974), p. 12.

section of the population. M. Paquet in his foreword to his Annual Report for 1975 summed up eloquently his conception of the future of the office:

> Demain . . . il reste beaucoup à faire.
> Préserver l'indépendance de l'institution.
> La rendre accessible à tous et d'abord aux plus humbles.
> Aider à adapter, à réformer ce qui doit l'être, surtout lorsque l'application de la Loi conduit à une injustice.
> Œuvrer au service de l'Homme.
> Cela exige beaucoup de patience, de tenacité, de courage et aussi de coeur.[1]

[1] *Rapport annuel du Médiateur* (1975), p. 5. The following is a free translation by the author: 'Tomorrow . . . there is still much to be done. To preserve the independence of the institution. To make it accessible to everyone and above all to the most humble. To help to adapt, to improve, especially when the application of the law leads to injustice. To work in the service of Man. That demands much patience, tenacity, courage, and also compassion.'

VII

THE UNITED KINGDOM: THE PARLIAMENTARY COMMISSIONER FOR ADMINISTRATION

THE Parliamentary Commissioner for Administration in the United Kingdom began to investigate complaints on 1 April 1967. The campaign which eventually led to the passage of the Parliamentary Commissioner Act, and the first four years of the operation of the Act, have been described by the author in *The British Ombudsman.* The account was continued, up to 1973, by Roy Gregory and Peter Hutchesson in their book, *The Parliamentary Ombudsman. A Study in the Control of Administrative Action.* What we shall therefore attempt to do in this chapter is to single out those features of the Parliamentary Commissioner which most distinguish him from the other Ombudsmen we have studied and examine the origins of these differences. We shall also assess the ways in which the office of Parliamentary Commissioner has developed in recent years.

IDEAS WHICH SHAPED THE PARLIAMENTARY COMMISSIONER SYSTEM IN BRITAIN

There were two principal sources from which the ideas which shaped the form of the office of Parliamentary Commissioner were drawn. The first was the report by a committee of 'Justice' published in 1961: *The Citizen and the Administration. The Redress of Grievances* (Stevens, 1961). The second was the experience of operating the office of Comptroller and Auditor-General, carried over into the office of Parliamentary Commissioner, by the first holder of that office, Sir Edmund Compton. Both these sources of influence have proved to be of major importance in shaping the scope and style of the office.

The 'Justice' Committee Report of 1961 is often known as the Whyatt Report since the Director of Research for the Committee was Sir John Whyatt, the former Chief Justice of Singapore. The chairman of the Committee was Norman Marsh who was at that time Director of the British Institute of International and Comparative Law and in 1976 was a member of the Law Commission.[1] The other members of the Committee were Sir Sydney Caine, who was then Director of the London School of Economics, and Dr. H. W. R. Wade, who was at that time a Fellow of Trinity College, Cambridge, and is one of the leading British authorities in administrative law.[2] The Committee's report was approved and published by the Council of 'Justice' which is an influential inter-party group of lawyers, working for reforms which promote the Rule of Law and individual liberties. It is the British Section of the International Commission of Jurists.[3]

It is important to take account of the climate in Britain on issues of this kind when the Whyatt Report was being drafted. The Franks Committee on Administrative Tribunals and Enquiries which reported in 1957 had made extensive proposals for the improvement of tribunal and inquiry procedures, and some of its proposals had been implemented with the passage of the Tribunals and Inquiries Act, 1958. But the Franks Committee had been prevented, by its terms of reference, from considering the wider problem of how more effective machinery could be provided for providing redress for citizens aggrieved by the action of public authorities, where there was no provision for appeal to an administrative tribunal. This led lawyers like F. H. Lawson, Professor of Comparative Law at Oxford University, to take an interest in the Scandinavian institution of the Ombudsman and to consider its relevance for Britain.

It was Professor Lawson's initiative which led 'Justice' to embark on the study which produced the Whyatt Report. But the members of the Committee which drafted the report were very aware that the Conservative Government at that time, headed by Harold Macmillan, was unlikely to implement proposals for a radical reform, setting up, for example, an Ombudsman with powers as

[1] The members of the Law Commission are appointed by the Lord Chancellor under the Law Commissions Act, 1965. Their function is to make proposals for reform of the law to the Lord Chancellor who then reports to Parliament.

[2] H. W. R. Wade was appointed Professor of English Law at Oxford University in 1961. His publications include *Administrative Law* (Clarendon Press, 3rd edn., 1971) and *Towards Administrative Justice* (Ann Arbor, Michigan Univ., 1963).

[3] See Stacey, *The British Ombudsman*, pp. 10–14 for a fuller account of the origins and role of 'Justice.' See also W. B. Gwyn 'Perspectives on Public Policy-Making' in *Tulane Studies in Political Science*, xv, 95–140.

extensive as those of the Swedish Ombudsmen. As a result they consciously shaped their proposals on cautious lines, reasoning that a more moderate reform stood a greater chance of acceptance by the Government of the day than a more radical reform.

They therefore proposed the appointment of a Parliamentary Commissioner who would investigate complaints from citizens forwarded to him by Members of the House of Commons or the House of Lords. They suggested that the system should be reviewed after an initial period of five years and consideration given to providing for direct access to him for members of the public. They suggested that Ministers should be able to veto investigation into complaints against their departments: this was to meet the objection that investigations by the Parliamentary Commissioner would undermine the principle of ministerial responsibility. They did not propose that the Parliamentary Commissioner should be empowered to see all the documents relevant to his investigations but only, as in Denmark, the incoming and outgoing correspondence in the Ministry pertaining to the case. Finally, they proposed that the Parliamentary Commissioner should be confined to investigating complaints about maladministration. Here also they argued that they were following Danish practice but, in fact, as we have seen in Chapter II, the Danish Ombudsman is not so precisely limited, although he does not have such wide powers, in practice, as the Swedish Ombudsmen to criticize unreasonable decisions by public authorities.[1] The Whyatt Committee proposed that the Parliamentary Commissioner should not be able to investigate discretionary decisions by government departments which did not involve maladministration. Complaints about such decisions should be examined through a much enlarged system of administrative tribunals. The Committee suggested that there should be provision for appeal to a tribunal in every main sphere of government activity and, where it was not possible for a specialized tribunal to be established, appeal should lie to a new general tribunal covering all those areas for which specialized tribunals had not been provided.

Despite the cautious nature of the Whyatt Committee's proposals, the Macmillan Government, after waiting for a year to consider the matter, turned down all its suggestions. In a statement issued in November 1962 the Government said that it rejected the proposal for a Parliamentary Commissioner because it would

[1] See above, pp. 19–20.

'seriously interfere with the prompt and efficient despatch of public business'. It similarly rejected the suggestion for extending the system of administrative tribunals on the grounds that it 'would lead to inflexibility and delays in administration'.[1]

There the matter would probably have rested had it not been for the fact that the Labour Opposition, soon after, took up the idea of an Ombudsman with some enthusiasm. The Labour Manifesto at the 1964 General Election included the statement that 'Labour has resolved to humanise the whole administration of the state and to set up the new office of Parliamentary Commissioner with the right and duty to investigate and expose any misuse of government power as it affects the citizen.'[2] The author of these words was Peter Shore who was, at that time, Research Secretary of the Labour Party and Secretary of the Home Policy Sub-committee of the National Executive Committee which had approved the proposal to make the appointment of a Parliamentary Commissioner part of the party platform at the general election.

When Labour won the election and came to power, they had some difficulty in translating their somewhat grandiloquent promise into action. Douglas Houghton, who was the Cabinet Minister entrusted with the task of preparing legislation to set up a Parliamentary Commissioner, has described to the author some of the difficulties which he encountered with government departments. Twenty-six departments were at first represented on the Cabinet Subcommittee which he chaired and whose function it was to draw up proposals for legislation. A great many of the representatives of departments, Ministers or junior Ministers, came briefed with a statement explaining why their department should be excluded from investigation by the Parliamentary Commissioner.[3] Houghton had to put his foot down and insist that the Labour Government had a manifesto commitment to proceed with the reform and it would go through. Significantly, however, many areas of government were excluded from scrutiny by the Commissioner. Schedule 2 of the Parliamentary Commissioner Act, 1967, lists almost all the departments of central government and other central authorities as being subject to investigation, in alphabetical order from 'Agriculture' to 'Welsh

[1] H.C. Deb., Vol. 666, Col. 1124.

[2] Labour Party, *Let's Go with Labour for a New Britain. Manifesto for the 1964 General Election*, p. 3.

[3] Stacey, op. cit., pp. 51–2.

Office'. But Schedule 3 of the Act, 'Matters not Subject to Investigation', eliminates large areas from investigation in many departments. Thus, although the Foreign Office is included in Schedule 2, action taken by the Foreign Secretary (or by other Ministers) in dealings with other countries is excluded by Schedule 3. So also are actions taken by British officials outside the United Kingdom. So a British citizen on holiday in France cannot complain to the Parliamentary Commissioner about, for example, the action or inaction of a British Embassy official in Paris and his failure to assist him in difficulties he is having with the Parisian police authorities, or in currency matters. Similarly, the Ministry of Health (now the Department of Health and Social Security) is included under Schedule 2, but action taken on behalf of the Minister of Health by any hospital authority in the National Health Service is excluded by Schedule 3. The Home Office is included under Schedule 2 but action taken by the Home Secretary (or by the Secretary of State for Scotland) for the purpose of investigating crime, or of protecting the security of the state, is excluded by Schedule 3. All contractual or commercial transactions by government departments or authorities are excluded by this schedule (except for transactions in the compulsory purchase or disposal of land). So are complaints in personnel matters by civil servants, by other people 'in office or employment' under the Crown, and by members of the armed forces. The nationalized industries and local authorities are not mentioned in Schedule 2 and are not therefore subject to investigation by the Parliamentary Commissioner.

All of these exclusions were to be strongly criticized during the passage of the Parliamentary Commissioner Bill through Parliament, and some of them have since been remedied. Thus under the National Health Service Reorganization Act, 1973, and the National Health Service, Scotland, Act, 1972, a Health Service Commissioner has been established to examine complaints against hospital authorities. Under Acts of 1974 and 1975, Local Commissioners for Administration were set up for England, Wales, and Scotland. Both these developments will be examined in subsequent chapters.

The exclusion of complaints against the police from the Parliamentary Commissioner's jurisdiction was partially remedied by the passage of the Police Act, 1976. This Act provides for three-man tribunals, consisting of two laymen and the Chief Officer of the police force concerned, to hear complaints against the police, where the case has not been referred to the Director of Public Prosecutions. But most of the other exclusions still remain. The contractual and commercial transactions of government departments are still excluded, although the Royal Commission on Standards of Conduct in Public Life recommended in July 1976 that they be brought within the Parliamentary Commissioner's purview.[1] The Select Committee of the House of Commons has several times recommended that complaints from civil servants in personnel matters should be open to investigation by the Parliamentary Commissioner, but no action has yet been taken on this recommendation.

Just as the influence of senior officials had an important effect in restricting the area of government about which the Parliamentary Commissioner may receive complaints, so officials, particularly in the Treasury, were influential in narrowing the role of the Parliamentary Commissioner in other ways. The Treasury in 1965–6 was still the department concerned with machinery of government. It was only in November 1968 that the Civil Service Department was set up and took over machinery of government functions. The Treasury was given charge of piloting the Parliamentary Commissioner Bill through Parliament and a senior official at the Treasury, Sir Philip Allen, was chairman of the Committee of Permanent Officials which paralleled the work in preparing for the bill which went on in the Cabinet Subcommittee chaired by Douglas Houghton. This Subcommittee, in effect, took the Whyatt Report as its starting-point and on a number of key issues it closely followed the Whyatt Report's recommendations.

On two important questions, however, the Cabinet Subcommittee decided to be less cautious than the Whyatt Committee had been. Douglas Houghton was convinced that the Parliamentary Commissioner could not be really effective if he did not have power to look at all the documents. Houghton had long experience of the Civil Service, having been Secretary of the Inland Revenue Staff Federation from 1922 to 1960. He wrote a memorandum to the Cabinet in 1965, urging the need to give the Parliamentary Commissioner access to all the files, and the Cabinet accepted his view. Although the Parliamentary Commissioner Act, 1967, empowers the Commissioner to see all the documents in the case, a Minister may, under Section 11 (3) instruct the Commissioner not to disclose

[1] Cmnd. 6524, *Report of the Royal Commission on Standards of Conduct in Public Life 1974–1976* (H.M.S.O., 1976), pp. 82–3.

the contents of a document he has seen, on the grounds that disclosure 'would be prejudicial to the safety of the State or otherwise contrary to the public interest'. But this power has been very rarely used by Ministers. All three Parliamentary Commissioners have, however, sought to respect the confidentiality of information about complainants which might be embarrassing to them if included in the reports of results.

The other cautious feature of the Whyatt Report which was abandoned by the Subcommittee was the proposal to give a Minister power to veto an investigation by the Commissioner. This also, Houghton thought, would seriously weaken his effectiveness and the suggestion was discarded. Indeed, the role of the Parliamentary Commissioner in relation to Ministers was made stronger than in many other Ombudsman systems. The Commissioner can criticize the actions of Ministers, on the same grounds as he can those of civil servants, and Commissioners have done so in practice on a number of occasions.[1] The New Zealand Ombudsman, whose powers are wider than those of the Parliamentary Commissioner in so many ways, is in this respect more restricted than the Parliamentary Commissioner. He can criticize the advice given to Ministers, but not the actions of Ministers themselves.

In other respects the Subcommittee's proposals were as cautious as those of the Whyatt Committee. In fact, on the question of access they were more restrictive. Whereas the Whyatt Committee had proposed that access should be only through M.P.s and peers, during a trial period of five years, after which direct access should be considered, the Act provides that access shall only be through M.P.s, peers are not a channel, and there is no provision in the Act for reviewing the situation after a trial period. The Subcommittee was influenced in its decision on this by two arguments. The first was that an Ombudsman had not yet been established in any country with a large population. Sweden, Finland, Denmark, Norway, and New Zealand were the only countries which had Ombudsmen at that time and all have relatively small populations. Sweden was the largest with a total population of around 8 million. But the United Kingdom has a population of more than 55 million. It was argued that if direct access to the Parliamentary Commissioner were to be permitted, in a country with so large a population, he would be swamped with cases. In fact, the volume of cases which it was

[1] See below, p. 164.

anticipated would result from the system of indirect access adopted in the Act proved to be of great overestimate. The first Parliamentary Commissioner, Sir Edmund Compton, told the press in April 1967 that he expected to receive between 6,000 and 7,000 complaints a year. In practice, in 1975 the Parliamentary Commissioner only received 928 complaints through M.P.s and this was the largest number he had received since 1968. Of this 928, a large proportion were, of course, not investigated because they were against authorities not listed in Schedule 2, or were excluded under Schedule 3, or by other provisions in the Act. The number of cases he did investigate in the year was only 244. There are strong grounds for saying, therefore, that the attempt to curtail the volume of complaints to the Parliamentary Commissioner, and to prevent it from becoming a flood, has been much too successful. The actual volume, while being more than a trickle, could not be described as anything more than a small river which the Parliamentary Commissioner and his staff are easily able to handle.

The other consideration which influenced the Subcommittee to decide against direct access was the belief that the majority opinion among M.P.s was against it. In fact, this was never tested in a free vote. The Legal and Judicial Group of the Parliamentary Labour Party had considered the question and had come up with the suggestion that access should be through an M.P., but that a member of the public should be allowed direct access to the Parliamentary Commissioner if he had already approached an M.P. without success.[1] This was in fact the formula eventually adopted for the Local Commissioners for Administration. The Legal and Judicial Group of the Parliamentary Labour Party had sent its suggestion to the Cabinet Subcommittee in a memorandum on the Ombudsman, but the Subcommittee did not canvass any wider section of M.P.s for their views.

In fact, when the Parliamentary Commissioner Bill come to be debated in the Commons, the predominant opinion heard, in both the second reading debate and the debates on the committee stage of the Bill in standing committee, was that the Parliamentary Commissioner was too restricted. There were several advocates of direct access to him by the public including three Conservative members of the standing committee, Dame Joan Vickers, Sir John Foster, and Cranley Onslow.[2] When a vote to amend the Bill, by

[1] Stacey, p. 54. [2] Ibid., p. 165.

providing for direct access, was taken in standing committee, the vote was lost. But the whip was on, on the Government side, and those Labour members of the committee who favoured direct access did not want to press their views to the extent of voting against the Government. The Treasury Minister in charge of the Bill at committee stage, Niall MacDermot, is himself now in favour of direct access. In 1965–6, when speaking on the issue, he argued the Government's case that providing for direct access might cause the Parliamentary Commissioner to be flooded with complaints. But in 1976 he wrote to the author that he would now be in favour of direct access. MacDermot was Financial Secretary to the Treasury when he was government spokesman on the Bill. He was Member of Parliament for Derby North, but did not seek re-election at the 1970 General Election. In December 1970 he was appointed Secretary-General of the International Commission of Jurists.

On all the other restrictive aspects of the Bill, there were M.P.s in the Commons who argued for wider powers for the Parliamentary Commissioner. There were many who pressed for the hospitals to be brought in. In fact, a majority in the standing committee approved an amendment to this effect. But the Government had this reversed at report stage. There were opponents of almost every other exclusion under Schedule 3. There were many critical of the Government's decision to limit the Parliamentary Commissioner to maladministration, and it is to this further respect in which the Government followed the Whyatt Committee's cautious proposals that we now turn. In fact, the Government was more cautious than the Whyatt Committee because not only did it limit the Parliamentary Commissioner to considering complaints about maladministration but it ignored the Whyatt Committee's proposed concomitant: an extension of the administrative tribunal system. It made no move, as the Whyatt Committee had suggested, to set up a comprehensive system of administrative tribunals including a general tribunal, or to give the Council on Tribunals power to recommend the setting-up of new tribunals. The only way in which it strengthened the position of the Council on Tribunals was through the introduction and passage of the Tribunals and Inquiries Act, 1966, which made it possible to bring non-statutory inquiries within the jurisdiction of the Council.

Meanwhile, 'Justice' had taken a second look at the maladministration question. In 1964 the Council of 'Justice' decided to reconstitute the Advisory Committee which had drawn up the Whyatt Report. Sir John Whyatt was not now available since he had been appointed Judge of the Chief Court for the Persian Gulf. The new Committee consisted of Norman Marsh, Professor H. W. R. Wade, Sir Sydney Caine, and Geoffrey Marshall, tutor and praelector in politics at the Queen's College, Oxford, and author of articles on the Ombudsman in *The Times*, *Public Law*, and *The Lawyer*. The Committee's report proposed three changes from the Whyatt Committee's recommendations. First, it suggested that Ministers should not be given the right to veto an investigation by the Parliamentary Commissioner, second that he should have the right to see all documents in the case, not merely the incoming and outgoing correspondence, and third that the Parliamentary Commissioner should not be limited to maladministration but should be given powers almost as wide as those of the New Zealand Ombudsman who can report on decisions which in his opinion are 'unreasonable, unjust, oppressive or improperly discriminatory'. The New Zealand Ombudsman can also report that, in his opinion, the decision was 'wrong'. The 'Justice' Advisory Committee proposed to substitute for 'wrong' the words 'shows a failure to conform with a proper standard of conduct on the part of an officer, employee or member of the Department or organization concerned'.[1] The Committee's report was not published, but a copy was sent to Lord Gardiner who became Lord Chancellor in the newly formed Labour administration in October 1974.[2]

The new 'Justice' report may well have helped influence the Wilson Cabinet to abandon the idea of a ministerial veto and to empower the Parliamentary Commissioner to see all the documents in the case. But it did not persuade the Government to give the Parliamentary Commissioner power to report on as wide a basis as that of the New Zealand Ombudsman. It remained firmly wedded to the idea that the Parliamentary Commissioner should be limited to maladministration. Indeed, the Treasury decided to make even clearer the limited role in investigation which the Parliamentary Commissioner would have by inserting a declaratory amendment to Section 5 of the Bill at report stage in the Commons. Section 5–(1) states that the Parliamentary Commissioner may investigate a

[1] See Stacey, pp. 43–6 for a fuller account of this second initiative by 'Justice'.

[2] Lord Gardiner was a founder member of 'Justice', from 1972 to 1975 he was chairman of its Council.

written complaint 'made to a member of the House of Commons by a member of the public who claims to have sustained injustice in consequence of maladministration' by a government department or other public authority named in the Act. During consideration of this section in standing committee, some members had argued that to confine the Parliamentary Commissioner to maladministration was too restrictive. Labour Members who took this view included David Weitzman and John Rankin.[1]

But one Conservative Member, Sir Hugh Lucas-Tooth, took a directly contrary view. He argued, as he had done at second reading, that the term 'maladministration' was capable of very wide interpretation and 'would be applicable to hundreds of thousands of cases which came in every year to Members of Parliament complaining simply about bad decisions'. He argued that this would allow the Commissioner to be 'a court of appeal for every ministerial act'.[2] The Treasury intended the word 'maladministration' to be limiting and clearly thought there was substance in Sir Hugh Lucas-Tooth's view, because the Financial Secretary to the Treasury introduced an amendment to Section 5 at report stage which read: '(4) Nothing in this section shall be construed as authorising or requiring the Commissioner to review by way of appeal any decision taken by a government department or other authority in the exercise of a discretion vested in that department or authority.'[3]

This amendment was approved at report stage but it created something of a storm, in both Parliament and the press. Many Conservatives criticized the amendment. For example, Sir John Hobson argued that its effect would be almost to exclude the Ombudsman from government documents. Since discretionary actions were to be excluded, then everything which a Minister said was done at his discretion would be excluded.[4] Quintin Hogg was even more emphatic, exclaiming that the Bill was shown to be the swindle which he had always thought it would be.[5]

[1] Stacey, p. 104.

[2] Official Report of Standing Committee B, 1966–7. The Parliamentary Commissioner Bill, col. 62.

[3] Stacey, p. 174.

[4] H.C. Deb., Vol. 739, Col. 1385.

[5] Ibid., Cols. 1392–3. There was a great variety of attitudes among Conservatives at this time on the Ombudsman. Some Conservative M.P.s, like Sir John Foster, were strong advocates of an Ombudsman, and Dr. Donald Johnson had put the original question to Harold Macmillan in 1959 which enabled 'Justice' to get funds for its inquiry. The Society of Individual Freedom, which had Conservative M.P.s among its

Criticisms on these lines were echoed, first in the quality press and then in the popular press culminating on 19 February 1966 in an article in the *Sunday Mirror* headlined: 'Ombudsboob—£8,600 for the Swordless Crusader'. The article said that as a result of the Government's amendment, the Ombudsman was shackled—'handcuffs, ball and chain, gag, the lot'. The Government should look again at its manifesto commitment to humanize the whole administration of the state by setting up a Parliamentary Commissioner who would be able to investigate and expose any misuse of government power as it affected the citizen.[1] Faced with such criticisms and with pressure from individual Liberal, Labour, and Conservative peers in the Lords, the Government decided to make a partial concession. At report stage in the Lords, Lord Gardiner introduced two related amendments. One deleted the new and much criticized subsection in Clause 5, and the other proposed to insert a new subsection into Clause 12: 'It is hereby declared that nothing in this Act authorises or requires the Commissioner to question the merits of a decision taken without maladministration by a government department or other authority in the exercise of a discretion vested in that department or authority.'

Both amendments were approved. It was not a major concession but it is a little less restrictive to say that the Parliamentary Commissioner cannot question the merits of a discretionary decision, taken without maladministration, than to say that he cannot review by way of appeal any decision taken by a government department in the exercise of a discretion. All was to hinge on what is meant by maladministration, and we shall discuss below what it has come to mean after ten years of the operation of the office of Parliamentary Commissioner.[2]

It is interesting at this point to notice how close the conception of the role of the Parliamentary Commissioner envisaged in the 1967 Act is to the role envisaged by the Whyatt Report. The

---

membership, commissioned T. E. Utley to write a book, *Occasion for Ombudsman* (Christopher Johnson, 1961), which advocated an Ombudsman for Britain. On the other hand, former Conservative Ministers in the Macmillan Government, like Quintin Hogg, tended to be dismissive of the Ombudsman idea. A group of Conservative lawyers, the Inns of Court Conservative and Unionist Society, published a pamphlet, *Let Right be Done* (Conservative Political Centre, 1966), advocating a British version of the Conseil d'État, rather than an Ombudsman, on the grounds that an Ombudsman would have no power to ensure that his recommendations were implemented.

[1] Stacey, p. 206.

[2] See below, pp. 154–64.

Whyatt conception was that the Parliamentary Commissioner should be limited to maladministration and that, as regards discretionary decisions taken without maladministration, he should not give his opinion that he would have exercised the discretion differently had he been sitting in the administrator's chair. The drafting of the Parliamentary Commissioner Act is clearly inspired by the same idea and government spokesmen on the Bill frequently reiterated this view.

We have seen that the second main influence on the scope and style of the office of Parliamentary Commissioner was the experience gained from his work as Comptroller and Auditor-General on which the first Parliamentary Commissioner, Sir Edmund Compton, was able to draw. When we say this, however, we must first acknowledge that the Whyatt Report had itself proposed that the office of Parliamentary Commissioner should be comparable to that of Comptroller and Auditor-General. But the Report advocated 'translating certain features of the Scandinavian Ombudsman system into the English idiom and combining them with the principle underlying the system of the Public Accounts Committee and the Comptroller and Auditor-General'.[1] In particular, it proposed that the Parliamentary Commissioner should be an independent officer of Parliament enjoying the same status and prestige as the Comptoller and Auditor-General.[2] This was achieved, in the Parliamentary Commissioner Act 1967, by providing that the Commissioner holds office during good behaviour and can only be removed from office by the Queen, before his retiring age of sixty-five, 'in consequence of Addresses from both Houses of Parliament'.[3]

A Select Committee of the House of Commons which would parallel, for the Parliamentary Commissioner, the work of the Public Accounts Committee was not mentioned in the Act. But during discussion of the Bill in the Commons the Government spokesman said that, after passage of the Act, the Government intended to ask the Commons to set up a Select Committee on the Parliamentary Commissioner. This was done in November 1967 and the Committee has ever since played an important role in the development of the office of Parliamentary Commissioner.[4]

[1] 'Justice', *The Citizen and the Administration*, p. 66 at para. 143.
[2] Ibid., p. 67 at para. 144.
[3] Parliamentary Commissioner Act, 1967, Sect. 1-(2) and 1-(3).
[4] See below, pp. 150-61.

The appointment of Sir Edmund Compton as the first Parliamentary Commissioner had, however, a more far-reaching influence in modelling the Parliamentary Commissioner system on the lines of the office of Comptroller and Auditor-General. Richard Crossman implied in his diaries that the choice of Sir Edmund Compton was determined by the fact that his place as Comptroller and Auditor-General was wanted for Sir Bruce Fraser who was without a job, since his post as Permanent Secretary at the Ministry of Land and National Resources had to come to an end with the absorption of that Ministry into the Ministry of Housing and Local Government.[1] The appointment of Sir Edmund Compton therefore solved an administrative conundrum, but it was not the only reason why this choice was attractive to the Prime Minister. As Leader of the Opposition, Harold Wilson had himself played a major part in projecting the proposal for a Parliamentary Commissioner, in speeches in April and July 1964. In the second of these speeches, at a public meeting at Stowmarket, he had said that the relationship of the Parliamentary Commissioner to a specially created committee of the Commons would be similar to the relationship between the Comptroller and Auditor-General and the Public Accounts Committee.[2] Harold Wilson had been chairman of the Public Accounts Committee from 1959 to 1963. During this period several reports of the Committee, including reports on the size of government expenditure on missiles and on the large profits being earned by drug firms supplying medicines under the National Health Service, attracted major publicity. Throughout this period Sir Edmund Compton was Comptroller and Auditor-General.

THE DISTINCTIVE ROLE OF THE PARLIAMENTARY COMMISSIONER'S OFFICE

Whatever the complex of reasons for his appointment as Parliamentary Commissioner, Sir Edmund Compton's previous experience as Comptroller and Auditor-General led him to make a special imprint on the office of Parliamentary Commissioner in two particular directions, first on the role of the office and second on its staffing. We need to look at each of these in turn. The distinctive

[1] Richard Crossman, *The Diaries of a Cabinet Minister, i: Minister of Housing, 1964–66* (Hamish Hamilton and Jonathan Cape, 1975), p. 499.

[2] Stacey, pp. 41–3.

feature of the office of Comptroller and Auditor-General is that its principal function is to carry out an audit of the accounts of government departments. This audit, although it is going on continuously, is an *ex post facto* review of expenditure to ascertain whether moneys have been spent as Parliament intended and whether the accounts reveal instances of 'waste or weakness of system'. This principle of *ex post facto* review was carried over by Sir Edmund Compton into the Parliamentary Commissioner's office and it is the concentration of his office on *ex post facto* investigations which most distinguishes the Parliamentary Commissioner from the other Ombudsmen we have studied. All other Ombudsmen carry out *ex post facto* investigations of complaints but they do not consider this to be their only, or main, function. They or their staff also try, where appropriate, to secure an immediate remedy for the complainant by writing to, or telephoning, the civil servant in the department concerned. The United Kingdom Parliamentary Commissioner, in the great majority of cases, acts as if he was precluded from trying to secure an immediate remedy for the complainant by the provision in the Act which states (at Section 7–(1)) that where 'the Commissioner proposes to conduct an investigation pursuant to a complaint under this Act, he shall afford to the principal officer of the department or authority concerned, and to any other person who is alleged in the complaint to have taken or authorised the action complained of, an opportunity to comment on any allegations contained in the complaint'.

The Parliamentary Commissioner takes the view that because he has to inform the permanent head of the department, and the officer concerned in the complaint, of his intention to carry out an investigation and afford them an opportunity to comment on the allegations in the complaint, he is normally prevented from securing an immediate remedy by asking the department concerned if it is prepared to review the case. Only in special circumstances will one of his staff telephone or write to the department before the formal notice of intention to investigate is sent. Such circumstances might be, for example, when a complainant was in danger of losing his rights if the statutory time for appeal had nearly expired, or when a complainant was facing immediate and serious financial consequences as a result of a mistake in the department. In the author's view, this is not the only possible interpretation of the words in the Act. It is always open to the Parliamentary Commissioner to see if he can secure an immediate remedy, without beginning an investigation, and without setting in motion the machinery of informing the department of his intention to undertake an investigation, and affording it an opportunity to comment on the allegations made in the complaint. This was not, however, how Sir Edmund Compton interpreted the Act. In fact he interpreted it, according to the style of the office of Comptroller and Auditor-General, as largely limiting his role to that of *ex post facto* review.

The Parliamentary Commissioner's review is also a high-level review in that every investigation must be brought to the attention of the Permanent Secretary of the department concerned. In Sir Idwal Pugh's words to the author in July 1976, it is a 'top hat investigation system'. This he saw as one of its strengths. It means that very close attention is paid to the Commissioner's comments in his reports, and a high priority is given in each department to responding to the investigation. The Parliamentary Commissioner's investigations are also high-quality investigations in the sense that the Parliamentary Commissioner sends his investigator to the department concerned to examine the relevant files in person and, where appropriate, to interview the civil servants concerned. All the other Ombudsmen we have studied depend, in a good proportion of cases, on staff in the departments to themselves review the files and see if they detect, in their own review, a failure to act according to the rules, or a failure to interpret the rules in a fair and reasonable way. The Ombudsmen's staff will only call for the files in the more difficult cases and will interview the civil servant concerned relatively rarely. In the great majority of cases the Parliamentary Commissioner's investigators go to the department to examine the files once an investigation has been decided upon, and in about 50 per cent of cases also interview the civil servant concerned. We can therefore see weaknesses and strengths in the Parliamentary Commissioner's system. It has weaknesses in that little scope is given for securing an immediate review in the department concerned and for securing rapid redress for the complainant. It has strengths in that every investigation should be thorough and is made by the Parliamentary Commissioner's own officers.

THE ORGANIZATION OF THE PARLIAMENTARY COMMISSIONER'S OFFICE

What we may call the 'Rolls-Royce' character of his investigations helps to account for the very high proportion of staff which the Parliamentary Commissioner has in relation to the number of investigations which he completes in a year. In 1975 he completed investigation of 244 cases. The total size of his staff at the time of writing (April 1977) is a little difficult to compute because he now doubles the role of Parliamentary Commissioner and Health Service Commissioner.[1] He has a staff of thirty-eight entirely on the Parliamentary Commissioner side and twenty-three on the Health Service Commissioner side. In addition, there are thirty-one support staff who are common to both sides of the office. If, purely arithmetically and somewhat arbitrarily, we allot this support staff to either side in proportion to the size of the investigating staff, we come up with the calculation that the Parliamentary Commissioner has a specialized staff of 38 plus 19 support staff, making a total staff of 57. The Health Service Commissioner has 23 specialized staff plus a support staff of 12, making a total staff of 35. If, then, we compare the Parliamentary Commissioner with the other Ombudsmen we have studied, he has the largest staff, 57, but investigates in a year a smaller number of cases than any other civil Ombudsman we have looked at, except for the New Brunswick and Manitoba provincial Ombudsmen.

It is not only, however, for the size of his staff that the Parliamentary Commissioner is distinctive but also for the kind of staff who are chosen for his office. The organization chart (see Fig. 1) of the staffs of the Parliamentary Commissioner and the Health Service Commissioner has been prepared by the author from information supplied in April 1977 by the Deputy to the Parliamentary Commissioner, Mr. Henry McKenzie Johnston.[2] It must be emphasized that, like all such charts, it is accurate only to the moment in time when it was drawn up. All organization diagrams become out of date very quickly as the needs of an office and the personnel change. What is particularly interesting for this study is that all the people

[1] See below, Ch. VIII on the Health Service Commissioner.

[2] Henry McKenzie Johnston has been Secretary to the Office of Parliamentary Commissioner, and Deputy to the Commissioner, since 1974. From 1973 to 1974 he was an Investigating Director in the Parliamentary Commissioner's office. He is on secondment from H.M. Diplomatic Service and from 1971 to 1973 was Consul-General in Munich.

included in the chart, the whole staff of the office, are on secondment from government departments or from the Health Service. In addition, all three Parliamentary Commissioners who have held office since 1967, Sir Edmund Compton, Sir Alan Marre, and Sir Idwal Pugh, are former civil servants.

To staff the office in this way is very much to follow on the model of the office of Comptroller and Auditor-General. The Comptroller and Auditor-General's staff are all civil servants and he himself is always a former civil servant. The bulk of his staff work continuously in the government departments whose accounts it is their function to scrutinize. Sir Edmund Compton adapted this idea as Parliamentary Commissioner and chose all his staff from civil servants, but instead of having them stationed in the departments they are on secondment from their departments, normally for a three-year period. This, in effect, carries over into the Parliamentary Commissioner's office the idea that the best people to investigate civil servants are civil servants themselves because they have the specialized administrative expertise which will make it easier for them to detect failings in the departments. The Parliamentary Commissioner does not hesitate to use civil servants on secondment from a department to investigate complaints against their 'parent' department. Both Sir Alan Marre and Sir Idwal Pugh have explained to the author that they consider it desirable, for example, for a civil servant on secondment from the Department of the Environment to investigate a complaint against that Department. He will then, it is reasoned, be able to bring his own experience to bear in assessing the case. He would not, however, be asked to investigate a complaint against the office within the Department in which he was previously employed.

In April 1977, as the organization chart shows, the Parliamentary Commissioner's staff included one person at Under-Secretary rank (his Deputy, H. McKenzie Johnston) and five at Assistant Secretary rank (four of them being Investigating Directors and one the Director of Administration for the whole office). Each Investigating Director is assigned a sector of government and is responsible for the work of either two or three investigating units, each one of which is headed by a Principal and includes, in addition, three Higher Executive Officers. There is also, on the Parliamentary Commissioner's side, a separate Screening Unit headed by a Principal and including three Higher Executive Officers. This unit

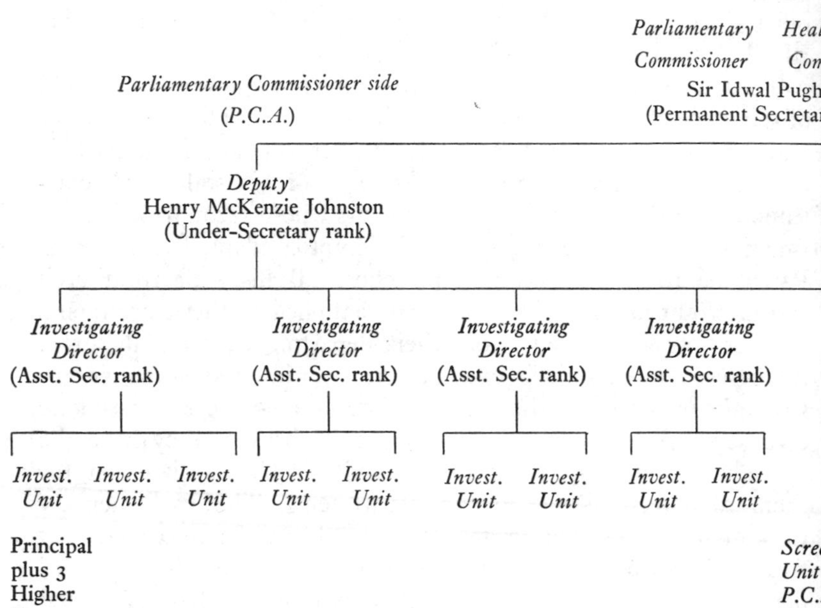

Compiled by the author from information given at interviews in the Parliamentary Commissioner's office. It is in no sense an official organization chart.

FIG. 1 Parliamentary Commissioner and

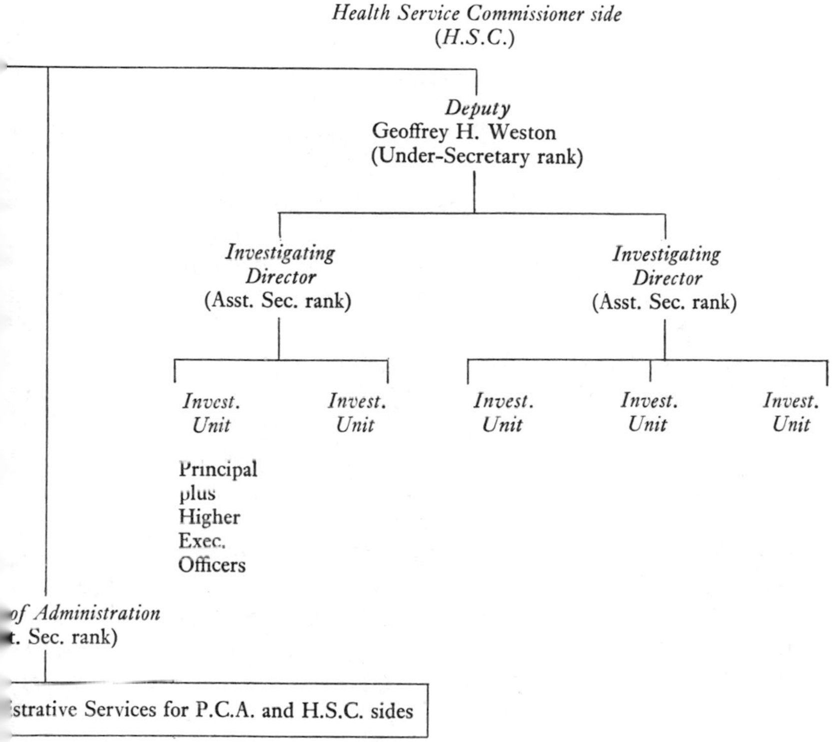

Health Service Commissioner side
(H.S.C.)

Deputy
Geoffrey H. Weston
(Under-Secretary rank)

Investigating Director
(Asst. Sec. rank)

Invest. Unit

Principal plus Higher Exec. Officers

Invest. Unit

Investigating Director
(Asst. Sec. rank)

Invest. Unit

Invest. Unit

Invest. Unit

of Administration
t. Sec. rank)

strative Services for P.C.A. and H.S.C. sides

Commissioner's Office, April 1977

screens all complaints to the Parliamentary Commissioner, as they reach the office, to decide which are, and which are not, eligible for investigation. The unit also deals with inquiries from members of the public about the Parliamentary Commissioner and the method of taking a complaint to him.

Another unique feature of the Parliamentary Commissioner's office is that he does not have any lawyers on his staff. He relies for legal advice on the Treasury Solicitor who advises the Government, and in particular on the Law Officers of the Crown on legal issues. The other Ombudsmen we have studied find it necessary, and appropriate, to have legally qualified people on their staff so that they have legal advice which is independent of the Government or in a few cases (for example, Manitoba) they do not have their own legal advisers but commission independent advice from lawyers in private practice. The Parliamentary Commissioner does neither.

The author discussed this question with Sir Edmund Compton in 1969. Sir Edmund Compton explained that, in his view, it was not necessary for the Parliamentary Commissioner to have his own legal adviser because what was needed in his staff was administrative expertise and not legal knowledge. This reinforces the view that Sir Edmund Compton saw the role of the Parliamentary Commissioner and his staff as that of a kind of internal Administrative Audit within the Civil Service. Like the office of Comptroller and Auditor-General, it is of course accountable to Parliament. The Select Committee on the Parliamentary Commissioner for Administration has a similar role to the Public Accounts Committee in scrutinizing the Commissioner's reports and examining senior civil servants about the failings revealed in their departments and about action being taken to implement his suggestions. Unlike the Comptroller and Auditor-General, the Parliamentary Commissioner also has a direct relationship with individual Members of Parliament since he reports to them on the results of his investigations, in the cases which they have referred to him. He has, however, very little direct contact with members of the public.

PUBLICITY FOR THE PARLIAMENTARY COMMISSIONER'S ACTIVITIES

It could be argued that the Parliamentary Commissioner Act does not envisage any such direct relationship with the public. As we have seen, the Wilson Government decided that access to him should only be through Members of Parliament. But experience of the Médiateur shows that an Ombudsman who can only be approached through parliamentarians can still make vigorous efforts to see that the public knows about him and his work, so that people will be stimulated to approach him through their representatives in the legislature. The three Parliamentary Commissioners who have held office since 1967 have not done this, although Sir Alan Marre and Sir Idwal Pugh have been more publicity-conscious than Sir Edmund Compton was.

In the author's view there are three main ways in which the Parliamentary Commissioner could seek greater publicity, all consistent with the provisions in the Act. These ways relate to his results reports on individual cases, the manner of presentation of his annual report, and the publicizing of his activities by, for example, issuing a brochure on the lines of the Médiateur's brochure on his activities in 1974.[1] The Parliamentary Commissioner Act, 1967, states, at Section 10, Subsections (1) and (2), that the Parliamentary Commissioner shall send a copy of his results report, when he has completed an investigation, to the Member of the House of Commons who asked him to investigate the complaint, to the principal officer of the department concerned, and to the civil servants who are alleged to have taken, or authorized, the action complained of. Section 10 also provides (at Subsection (4)) that the Commissioner shall make an annual report to Parliament on the performance of his functions and 'may from time to time lay before each House of Parliament such other reports with respect to those functions as he thinks fit'.

The Act also provides, at Section 10–(3), that if after making a report on an investigation, it appears to him that the injustice caused to the complainant has not been, or will not be, remedied, he may make a special report to Parliament. However, in the nine and a half years of the operation of the office no Parliamentary Commissioner has thought it necessary to make a report under this subsection. It remains, of course, an important reserve power for the Parliamentary Commissioner if faced by a recalcitrant department. So far, as we shall see, Parliamentary Commissioners have found that the Select Committee has given them sufficient support when a department has raised difficulties about implementing their recommendations.[2]

[1] See above, pp. 101–2.

[2] See below, pp. 150–61.

The Parliamentary Commissioner's interpretation of Subsections (1) and (2) of Section 10 is that he should normally only send a copy of his results report in an investigation to the M.P. forwarding the complaint, to the principal officer of the department, and to the civil servants concerned in the complaint. This means, in practice, that his results reports receive only very patchy publicity. It is left to the individual M.P. to decide whether to communicate with the press about one of the Commissioner's results reports. Some M.P.s inform the press and some do not, and those who do inform the press usually contact their local newspaper, which is not surprising because it is in the local newspaper that M.P.s want to see their activities on behalf of constituents well publicized.

Since August 1972 the Parliamentary Commissioner, has, in fact, published all his results reports, collected in quarterly volumes. But the overwhelming majority of the reports in these volumes are in an 'anonymized' form. This means that the name of the complainant is omitted, as is the name of the M.P. who forwarded the complaint. This 'anonymizing' process makes the report much less informative than when a report is sent to the press by an M.P. since the journalist who writes up the report is then able to say who made the complaint, and can often say also whether the complainant was satisfied with the report and give other background information such as whether he made the complaint on behalf of an amenity society and what its reaction was to the report.

Similarly, when the Commissioner makes a special report to Parliament on an individual investigation under Section 10–(4), he sometimes gives the name of the complainant and of the Member of Parliament forwarding the complaint. His reports in this category are, in general, much more informative than the anonymous reports. But Commissioners only make such reports relatively rarely. For example, they have reported individually on the Sachsenhausen case (H.C. 54 of 1967–8), a complaint about aircraft noise (H.C. 47 of 1967–8), the Duccio painting case (H.C. 316 of 1968–9), the claim to a disability (war) pension by Captain R. C. Horsley (H.C. 581 of 1970–1), the census form case (H.C. 304 of 1971–2), the Court Line case (H.C. 498 of 1974–5), the application of increased television licence fees (H.C. 680 of 1974–5), and the Nation Life Insurance Co. case (H.C. 485 of 1975–6).

The Parliamentary Commissioner could, in the author's view, secure much more publicity for his results reports in two main ways.

First, he could, as a matter of routine, send a copy of each of his results reports to the press, or allow the results reports to be scrutinized by journalists in his office as the Scandinavian Ombudsmen do, unless the M.P. or the complainant objected to publicity on grounds of the confidential nature of the complaint. It has been suggested to the author that the Commissioner is precluded from doing this by Section 11–(2) of the Act which provides that the Commissioner, or his officers, shall not disclose information obtained during the course of an investigation except (a) for the purposes of the investigation and of any report to be made thereon under the act, (b) for the purposes of proceedings under the Official Secrets Act for an offence alleged to have been committed by the Commissioner, or one of his officers, in respect of information gained by them or for proceedings for an offence of perjury alleged to have been committed in the course of an investigation, or (c) for purposes of a proceeding under Section 9 of the Act which enables the Commissioner to proceed against anyone who obstructs him, or one of his officers, in the performance of his functions under the Act.

In the author's view, this section does not prevent the Commissioner from disclosing the contents of one of his results reports to the press. It inhibits him from disclosing information which he obtained in the course of investigation for purposes other than making the reports which he is empowered to make under the Act. In particular, it says specifically that he shall not be called upon to give evidence in any judicial proceedings (other than in proceedings under the Official Secrets Act, or for perjury in the course of his investigations, or for proceedings against someone who is obstructing him in his functions). If the author is wrong, and this part of Section 11 can be construed to mean that the Commissioner cannot disclose the contents of a results report to the press, the obvious remedy is to amend this part of the Act.

Short of this being done, there is another way in which the Commissioner could secure greater publicity for his results reports. He could issue many more of them as individual reports to Parliament under Section 10–(4). The objections to doing this on the part of the Parliamentary Commissioner's office seems to be that this might, in a sense, devalue these individual reports. As things stand, these reports have a bigger impact than the Commissioner's other results reports because they are brought individually to the notice of Parliament, because they are often about identifiable persons, and because they receive much more attention in the press. Senior civil servants are said metaphorically, and perhaps actually, to 'shiver in their shoes' until they see the contents of an individual report and the public reaction to it. But to argue in this way is, in effect, to admit that other results reports often receive insufficient publicity.

The Parliamentary Commissioner could do a great deal to make his quarterly volumes of results reports more readily intelligible to the press and the interested public. These quarterly reports are also laid before Parliament under Section 10–(4) and each volume includes a great many results reports. Thus Sir Idwal Pugh's quarterly volume published in June 1976 contained 73 separate results reports.[1] Very little is done to enable the reader to see which reports best illustrate the impact the Commissioner is making on government departments. Exceptionally, the Parliamentary Commissioner does draw attention to one of the results reports in his brief introduction. For example, in the volume published in March 1976 he drew attention to the inclusion of his results report on a complaint involving the enforcement of the Asbestos Regulations, and in the volume of September 1975 to the inclusion of his results report on a complaint about the three-wheeled vehicles used by disabled people. Although each of these reports had been completed after the end of the quarterly period, he brought them forward for earlier publication because of public interest in the subject-matter of the report. In his quarterly volume of March 1974 he drew attention to his results report on a complaint about Turnhouse Airport in Scotland. On this occasion it was because he had decided exceptionally not to 'anonymize' the report, because the publicity which had already attached to the case meant that people concerned in the case were already known.

With these rare exceptions, the Commissioner does nothing at all to single out any results report as being of particular significance or interest to the reader. Not even a table of contents or an index is provided to help the reader find his way about the reports. They are published by department in chronological order, with no attempt made to separate out or highlight those in which the Commissioner finds there has been a failing in the department or to distinguish

[1] H.C. 496 of 1975–6. Fifth Report of the Parliamentary Commissioner for Administration.

them from the reports in which he finds there has been no maladministration in the department. There is no linking text or comment by the Parliamentary Commissioner about the trend of cases which he has investigated, or the impact his reports are, or are not, having on administration in the departments.

When a quarterly report is published, the press does receive a hand-out from the Parliamentary Commissioner's office pointing to cases in the report which are of special interest. But the office is somewhat naïve to assume that newspapers will follow its guidance and select stories from these cases for publication. A sub-editor will use his discretion in deciding what is newsworthy, and anyway pressure of other news may force out of the paper items from these cases which he might otherwise have included. It would surely be better if the Parliamentary Commissioner, instead of issuing a hand-out to the press highlighting the most important cases, prefaced the text of each quarterly report with some comments on the cases which he considers to have been most important and interesting during the quarterly period.

The Parliamentary Commissioner's annual reports are also far from satisfactory. He now includes some comments on cases which he has investigated in the year and some discussion of developments in the departments. But there is no systematic discussion, by department, of the trend of cases and the improvements in administration he has suggested, followed by a selection of illustrative cases relative to that department, as is provided, for example, in the Quebec Public Protector's annual report. The Quebec Ombudsman's reports are much more informative than the Parliamentary Commissioner's reports. They also provide much more, and more readily assimilable, statistical material. The Quebec Ombudsman provides three pages of statistics clearly printed and set out in which he lists, by department, the number of cases he has investigated each year and the numbers where he did not recommend a changed decision, where he made a formal recommendation, and where he made a non-formal recommendation. He also gives in another table an analysis of his reasons for not investigating cases which were outside his jurisdiction, etc.[1] The Parliamentary Commissioner provides only one table, in tiny print which makes it very hard to follow, giving the statutory categories, by department, for the cases which he rejected or discontinued after partial investigation. Even

[1] See above, p. 57 et seq.

those categories are not properly explained. Instead of giving the reason for discontinuance or rejection at the head of the column, for example 'Not submitted through an M.P.', he merely gives the number of the section and subsection of the Parliamentary Commissioner Act under which the complaint was rejected. The reader must therefore hold the Act in his hand and thumb through it in order to piece together the information given in the table. Furthermore, the table does not give the number of cases, by department, in which the Parliamentary Commissioner has found maladministration and the number of cases in which he has found no failing in the department.

In respect therefore of his individual results reports, of the quarterly reports in which his results reports are collected together, and of his annual reports, the Parliamentary Commissioner is insufficiently aware of the need to secure publicity for his reports and activities. This confirms the impression that he sees his function to be more one of providing an internal administrative audit than of acting as a ready channel for uncovering and investigating citizens' grievances. Or, at the least, that the first Parliamentary Commissioner, Sir Edmund Compton, saw his function in this way and that his two successors have not done a great deal to modify the atmosphere of the office.

It is true that they have shown themselves to be more publicity-conscious than Sir Edmund Compton was and this brings us to the third main aspect of publicity, the degree to which Parliamentary Commissioners have attempted to secure publicity for their office, apart from the publicity gained through their results reports and annual reports. Sir Alan Marre and Sir Idwal Pugh have shown themselves more willing to appear on radio and television programmes than their predecessor was and more communicative when they have taken part in programmes. For example, Sir Alan Marre took part in a very good 'It's your Line' programme on BBC Radio 4 on 1 October 1975. He answered listeners' questions about problems of access to him and about his limited jurisdiction in a forthright and informative manner. For example, one questioner complained that he had asked his local M.P. to take up his case with the Parliamentary Commissioner but the M.P. had refused to do so. When he had then taken his case to another M.P., that M.P. had forwarded his letter to the original M.P. who maintained his refusal to take it to the Parliamentary Commissioner. Sir Alan Marre did not attempt to gloss over the fact that this is a real defect of the present system of access to him through M.P.s. Similarly, Sir Idwal Pugh, since taking office in April 1976, has appeared on radio programmes such as the Jimmy Young programme which is a 'records and chat programme' each weekday morning on Radio 2. This programme, despite its bland and breezy manner, includes a fairly high content of serious discussion of current affairs and consumer problems and has a wide audience.

It may be that the greater awareness of the need for publicity shown by Sir Alan Marre and Sir Idwal Pugh is partly explained by their earlier career patterns in the Civil Service which were considerably different from that of Sir Edmund Compton. Before becoming Comptroller and Auditor-General, which office he held for eight years, he had spent almost all of his career in the Civil Service, in the Treasury. Sir Alan Marre entered the Ministry of Health in 1936 as an Assistant Principal and served there continuously until 1963, rising to the rank of Under-Secretary. He then spent five years at the Ministry of Labour, until 1968, when he was appointed Second Permanent Secretary at the Department of Health and Social Security. Sir Idwal Pugh has had a varied experience in departments with dealings with several different sections of the public. His original appointment was in the Ministry of Civil Aviation in 1946. After serving as Civil Air Attaché in Washington from 1957 to 1959, he was appointed Under-Secretary in the Ministry of Transport where he remained until 1961. He then spent eight years at the Ministry of Housing and Local Government, until 1969, when he was appointed Permanent Secretary to the Welsh Office. The Welsh Office is concerned with a range of functions exercised in England by several different departments including housing and local government, health, education, transport, forestry, and agriculture. In 1972 he was appointed Second Permanent Secretary at the Department of the Environment.

While Sir Alan Marre and Sir Idwal Pugh have been more publicity conscious than their predecessor was, it remains true that when compared, for example, with the French Médiateur, Parliamentary Commissioners have done relatively little to secure publicity for their office. The Médiateur, as we have seen, has shown himself to be very conscious of the need to gain publicity for his office so that as high a proportion as possible of citizens who have grievances will be able to get them to him. He has issued an attractive brochure about his work and combined this with a programme of regional visits and meetings with leaders of opinion. Parliamentary Commissioners, on the other hand, seem to be quite unaware of this need and have never issucd a popular brochure. The leaflet provided to inquirers by the Parliamentary Commissioner's office is a depressing document. Like so many of his publications, it is in tiny print and a large part of the leaflet is taken up in explaining what the Parliamentary Commissioner cannot do. It could be argued that this gives an accurate picture of the way in which the Commissioner is circumscribed by his legislation. Nevertheless, the over-all impression is misleading since within his restricted frame of reference he can be very effective, but few members of the general public can be aware of this. He does good by stealth, in one of the strongest, if not one of the best, traditions of the British Civil Service.

THE COMMONS SELECT COMMITTEE AND ITS SUPPORT FOR THE PARLIAMENTARY COMMISSIONER

One of the factors which has helped to enhance his effectiveness has been the support and encouragement provided by the House of Commons Select Committee on the Parliamentary Commissioner. We have up to this point been mostly critical of the package in which the Parliamentary Commissioner was designed as something as closely as possible paralleling the Comptroller and Auditor-General and his office. We have condemned the practice of staffing his office only with civil servants and of acting only as an *ex post facto* review system and the relative shunning of publicity for his reports and activities. But the appointment of a Select Committee of the Commons to examine his reports, which was also taken over from the Comptroller and Auditor-General's system, has proved most valuable. The Select Committee on the Parliamentary Commissioner for Administration, to give it its full title, has eight members and its composition is always related to the party composition of the House of Commons. Originally it had eleven members, but the membership was by stages reduced to eight. This did not reflect a lack of interest by its members in the work of the Committee, but the general difficulty experienced by the Commons in manning its committee system, as the use made of Commons committees has developed. The chairman of the Committee, like the chairman of the Public Accounts Committee, is always a member of the Opposition. This is also the convention in choosing the chairman of the Select Committee on Statutory Instruments. It helps to indicate that each of these three committees is, so to speak, a 'constitutional' committee concerned with safeguarding the rights of citizens and of the non-governmental point of view.

The Select Committee receives the Parliamentary Commissioner's reports and then decides which senior civil servants to summon for examination on issues arising from his reports. The Commissioner himself is always present when these witnesses are examined and himself frequently gives evidence. The Committee does not receive any documents additional to those which are available to other M.P.s and to the general public. It therefore works from the Commissioner's quarterly reports, special individual reports, and his annual reports. The Committee does not have its own staff apart from a House of Commons Clerk who also acts as Clerk to other Commons committees. Exceptionally, it was empowered to appoint a special part-time adviser for the inquiry which the Government asked it to conduct in 1976 into the best method of examining complaints against hospital doctors in clinical questions.[1] The Committee meets about once a month, but in certain parts of the session more frequently. Thus during the session 1974–5 it met once in each of the following months: December, January, May, June, and July and twice in each of the following months: February, March, and April.

The Committee has been concerned, over its nine-year life, with three main areas of inquiry. First, it has been concerned to find out how far the Commissioner's recommendations are being implemented in the departments, and what are the effects of the Commissioner's investigations on administration in the departments. Second, it has considered whether his powers in investigation should be strengthened within his allotted jurisdiction. Third, it has sought evidence on whether his jurisdiction should be widened. In general, it has given steady support to the Commissioner and its influence has been consistently towards widening his jurisdiction and strengthening his position in investigations.

The Committee started off, however, on a somewhat stormy note. One of the Commissioner's earliest investigations, and still perhaps his most notable, was his inquiry into a complaint against

[1] See below, p. 176 et seq.

the Foreign Office in the Sachsenhausen case. This was a case in which four individuals complained to the Parliamentary Commissioner that they had been unjustly denied compensation from a fund, provided by the West German Government and administered by the United Kingdom Government, for British nationals or their dependents who had suffered loss of liberty, damage to their health, or death as a result of Nazi persecution during the Second World War. The Foreign Office decided that for compensation to be paid, applicants had to show either that they had been detained in a Nazi concentration camp, or that the conditions they had experienced were comparable to those in a concentration camp. The four complainants had been denied compensation on the grounds that they were not held in the main part of Sachsenhausen concentration camp but either in the *Zellenbau* (cell block) or the *Sonderlager* which was a subsidiary camp on the borders of the main camp.

The Foreign Office maintained that conditions in the *Zellenbau* and the *Sonderlager* were not so bad as in the main camp. But when the Parliamentary Commissioner examined the files, and looked at other sources, he found that there was evidence that some of the prisoners in the main compound were well treated, while some occupants of the cell block were chained to the floor and were kept under constant threat of immediate execution. He found that there had been maladministration by the Foreign Office, in that the complainants' claims to compensation had been rejected in terms which were damaging to their standing and reputation. He found that their claims were well based and recommended that the Foreign Office should review its decision.

Compensation was then paid, although the Foreign Secretary, George Brown, inexplicably maintained that the original decision had been correct and that he was only paying compensation out of respect for the Parliamentary Commissioner and belief in the value of his office. The case made a big impact in the House of Commons and in the press, and it did a lot to convince doubters, particularly on the Conservative side of the House of Commons, that the Parliamentary Commissioner could be effective.[1] The Select Committee was concerned to take up a number of issues raised by the Parliamentary Commissioner's investigation, but the one which gave rise to the strongest controversy was its attempt to interview the civil servants in the Foreign Office who had made the original

[1] See Stacey, pp. 256–7.

decision not to pay compensation to the complainants, and who went on recommending to Ministers that the complainants had no case and the decision should not be reviewed. One of the features of the case was the way in which, despite a determined campaign by Conservative and Labour back-benchers, a succession of Ministers, the Ministers of State, George Thomson and Eirene White, then the Foreign Secretary, and finally the Prime Minister all said, on the advice of their civil servants, that there were no grounds for looking at the case again. Only when the complainants went to the Parliamentary Commissioner was Sir Emund Compton able to go to the files and uncover evidence to show that the original decision was unsound. It was the fact that he was able to do this and so secure redress, which had been so emphatically and repeatedly denied, that convinced doubters that the Parliamentary Commissioner could really be effective.

The Select Committee thought, not unreasonably, that it should try to find out why the deicision had been wrongly made in the first place and why advice was then given, on repeated occasions, to Ministers that there was no case for a review. But the Select Committee came up against a stubborn refusal by the Foreign Office to allow the civil servants concerned to appear before the Committee. In fact, as one member of the Committee said in private: 'We have powers to send for civil servants to give evidence to the Committee, but we have no power to make them come.' (This is of course true for all Committees of the Commons of their power 'to send for persons, papers and records'.) Eventually, the Attorney-General, Sir Elwyn Jones, appeared before the Committee to explain the Government's position. He argued that the Committee should follow the practice of the Public Accounts Committee and call for evidence from the principal officer of the department and from anyone else he chose to nominate. The decision then as to which officials would appear to give evidence would always be made by the principal officer of the department. He argued that it would 'corrode' the sense of ministerial responsibility if the Committee were able to go down the lower echelons of a department and single out the civil servant whom they held to be blameworthy.[1]

The Committee noted this advice and has not since attempted to summon a civil servant to give evidence when the principal officer

[1] H.C. 350 of 1967–8. Second Report from the Select Committee on the Parliamentary Commissioner for Administration, p. 77 at question 556.

of the department has been unwilling for him to appear. It has thus avoided any further confrontation with the Government of the day on this issue. But it has had an important influence in pressing for implementation of the Commissioner's recommendations where they have not been accepted in full by the department concerned, in urging a broad interpretation of his powers within his allotted jurisdiction, and in advocating extension of his jurisdiction in a number of ways.

Two examples will be given of instances of the Select Committee taking up what it thought to be an unsatisfactory response by a government department to an investigation by the Parliamentary Commissioner, and pressing for and securing reform: one relates to the Home Office and one to the Inland Revenue. In the session 1970–1 the Select Committee followed up a report from the Parliamentary Commissioner which had found that the Home Office had not allowed a prisoner to receive legal advice to enable him to take proceedings against the prison medical service. The prisoner claimed that negligent treatment by prison medical officers had caused him to lose a leg. When the Committee took evidence on the case from the Permanent Under-Secretary at the Home Office, it was told that it was not the practice of the Home Office to allow a prisoner to seek legal advice about alleged negligence unless there was a prima facie case, and the Home Office did not consider that the prisoner concerned in the complaint had been able to show there had been a prima facie case of negligence.

The Select Committee was very dissatisfied with this reply and in its report to Parliament argued that, in a situation of this kind, the Home Office should take independent advice on whether or not the prisoner had a prima facie case.[1] The Home Secretary then made a partial concession to the view that the Home Office was wrong to insist on being judge in its own cause in this kind of case. He announced in December 1971, in his published reply to the Committee's observations, that he and the Secretary of State for Scotland had decided to 'liberalise existing practice' in such cases. Instructions had been given, with immediate effect, that where a prisoner had suffered some physical injury or disablement and claimed damage for alleged negligence by the prison authorities or staff, he would be allowed to consult a solicitor and begin legal

[1] H.C. 513 of 1970–1. Second Report from the Select Committee on the Parliamentary Commissioner for Administration, pp. xi–xii.

proceedings, unless there were overriding considerations of security which would make this inadvisable.[1]

In the example which we shall choose from the Commissioner's investigations into complaints against the Inland Revenue the Committee had to campaign a good deal longer before the reform which it advocated was at last implemented. The Committee found, as a result of reports by the Commissioner, that it was not the practice of the Inland Revenue to pay interest on tax which had been overpaid and was only repaid after some delay. This was in the Committee's view unjustifiable particularly since the Inland Revenue requires the payment of interest by the taxpayer on tax underpaid and not paid promptly on demand.

The Committee heard evidence from the Inland Revenue that it was not allowed to pay interest on tax overpaid, and that it would require new legislation to make this possible. After the Committee and the Parliamentary Commissioner had, on several occasions, reiterated their dissatisfaction with the situation, the Government eventually decided to provide redress. In the Finance Bill, introduced in the session 1974–5, the Government made provision for payment of interest by the Inland Revenue on delayed repayments of income tax and estate duty. This became law in 1975.

ENLARGEMENT IN PRACTICE OF THE PARLIAMENTARY COMMISSIONER'S POWERS

This example leads on to the second main area in which the Committee has been active: in suggesting ways in which the Commissioner's powers can be strengthened within his allotted sphere of jurisdiction. What was interesting about this interchange with the Inland Revenue was that when the Parliamentary Commissioner system was set up in 1967, there was no suggestion that he would be able to recommend changes in legislation. He is not given any such power in the 1967 Act, as we have seen the Canadian provincial Ombudsmen are by their legislation. But by 1973 we find the Select Committee, and the Parliamentary Commissioner, together pressing for a change in legislation to permit redress to a class of complainants who would otherwise have been denied redress. It is now one of the achievements of the Parliamentary Commissioner that he has secured

[1] Cmnd. 4846. Second Report from the Select Committee on the Parliamentary Commissioner for Administration 1970–71, Observations by the Government, H.M.S.O. London at para. 3.

this reform for the taxpayer and the fact that it required new legislation to bring it about has meant, by implication, that the Parliamentary Commissioner has to some extent demonstrated his right to recommend changes in legislation, although this has not as yet been clearly recognized.

The same gradual enlargement of role for the Parliamentary Commissioner has taken place in relation to the rule-making powers of government departments. In his report on Sachsenhausen Sir Edmund Compton had said: 'I may not question the merits of the general ruling as applied throughout the compensation scheme that claimants judged not to have been held in a concentration camp had to establish detention in conditions comparable with those in a concentration camp "as generally understood", meaning severe forms of Nazi persecution treatment. I record that this ruling could mean that a non-camp claimant had to pass a more severe test than a camp claimant, and that this actually happened at Sachsenhausen'.[1] The Committee thought that the Parliamentary Commissioner here took too narrow an interpretation of his power to criticize a departmental rule. On 22 May 1968 Sir Edmund Compton discussed this question with the Committee and asked for its 'assistance and guidance'. He asked whether when he found a rule was causing hardship he should 'test the department administratively for not having taken action to review this rule'.[2] In its report the Committee confirmed that it had approved this suggestion, and it has since remained the position that if the Commissioner has found that a departmental rule has been causing hardship he can criticize the department for not reviewing the rule. But to criticize the department for not reviewing a rule is, in practice, not very different from crititicizing the substance of that rule. Inevitably the distinction has become blurred. So, whereas the Commissioner began by saying that he did not have power to criticize a departmental rule, he has, with the encouragement of the Committee, in practice come to exercise that power.

THE DEVELOPING CONCEPT OF MALADMINISTRATION

A parallel and even more important development has taken place in the concept of maladministration. Sir Edmund Compton began

[1] H.C. 54 of 1967–8. Third Report of the Parliamentary Commissioner for Administration, p. 18.

[2] H.C. 350 of 1967–8. Second Report from the Select Committee on the Parliamentary Commissioner for Administration, pp. 90–1 at question 611.

by interpreting it almost exclusively in procedural terms. In evidence to the Committee he reiterated the view, put forward by Ministers during the passage of the Parliamentary Commissioner Act, that he should not review discretionary decisions taken without maladministration.[1] The Permanent Secretary to the Treasury, Sir William Armstrong, gave evidence to the Committee in May 1968 that the Treasury distinguished ten kinds of maladministration in the cases of maladministration which the Parliamentary Commissioner had found in his first year. Nine of these categories were procedural, varying from delays, or failing to reply to a letter, to unclear or ambiguous circulars sent to local authorities, failure to take relevant facts into consideration, and misleading advice given to the complainant. The tenth category was bias on the part of the official, and only one case came in this category.[2]

The Committee was dissatisfied with this largely procedural interpretation of maladministration. In a report in 1968 it recommended that if the Parliamentary Commissioner 'finds a decision which, judged by its effect upon the aggrieved person appears to him to be thoroughly bad in quality, he might infer from the quality of the decision itself that there had been an element of maladministration in the taking of it and ask for its review'.[3] In other words, even a decision which was procedurally correct could be adjudged maladministration if it was thoroughly bad in its effects.

Sir Edmund Compton accepted the Committee's recommendation that he should consider the quality of a decision, but it seemed to have little impact in widening his interpretation of what constituted maladministration. His successor, Sir Alan Marre, took a different line. In an interview with the author in May 1973 he expressed some scepticism about the advantages of considering the quality of a decision. But he said that he distinguished two broad types of maladministration. The first was procedural, and we have already considered some of the procedural failures in administration which fall within this type. The second main category was when the decision, although procedurally correct, was one which no reasonable person could have made on the evidence. This was to widen appreciably the concept of maladministration

[1] Ibid., p. 39 at question 135.

[2] Ibid., pp. 100–1 at question 643. See also Stacey, pp. 278–9.

[3] H.C. 350 of 1967–8, viii at para. 14.

and to move towards the New Zealand and Canadian concept of an unreasonable decision.

A close scrutiny of some of the recent major cases on which the Parliamentary Commissioner has reported brings to light a further development. We find in a number of cases that the Commissioner has not said whether or not he found maladministration, but has said that he found some failing on the part of a government department. For example, in the Court Line case he said, in the final paragraph of his report: 'In my view, therefore, the Government cannot be absolved of all responsibility for holidaymakers' losses arising from the Court Line collapse'.[1] He considered that statements to the Commons by the Secretary of State for Industry, Tony Benn, had indicated that the Department had a degree of confidence in the viability of the Court Line Company which was not justified by its knowledge of the position in which the Company then stood.

He acknowledged that the Secretary of State had grounds for saying to him that had he made public his reservations about the future of the business, that might have led to an earlier collapse of the Company. But Sir Alan Marre concluded that Tony Benn's statements had led some holiday-makers not to cancel their holidays with Court Line, and so placed them in a position in which they lost their holidays and the money they had paid to the Company. They were eventually compensated under the Air Travel Reserve Fund Act which was passed by Parliament in 1975 as a response to the Court Line case. The Fund is financed by a levy on the travel companies, and ultimately therefore by all holiday-makers who contribute to the fund in the cost of their holiday. The Fund was started off by an interest-free loan from the Government.

The Parliamentary Commissioner's report on the three-wheeled vehicles for the disabled case also included several criticisms of the Department of Health and Social Security but did not say whether or not he had found maladministration. This case was concerned with complaints about the handling by the Department of Health and Social Security of representations that the three-wheeled vehicles, vehicles supplied to disabled people under the National Health Service, were unsafe to drive. Sir Alan Marre concluded in his report that the Department was slow in deciding to commission

[1] H.C. 498 of 1974–5. Fifth Report of the Parliamentary Commissioner for Administration, p. 28 at para. 92.

tests of these vehicles by the Motor Industry Research Association, that the Department was unwise to refuse initially to publish the results of these tests, and that some of the replies given to questions asked in the House about the safety of the vehicles were less than frank. He found, in his own words, 'an attitude of defensiveness over the Department's actions and policy with regard to three-wheelers which was, in the circumstances, unwarranted and unwise'. But he said that he was satisfied that throughout the period during which the safety of the vehicles was under consideration 'both officials and Ministers were in fact concerned to arrive at a balanced judgement of the provision which ought to be made for disabled people'.[1]

We find a further example of an important report which did not mention maladministration in its conclusions in the Commissioner's report in 1976 on the asbestosis case. This report was on a complaint that the Factory Inspectorate of the Department of Employment (subsequently incorporated in the Health and Safety Executive) had not adequately carried out its responsibility of enforcing the Asbestos Regulations in an asbestos factory at Acre Mill at Hebden Bridge, Yorkshire. A former employee at the factory contended that he had contracted asbestosis as a result of the failure of the Inspectorate to enforce the regulations there.

The Commissioner found that the quality of attention given to Acre Mill was not as high as it should have been. The need for decisive action there was not recognized soon enough. There had been a failure to appreciate the significance of statistics of asbestosis. There had been organizational failures. In particular, there had been little co-ordination between the Chemical Branch of the Department, which analysed concentrations of asbestos dust, and the Engineering Branch, which tried to help firms find practical ways of eliminating them. Between them they did not always give consistent advice to district staff. On one occasion, the Chemical Branch gave advice which seemed to justify prosecution of the firm at Acre Mill, but the Engineering Branch gave contrary advice.[2]

In these three reports, therefore, we find the Commissioner pointing to failings in the departments concerned: failure to warn

[1] H.C. 529 of 1974–5. Sixth Report of the Parliamentary Commissioner for Administration, p. 182 at para. 88.

[2] H.C. 259 of 1975–6. Third Report of the Parliamentary Commissioner for Administration, p. 209.

the public of the shaky situation in the Court Line Company, failure at first to commission tests on the safety of three-wheeled vehicles for the disabled followed by reluctance to publish the results of those tests, failure to act soon enough in the Acre Mill case coupled with failings in intelligence and organization in the Factory Inspectorate. In none of these reports are these failings characterized as maladministration by the Commissioner. This prompts three main reflections. First, we should note that the Commissioner is not required by the Act to say in his report whether or not he finds maladministration. He investigates complaints that members of the public have sustained injustice in consequence of maladministration and he is required to report on these investigations. But the Act does not say that he must report that he has, or has not, found maladministration. Second, there may be considerable advantages in the Commissioner finding that there have been failings, but not discussing whether or not there has been maladministration. He is then able to say simply what, in his opinion, has gone wrong. His findings may also help to indicate how a remedy may be provided, either directly to the complainant, or indirectly by pointing to ways in which the administration of the question can be improved. Third, by acting in this way the Commissioner is in practice widening his investigatory powers because he is in effect saying: 'I am concerned with maladministration but when I am asked to investigate I report on what I find and do not have to define whether or not the failures I find are, or are not, maladministration.' This development is perhaps even more important than Sir Alan Marre's decision to consider unreasonable interpretation of the evidence as maladministration. It means that the original rather narrow conception of the role of the office of Parliamentary Commissioner, put forward by Sir Edmund Compton, has been considerably widened. The Commissioner is now reporting on administrative failures and therefore his role, in practice, is not so far as it might seem, in law, from the role of the Médiateur in reporting on the failure of a public authority to act according to its mission of public service.

This does not mean that it would not be better to amend the Parliamentary Commissioner Act, 1967, by enabling the Commissioner to report broadly, as the New Zealand and Canadian Ombudsmen can do, on actions or omissions by government departments that are unreasonable, unjust, or oppressive and to give him power to report on administrative failures. The disadvantage of leaving the Act as it stands is that it gives the impression that the Parliamentary Commissioner is very limited in his power to investigate and report. In practice, he is not nearly so limited, and credit must go to successive Commissioners, and to the Select Committee, for widening his powers. But knowledge of the extent of his powers has not seeped through very much to the general public. So we come to the same general criticism of the Parliamentary Commissioner that we did over publicity. Too little is known by the public of the extent of his powers and, as a result, he is too little used by people who are dissatisfied with their treatment by a government department.

RECENT REPORTS PRODUCE GREATER PUBLICITY FOR THE COMMISSIONER'S ACTIVITIES

There are some indications, however, that there is growing awareness that the Parliamentary Commissioner can be effective in securing redress for aggrieved groups and individuals. The publicity which greeted his report on the Court Line case seems to have stimulated a considerable increase in the flow of complaints to him. Here the Commissioner's ability to criticize the Minister was important. As we have seen, he roundly criticized the Minister's statements about the viability of Court Line. Tony Benn defended himself in the Commons and said that he rejected the Commissioner's criticisms. This was not, as some newspapers said at the time, a defeat for the Parliamentary Commissioner. It was, in an important sense, a victory because this debate with the Minister brought much more publicity to the Commissioner and his office than he had received since the Sachsenhausen case in 1968. There must be a very strong presumption that it was publicity over his report on Court Line, and the Government's response to it, which stimulated a much greater flow of complaints to him in the months which followed. As Table XII shows, in 1974 he received 704 complaints through M.P.s and investigated 252 cases. In 1975 the number of complaints he received through M.P.s rose to 928 and he investigated 244 cases. The number of complaints he received directly from members of the public, which he of course sent back telling them to ask an M.P. to take up the complaint with him, rose even more sharply from 724 in 1974 to 1,068 in 1975.

The Court Line case was not the only case to attract a great deal of publicity at this time. His special report on the Court Line case was published on 29 July 1975. Two days later his report on the case of vehicles for the disabled appeared in his quarterly volume of reports. The Parliamentary Commissioner's report on this case was bound to receive a lot of publicity because the campaign for replacement of the existing design of three wheeled vehicles for the disabled had already won a lot of sympathy and support. The former racing driver and racing team manager, Graham Hill, had taken part in the campaign before his tragic death in an air crash, and Lord Snowdon had spoken on the question in the House of Lords. He emphasized the dangerous handling characteristics of the vehicle, particularly in cross winds. The Disabled Drivers' Action Group, which was formed to press for replacement of the existing three wheeler had been active in securing publicity for the campaign and it was their Co-ordinator who referred complaints about the vehicle to the Parliamentary Commissioner.

In November 1975 the Parliamentary Commissioner published another report on an issue of acute controversy. This was his report in the television licence fee case. No less than twenty-five M.P.s had referred complaints to him about the action of the Home Office in relation to an increase of the television licence fee on 1 April 1975. After the increase was announced in January 1975, 26,000 people had the bright idea that by taking out a new licence before the increased charges came into effect, and having this licence overlapping with their existing licence, they could make a considerable saving. When the increased licence fee came into effect, the Home Office informed people holding overlapping licences that they must pay the difference between the cost of the licence at the old rate and its cost at the new rate, so that the stratagem to effect a saving would be nullified.

In his report Sir Alan Marre said that the Home Office was at fault in three respects. First, when it announced the increased charges in January 1975 it did not send notices to post offices instructing them that the facility to renew licences, in advance of the expiry of the old licence, had been withdrawn. Second, it did not announce its intention to disallow overlapping licences. Third, after two national newspapers had carried articles describing the procedures relating to overlapping licence, the Home Office made no statement to the press saying that these procedures would be made inoperative. The Commissioner concluded that in deliberately

TABLE XII

United Kingdom Parliamentary Commissioner, 1967–1975

	1967	1968	1969	1970	1971	1972	1973	1974	1975
Complaints received through M.P.s	1,069	1,120	761	645	548	573	571	704	928
Outside jurisdiction	561	727	445	362	295	318	285	374	576
Investigation discontinued	100	80	43	30	39	17	12	27	19
Investigation completed	188	374	302	259	182	261	239	252	244*
Elements of maladministration found	19	38	48	59	67	79	88	94	90
Percentage of cases investigated in which maladministration was found	10%	10%	16%	23%	37%	30%	37%	37%	37%
Complaints received direct from members of the public	743	808	814	645	505	661	676	724	1,068

* In 1975 the Commissioner investigated 321 cases but since these included 79 multiple complaints on the same issue (49 about Court Line and 30 on overlapping TV licences) he reduced the figure to 244 in his statistical review.

Source: Compiled from Parliamentary Commissioner's Reports 1967 to 1975.

deciding not to give general publicity to its intention to recover the difference between the licence at the old rate and at the new rate, it made a serious error which exposed it to a charge of lack of sufficient frankness with the public. The Home Office's actions were not, in the opinion of its own legal advisers, illegal, but he pointed out that any dispute about the legality of the Home Office's action in requiring an additional payment from holders of overlapping licences could only be settled in the courts.[1] One of the aggrieved licence holders did, in fact, take his case to the courts who ruled that the Home Office's action was illegal. The Home Office then repaid to the holders of overlapping licences all the additional payments that it had illegally required them to make.

Of none of these four recent major cases could it be said that the Commissioner's report produced an immediate remedy for the complainants, as his report on the Sachsenhausen case did. But in some cases his investigation gave considerable assistance to the people who were campaigning for compensation or a change of policy. In the Court Line case his investigation helped to stimulate the Government into introducing legislation to set up a fund to finance compensation for people, including the Court Line victims,

[1] H.C. 680 of 1974–5, pp. 13–14 at para. 29.

who have lost as the result of the failure of a travel company, and to launch the fund with an interest-free loan from government funds. In the invalid vehicle case the Commissioner's report was followed by a decision by the Minister to phase out the three-wheelers and provide instead an increased allowance to disabled people towards the cost of a car. Following the Commissioner's report on the asbestosis case, the Minister concerned, Michael Foot, who was then Secretary of State for Employment, announced in the Commons on 30 March 1976 that the Health and Safety Commission had decided to set up a committee to review the health risks associated with asbestos. He thanked Max Madden, the M.P. for Sowerby, who had taken the complaint to the Parliamentary Commissioner and said that his skill and persistence in raising the matter had been of great importance for his own constituents and for many others besides.[1] The Under-Secretary for Employment, Harold Walker, had the previous day made a statement accepting the Parliamentary Commissioner's criticisms of the Department, adding that the Chief Inspector of Factories agreed, with hindsight, that even with the existing difficulties the regulations could have been enforced more rigorously.[2] Finally, in the television licence case, although the Commissioner in some respects defended the Home Office decision and did not challenge its legality, he said that it was open to the complainants to test the decision in the courts which one of them did successfully.

THE NEED TO MAKE THE PARLIAMENTARY COMMISSIONER'S OFFICE INDEPENDENT OF THE CIVIL SERVICE

In each of these four cases the Commissioner found things to say in the department's favour. In the Court Line case he acknowledged the force of Tony Benn's argument, but came down on balance against it. In the invalid vehicle case he said that officials and Ministers were concerned to arrive at a balanced judgement of the provision which ought to be made for disabled people, although they had been inept in not commissioning tests early enough, in not at first communicating results of the tests to the public, and in being evasive in reply to parliamentary questions. In the asbestosis case he pointed out that the dangers involved in processing asbestos were not fully realized until the early 1960s, and that visits to the

[1] H.C. Deb., Vol. 908. Col. 1105.
[2] Report in *The Times*, 30 Mar. 1976.

Acre Mill site were more frequent from this period onwards. In the television licence case he accepted the Home Office's contention that most people, about two million of them, who did not seek to avoid the higher fees by obtaining an overlapping licence would have a legitimate grievance if the minority escaped paying part of the higher fee.

It is right that the Parliamentary Commissioner should be scrupulously fair between the complainant and the civil servant and give full weight and credit to the arguments put forward on the department's side. But there is a danger that because the Parliamentary Commissioner himself has always had a Civil Service background, and all his staff are civil servants, they will be thought by complainants to be biased towards the side of the Civil Service. This was certainly what happened in the disabled persons' vehicle case. The Disabled Drivers' Action Group clearly hoped that the Parliamentary Commissioner would report that the existing three-wheeled vehicle was unsafe and should be replaced by cars provided at government expense. Instead, the Parliamentary Commissioner reported that the Government had decided not to provide cars instead of three wheelers but would increase the mobility allowance for disabled people.

He did not say that he found this an unreasonable outcome, indeed he said that he was satisfied that the new policy had been 'settled in the light of all the relevant considerations, including those advanced by D.D.A.G. and other organisations'.[1] The Co-ordinator of the Disabled Drivers' Action Group did think that the decision was unreasonable and in January 1976 he wrote to the Select Committee on the Parliamentary Commissioner complaining that Sir Alan Marre had been less critical of the Department of Health and Social Security than the facts warranted, because of his previous association with the Department as Second Permanent Secretary from 1968 to 1971. The Select Committee, in a special report published in February 1976, rejected the criticism. It said that it had 'the fullest confidence in the way Sir Alan Marre, in fulfilling his role of an independent investigator, has served this House and its individual Members'.[2] It was satisfied that his investigation in

[1] H.C. 529 of 1974–5. Sixth Report of the Parliamentary Commissioner for Administration, p. 182 at para. 89.

[2] H.C. 166 of 1975–6. First Special Report on the Parliamentary Commissioner for Administration, p. iv at para. 6.

the case was conducted with the fairness and impartiality with which he had carried out his other investigations as Parliamentary Commissioner and Health Service Commissioner, including those involving his former department.

Members of the disabled drivers' lobby were still not satisfied. On 9 August 1976 Adam Fergusson wrote in an article in *The Times*: 'Two ombudsmen, at length persuaded to investigate the drivers' complaints, have turned out to have had close personal responsibility for administering the tricycle service or for the road safety policies in respect of it before being appointed (a fact which may not have affected their judgements, but which certainly convinced the drivers that justice was not obtainable in Westminster).' The reference to two Ombudsmen is of course explained by Sir Idwal Pugh's previous appointment. Before becoming Parliamentary Commissioner in April 1976 he was Second Permanent Secretary at the Department of the Environment, and that Department included responsibility for transport and road safety among its many functions.

This case well illustrates the lack of confidence which can develop when an investigating institution is not seen to be fully independent of the government department concerned. It is not the only instance of such ambiguity. In June 1976 George Rodgers, the Labour M.P. for Chorley, commented on the disturbing aspects of a report by Sir Idwal Pugh, as Parliamentary Commissioner, on his investigation of a complaint made on behalf of a severely disabled girl. The disturbing aspects of the report, as George Rodgers saw them, included criticisms made by Sir Idwal Pugh of a departmental circular, issued to local authorities, and signed by Sir Alan Marre when he was Second Permanent Secretary at the Department of Health and Social Security.[1] The circular said that local authorities had to determine critieria of need in the light of their resources. Sir Idwal Pugh said this circular might have 'muddied the waters' and led to the local authority not recognizing its duty under the Chronically Sick and Disabled Persons Act, 1970, to help with provision for the disabled girl. Nevertheless, he decided that the complaint was unfounded. It was clearly an invidious position for him to have to comment on a circular issued, when he was an administrator, by his predecessor as Parliamentary Commissioner.

There is a great deal to be said for ending the practice, followed

[1] Report in *The Times*, 11 June 1976.

in the appointment of the first three Parliamentary Commissioners, of appointing only senior civil servants to the office of Parliamentary Commissioner. It would not be right, on the other hand, to exclude civil servants from appointment as Parliamentary Commissioner. Some civil servants have the necessary combination of qualities to serve as Ombudsmen and in this survey we have seen instances in other countries of Ombudsmen being chosen from among the ranks of civil servants. For example, the Danish Ombudsman, Mr. Nordskov Nielsen, was a civil servant before being appointed Ombudsman. He was the chief administrator of the Danish prison service. But significantly his predecessor was a Professor of Law. What is necessary in Britain is to show the public that the Parliamentary Commissioner's office is independent of the Civil Service. It would therefore be highly desirable to choose as successor to Sir Idwal Pugh, when his date for retirement comes round, someone who is not associated with the Civil Service.

It would also be desirable for the Select Committee on the Parliamentary Commissioner to have a role in the appointment of the Parliamentary Commissioner. Ian Gow, the Conservative Member for Eastbourne, introduced, in the session 1975 6, a Private Member's bill including a provision that the Select Committee must be consulted on appointment of a Parliamentary Commissioner. This was not enacted, but it would be advantageous if legislation on these lines were passed and important that such legislation should include a requirement for nomination of candidates for the office of Parliamentary Commissioner by the Select Committee. It would be unsatisfactory if consultation with the Select Committee came to mean only that the Prime Minister gave advanced notice to the Select Committee of his choice of a Parliamentary Commissioner and continued to treat the appointment as part of the internal promotion network in the higher ranks of the Civil Service.

In its report in May 1976 the Select Committee on the Parliamentary Commissioner gave its opinion in strong terms that the House of Commons should be consulted on the appointment of a Parliamentary Commissioner. It thought that Ian Gow's proposal that the chairman of the Select Committee should be asked to give his views on the candidates for the post, and that the appointment should be confirmed by a resolution in each House of Parliament, was the minimum requirement for consultation. It also suggested that the House of Commons should have an opportunity of discussing whether or not the person appointed should invariably be a former civil servant.[1]

The Callaghan Government did not accept all of the Select Committee's proposals on the appointment of a Parliamentary Commissioner. But it announced in March 1977 that when a vacancy next occurred in the post the Government would arrange for the chairman of the Select Committee to be consulted 'about the experience and qualities desirable in candidates', and any names the chairman wished to recommend would be taken into consideration at that stage. At a later stage the chairman would be shown the list of two or three names from which the Prime Minister intended to make his recommendation to the Queen.[2] The Government also said that in its view it was desirable for successive holders of the post 'to bring to it diverse experience of relevant fields of public administration'. Since the three appointees to that date had been from the Civil Service, the Government said that the next appointee would be someone with substantially different experience, perhaps from local government or the nationalized industries.[3] This represented a very considerable advance by the Government towards the Select Committee's position on appointment of the Parliamentary Commissioner.

Just as it would be advantageous if the Parliamentary Commissioner was not always a former civil servant, so it would be an advantage if not all his staff were civil servants. It is clearly desirable to have some members of his staff who have Civil Service experience but they should be intermixed with people who have experience, for example, in local government, social work, or business. Such people would, on occasion, be prepared to question Civil Service standards and attitudes, in a way which civil servants might not.

The present practice whereby all the staff are on secondment from their departments is also of dubious value. Again, it would not be sensible to exclude such secondments, but there is a strong argument for saying that the bulk of appointments to the Commissioner's staff, of people from both inside and outside the Civil

[1] H.C. 480 of 1975–6. Second Report from the Select Committee on the Parliamentary Commissioner for Administration, pp. xiv–xv at paras. 29–31.

[2] Cmnd. 6764, Second Report from the Select Committee on the Parliamentary Commissioner for Administration, Session 1975–6, Observations by the Government, H.M.S.O., 1977, p. 3 at para. 7.

[3] Ibid., at para. 8.

Service, should be permanent appointments. The Commissioner's staff is large enough and the work is varied enough for there to be a career structure within his own staff. It would also be an advantage to have most of the senior positions on the Commissioner's staff, such as the Heads of Investigating Units and the Investigating Directors, filled from within his staff by people who have had investigating experience. There could also be some interchange between the Parliamentary Commissioner's staff and the staff of the Local Commissioners for Administration which, as we shall see, is composed of people with a varied experience and background.

The Parliamentary Commissioner should also have his own legal adviser, independent of the government service. It is not satisfactory that he should receive legal advice from the Government's own adviser, the Treasury Solicitor. It raises doubts, for example, about the quality of advice which the Commissioner received in the television licence case and which led him to state that he did not feel able to question the Home Office's actions since it had been told by its legal advisers that they were not illegal: a view which was promptly shown to be wrong by a successful appeal to the courts. It may well be that an independent lawyer would have given him the same advice, but then it would have been known that the advice was independent.

We come then to the conclusion that it was a mistake to have set up the Parliamentary Commissioner and his staff as a kind of internal administrative audit rather than as an independent investigating service. The question is whether anything significant would be lost by normally not appointing a civil servant as Parliamentary Commissioner, by having his staff composed of people with a varied background, not exclusively from the Civil Service, and by giving him his own independent legal adviser. The one danger is that the relationship with the permanent heads of department might deteriorate to some extent. But all the other Ombudsmen we have studied, except the Médiateur, have staff who are entirely independent of the Civil Service and they all have good relations with the heads of departments with whom they have to deal. The Médiateur is in a kind of midway position since some of his staff are permanently appointed to his office while others are part-time and he also makes extensive use of the specialized government inspectorates for which we have no clear parallel in this country.[1]

[1] See above, pp. 98–9.

A number of important gains would result from making the Parliamentary Commissioner's office a truly independent service. First, it would produce greater public confidence in the really independent character of his judgement. Second, it would make the Parliamentary Commissioner's office more publicity-conscious and more aware of the need to be communicating constantly with the public about the Commissioner's activities and his potentialities for helping to produce redress. We have seen that one of the chief weaknesses of the present Parliamentary Commissioner system is the poor publicity attendant on the Commissioner's activities so that his on the whole highly creditable achievements for complainants are little known about or understood.

THE NEED TO PROVIDE FOR DIRECT ACCESS TO THE COMMISSIONER

The other great weakness of the present Parliamentary Commissioner system is that so few people take their complaints to him. We have seen that he is by far the least used, in terms of population, of any of the Ombudsmen we have surveyed. In part this is due to the inadequate publicity secured for his work. But it is even more clearly due to the fact that he has to be approached through Members of Parliament and cannot take up a complaint direct from a member of the public. We see from Table XII that in every year since 1972 more people have gone direct to the Commissioner with their complaints, and have had to be rebuffed, than have gone to him through an M.P. But the figure of those who at present approach him direct probably greatly underestimates the potential volume of complaints. The Royal Commission on the Constitution (the Kilbrandon Commission) organized a random sample survey which shed some light on this question. Two-thirds of the people questioned in the survey said that they had had grievances, at some time, against an agency of central or local government, the health service, or a nationalized industry. No less than one-half of such people also said that their grievance had not been resolved, either because they had not received satisfaction of their complaint or because they thought it would be useless to complain.[1] The Swedish experience is also highly relevant here since Sweden, like the United Kingdom, is on the whole a well-administered country but the volume of

[1] Cmnd. 5460–1, Royal Commission on the Constitution, 1969–1973 (H.M.S.O., 1973), vol. ii, p. 16.

complaints received each year by the Swedish Ombudsmen is far greater than the volume of complaints reaching the Parliamentary Commissioner. There is a strong likelihood, therefore, that direct access to the Parliamentary Commissioner would greatly increase the flow of complaints to him. This could be assisted by making the Citizens' Advice Bureaux some of the main pick-up points for the Parliamentary Commissioner. The Bureaux could be circularized by the Parliamentary Commissioner with details of ways in which they could help citizens in presenting their complaints to him. For example, Bureaux staff could assist the complainant to put his complaint into writing, and could advise on the eligibility of the complaint.

The Parliamentary Commissioner's office could also, with direct access, be much more receptive to complainants than it is at present. The Commissioner's office is in Church House, Westminister, which is used for a group of small government offices and is just beyond Westminster Abbey, in Great Smith Street. It is therefore, like other Ombudsman's offices we have surveyed, centrally placed in the capital, and it is near to the Houses of Parliament. But unlike other Ombudsman's offices it is not much visited by members of the public. Complainants are sometimes invited to go to the office during the course of an investigation, but this is infrequent and usually occurs in the more serious cases when the Parliamentary Commissioner himself, or his Deputy, is carrying out the investigation. Examples of recent cases which the Parliamentary Commissioner has himself investigated are the Court Line case and the Edinburgh (Turnhouse) Airport case. In the latter case the Parliamentary Commissioner in fact went to Edinburgh to interview the parties in the case. A recent case investigated by the Deputy to the Commissioner was the asbestosis case and, in this instance, he decided to visit Yorkshire to interview the complainant and the regional staff of the Factory Inspectorate. In the more run of the mill case it is normal for the investigator, if he decides to interview the complainant, to go to the complainant's home to see him.

Visits by members of the public to the Parliamentary Commissioner's office are therefore relatively rare and potential complainants are not encouraged to visit the office or to telephone details of their complaints (as they do to the Quebec Public Protector) because the statutory channel to the Parliamentary Commissioner at present is through an M.P. If access were direct the office staff could make themselves much more available to complainants. Direct access would of course mean that complainants would still be able to go through an M.P. to the Commissioner, but they would have a choice of channel: either direct to him or through an M.P.

There is some indication that the present complicated method of access to the Commissioner not only reduces the flow of complaints but also to some extent favours the more articulate middle-class person and is to the disadvantage of the less articulate and the less affluent. Table XIII lists the numbers of complaints investigated by the Parliamentary Commissioner in 1974 and 1975, ranked by department. What is clear from the table is that a high proportion of complaints investigated by the Parliamentary Commissioner in

TABLE XIII

United Kingdom Parliamentary Commissioner, 1974–1975

Complaints investigated (ranked by department)*

	1974	1975	Total in the 2 years
Department of Health and Social Security	51	75	126
Inland Revenue	60	49	109
Department of the Environment	54	46	100
Trade and Industry (including separate Department of Industry after April 1974)	8	58	66
Home Office	20	41	61
Department of Employment	14	9	23
Customs and Excise	11	4	15
Ministry of Agriculture	7	8	15
Department of Education and Science	6	8	14
Scottish Office	5	8	13
Welsh Office	7	5	12
Foreign and Commonwealth Office	3	3	6

* Departments against which less than 5 complaints were investigated in the two-year period are not included in this table.

Source: Compiled from Parliamentary Commissioner's Annual Reports for 1974 and 1975 (H.C. 126 of 1974–5 and H.C. 141 of 1975–6).

those years were against three departments: the Inland Revenue, the Department of the Environment, and Trade and Industry (which during part of this period consisted of separate departments, and for part of the time was one department). Together these three departments accounted for 275 of the investigations carried out by the Commissioner. Complaints against these departments are predominantly from relatively well-to-do people or from business firms. On the other hand, complaints investigated against the Department of Health and Security, where a good proportion of complaints are about pension rights and come in many cases from less well-to-do people, numbered only 126, although this was the largest single group of complaints. It is of course true that some complaints against the Inland Revenue come from less well-to-do people and it is certain that some of the Commissioner's investigations in Inland Revenue cases have brought major benefits to such people. For example, in 1972 the Select Committee was able to report that the Inland Revenue had responded to suggestions put forward by the Commissioner and the Committee about demands for arrears of tax due to departmental error. The Inland Revenue had decided to remit, partially or completely, demands for such arrears where the individual concerned could show that it would cause hardship.[1] This concession in particular benefits people on retirement pension who would find it difficult to meet arrears which had accrued while they were wage-earners. Nevertheless, it is undeniable that the bulk of people who employ tax consultants, and therefore may be advised to take their case to the Parliamentary Commissioner via an M.P., are members of the middle class.

The contrast here with other Ombudsmen we have surveyed, and particularly with the Swedish Ombudsmen, is quite striking. In Sweden a large number of complaints to the Ombudsmen come from middle-class people. Thus in 1974 the Swedish Ombudsmen investigated 251 complaints against the departments concerned with taxation and revenue and 85 complaints against planning. But the volume of complaints they investigated from the less affluent sections of the population was much greater. Thus in 1974 they investigated 321 complaints against the police, 312 complaints about social services, 257 complaints about medical care, and 236 complaints against prisons. The contrast in this last category is particularly notable. The Parliamentary Commissioner investigates very few complaints from prisoners. In 1974 the total number of complaints which he investigated against the Home Office, and this includes complaints from prisoners, was only 20. It is true that he has secured redress for prisoners in some important cases but this

[1] H.C. 334 of 1971–2. Second Report from the Select Committee on the Parliamentary Commissioner for Administration, pp. ix–x at paras. 19–21.

only strengthens the argument that his services should be more widely used by prisoners.[1] The presumption must be that very few prisoners know about the Parliamentary Commissioner, or think it would be worth while to complain to him. We should also note that whereas in Sweden, and in the Canadian provinces, prisoners' letters must be forwarded unopened to the Ombudsman, in the United Kingdom not only do prisoners not have direct access to the Ombudsman, but their letters to M.P.s are opened and examined by the prison authorities.

How would the increased flow of complaints which would result from providing for direct access to the Commissioner affect the organization of his office and the character of the Parliamentary Commissioner system in the United Kingdom? Clearly, the 'Rolls-Royce' kind of investigations which the Commissioner uses for all complaints could not then be used in every case. The present system of investigation in which he sends the investigator to the department concerned to examine the files and, if necessary, interview the officials concerned would have to be confined to the more serious and complex cases. More routine cases would be handled, as they are by other Ombudsmen and their staff, by simpler methods such as telephone or written inquiry to the department concerned. This transition would make it even more appropriate for the Commissioner not to confine himself to *ex post facto* review but to try and secure immediate redress for the complainant.

The value and the feasibility of retaining the present investigation procedures for the more serious cases deserve emphasis. It is one of the strong points of the Parliamentary Commissioner system that the investigators, including in the major cases the Commissioner himself or his Deputy, themselves interview the civil servants concerned. Another strong point which could also be retained is the Commissioner's power to criticize Ministers. The three main reports in which the Commissioner has exercised his power in this way, to good effect, have been the Sachsenhausen case, the Duccio painting case, and the Court Line case. But of course these have not been the only occasions when the Commissioner has interviewed Ministers. When he interviews a Minister he normally goes to the department concerned and interviews the Minister in his own room.

Another excellent feature of the Parliamentary Commissioner system is his link with the Select Committee of the Commons. This

[1] See above, pp. 86, 154.

also would be retained if direct access to the Commissioner were permitted. His responsibility to Parliament would remain, as would the Members' own role as a channel to the Commissioner. The interest taken by the Committee in his activities would, if anything, probably be enhanced because of the increased volume and range of cases which would come to him following direct access.

It would be wrong to assume that the Parliamentary Commissioner's office is complacent about the present limitation of access to the Commissioner through M.P.s. In an interview to *C.H.C. News*, the journal published for Community Health Councils, Sir Alan Marre said, just after his retirement from the posts of Parliamentary Commissioner and Health Service Commissioner: 'I think it is confusing to the member of public not only that there are a number of different commissioners, but that the method of access is different to each of them.'[1] At present, a member of the public must go through an M.P. to the Parliamentary Commissioner, he can go direct to the Health Service Commissioner without an intermediary, and he must apply to a Local Commissioner for Administration, in the first instance through a local councillor, but if a councillor refuses to forward his complaint he can complain direct to the Local Commissioner.

Before we consider how the problems created by the proliferation of Ombudsmen in the United Kingdom can best be tackled, it is appropriate to assess the development and operation of the Health Service Commissioner and the Local Commissioners for Administration. This we shall do in the chapters which follow.

[1] *C.H.C. News*, Apr. 1976.

VIII

THE UNITED KINGDOM: THE HEALTH SERVICE COMMISSIONER

WHEN the Parliamentary Commissioner Bill was being debated in Parliament in 1966 and 1967, the most strongly criticized feature was the provision in Schedule 3 which excluded National Health Service hospitals from scrutiny by the Parliamentary Commissioner. The Government was defeated on this issue at committee stage of the Bill in the Commons, but it had the provision to exclude the hospitals restored at report stage, and although it promised to look at the question again it successfully resisted an amendment to bring the hospitals back in during discussion of the Bill in the Lords.

In the Commons numerous M.P.s from the Conservative and Labour sides of the House had argued strongly for inclusion of the hospitals, principally on the grounds that the existing procedure for complaints in the hospital service was very unsatisfactory and that there was a great deal of evidence available to M.P.s of disquiet amongst users of the service about the handling of complaints.[1] It was therefore to be expected that the Select Committee on the Parliamentary Commissioner would early on review the arguments for continuing to exclude the hospitals. On 12 June 1968 it heard evidence from the Permanent Secretary at the Ministry of Health, Sir Arnold France, and from the Secretary of the Scottish Home and Health Department, Mr. R. E. C. Johnson. Members of the Committee were not convinced by the arguments put forward by the Ministries for continued exclusion of the hospitals and the Committee reported to the Commons in July 1968 that, in its view the Parliamentary Commissioner should be empowered to examine complaints about the hospitals.[2]

Just at this time, the Minister of Health, Kenneth Robinson,

[1] Stacey, *The British Ombudsman*, pp. 153–9 and 184–7.

[2] H.C. 350 of 1967–8. Second Report from the Select Committee on the Parliamentary Commissioner for Administration, p. xiv at para. 37.

published a discussion document on reorganization of the Health Service and included in this document the suggestion that either the Parliamentary Commissioner's jurisdiction should be extended to include the hospitals, or a separate Health Service Commissioner should be appointed.[1] Other features of his scheme for reorganization came in for much criticism and his successor as Minister responsible for the Health Service, Richard Crossman, published a much revised series of proposals in June 1970. Crossman's Green Paper included the statement that consultation with professional and other interests was continuing about the proposal for a Health Service Commissioner.

Many voluntary organizations concerned with the Health Service were in favour of an Ombudsman for the hospitals. For example, a book published by Aid for the Elderly in Government Institutions (A.E.G.I.S.) in 1967 concluded with a strong plea for a Health Service Ombudsman.[2] But the doctors' organizations were generally critical, and the idea might not have got off the ground had it not been for a series of reports of inquiries into allegations of ill-treatment of patients in psychiatric hospitals at Ely in 1969, and at Farleigh and Whittingham Hospitals in 1971 and 1972. The report of the Farleigh Hospital Inquiry recommended that 'A Health Service Commissioner, given the widest possible powers, should be appointed urgently to meet public anxiety about the investigation of complaints in the health service.'[3] In February 1972 the Heath Government announced that it intended to set up Health Service Commissioners for England, Wales, and Scotland. The proposals were implemented in the National Health Service, Scotland, Act, 1972, and the National Health Service Reorganization Act, 1973.

These Acts provide for separate Health Service Commissioners for England, Wales, and Scotland but the Government decided that, in the first instance, all three offices would be held by the Parliamentary Commissioner. As we have seen in Chapter VII, the actual volume of complaints reaching the Parliamentary Commissioner through M.P.s had proved much smaller than had been anticipated. Sir Edmund Compton had estimated in April 1967 that

[1] Ministry of Health, *National Health Service. The Administrative Structure of the Medical and Related Services in England and Wales* (H.M.S.O., 1968), pp. 24–5.

[2] Barbara Robb, *Sans Everything* (Nelson, 1967). See the concluding section by Brian Abel-Smith, pp. 128–35.

[3] Cmnd. 4557, Report of the Farleigh Hospital Committee of Inquiry, p. 29, recommendation 12.

he might receive between 6,000 and 7,000 complaints a year. In fact, in 1973 Sir Alan Marre received only 571 complaints as Parliamentary Commissioner. He therefore had spare capacity to take on, in addition, his new roles as Health Service Commissioner for England, Wales, and Scotland, and he began to receive complaints in his new functions in October 1973.

The Health Service Commissioner has a different relationship with complainants from the relationship which the Parliamentary Commissioner has. People complaining against the health authorities for example the Regional and Area Health Authorities in England, or the Health Boards in Scotland, as well as the Family Practitioner Committees, can complain direct to the Health Service Commissioner. They do not have to go through a Member of Parliament or other intermediary. They do, however, have to have made their complaint, in the first place, to the health authority concerned and to have given that authority an adequate opportunity to investigate it, before the Health Service Commissioner can investigate. The one exception to this requirement is when a complaint is made by a member of staff of a hospital or health authority, acting on behalf of a patient who is not able to complain himself. This provision was put into the legislation, during its passage through Parliament, and is intended to allow a nurse, for example, to complain directly to the Commissioner, on behalf of a mental patient, where complaint to the relevant authority might result in victimization, or blocking of the complaint.

The Health Service Commissioner also has a wider frame of reference than the Parliamentary Commissioner in making his investigations. He is empowered to investigate 'an alleged failure in a service provided by a relevant body' or 'an alleged failure of a relevant body to provide a service which it was a function of the body to provide', where someone complains to him that he has sustained injustice or hardship as a result of this failure or as a result of maladministration.[1]

In other respects, his powers are very similar to those of the Parliamentary Commissioner. He can require the production of documents by the health authority. He is instructed not to investigate any action where the aggrieved person has a right of appeal to an administrative tribunal or to a court of law. But, like the Parliamentary Commissioner, he may waive this instruction where he thinks

[1] National Health Service Reorganization Act, 1973, Sect. 34–(3).

it is not reasonable for the complainant to go to a court or tribunal. The National Health Service Reorganization Act also almost exactly reproduces the limitation on the Parliamentary Commissioner as regards questioning the merits of discretionary decisions. The Act states at Section 39–(2): 'It is hereby declared that nothing in this Part of this Act authorises or requires a Commissioner to question the merits of a decision taken without maladministration by a relevant body in the exercise of a discretion vested in that body.' This is exactly the phraseology used in the Parliamentary Commissioner Act, merely substituting the words 'relevant body' for 'government department' or 'authority'.

The provision for direct access to the Health Service Commissioner, and his wider frame of reference, constitute a considerable advance on the role and powers of the Parliamentary Commissioner. But his effectiveness is reduced by two limitations which are placed upon him by the Acts. First, he is not allowed to investigate complaints, or aspects of complaints, in which the clinical judgement of Health Service staff is in question.[1] Second, he is expressly excluded from investigating complaints about the operation of Medical Service Committees, or of the Dental and other Service Committees of Family Practitioner Committees. These are the administrative tribunals which examine complaints against doctors, dentists, pharmacists, and opticians practising in the Health Service. We shall consider, in turn, the implications for the effectiveness of the Health Service Commissioner of these two major exclusions.

The provision which excludes the Commissioner from investigating complaints which involve clinical judgement was written into the Acts at the insistence of the British Medical Association. It is a limitation which is hard to justify particularly since the Parliamentary Commissioner is able to investigate complaints which come to him from patients in hospitals under the direct control of government departments, and is not then excluded from looking at clinical questions. These are the top-security hospitals at Broadmoor, Rampton, Moss Side, and Carstairs and the Ministry of Defence hospitals provided for members of the armed forces. The Select Committee on the Parliamentary Commissioner was told in 1968 that when the Parliamentary Commissioner investigated a

[1] The Health Service Commissioner himself decides whether or not the action complained about was a matter of clinical judgement. See National Health Service Reorganization Act, Schedule 3–(1).

complaint which had a clinical aspect, from one of the top-security hospitals, he took medical advice on the clinical aspect of the case.[1] The Health Service Commissioner could do this perfectly well in Health Service cases, and the National Health Service Reorganization Act specificially empowers him, at Section 33–(3), to 'obtain advice from any person who is qualified to give it' and pay a fee for the advice given.

This exclusion from considering clinical questions is one factor which helps to account for the high proportion of complaints which he has to decline to investigate. From Table XIII we see, for example, that in the year 1974–5 he had to reject, as outside his jurisdiction, 354 of the 612 complaints which were sent to him during the year (or were carried forward from the previous part year). He told the Select Committee in 1975 that about one-sixth of these 354 cases were outside his jurisdiction because they were complaints about the diagnosis or the treatment of patients solely concerned with the exercise of clinical judgement by medical staff.[2] Perhaps even more serious than this is the dissatisfaction caused to complainants when they find that the Health Service Commissioner can only look at part of their complaint because he is excluded from looking at the clinical aspects. The Commissioner is fully aware of this dissatisfaction. Sir Alan Marre told the Select Committee in 1975 that 'from the complainants' point of view he often feels that I have done only half or less than half the job'.[3]

This can be well illustrated from a case of which the author had first-hand knowledge. A lady complained to the Health Service Commissioner about the treatment which her brother had received when taken to hospital suffering from pneumonia. She complained that he was kept cold in bed with very few blankets, although he had a high temperature, and that this treatment led to a worsening of his condition which resulted in his death in hospital. She also complained that a student nurse was given a test on the care of her brother shortly before his death, that she was not allowed to be at his bedside when he died, and that a post-mortem was carried out on him without her consent. The Health Service Commissioner was only able to investigate these latter aspects of her complaint which

[1] H.C. 350 of 1967–8. Second Report from the Select Committee on the Parliamentary Commissioner for Administration, p. 130 at question 742.

[2] H.C. 282 of 1975–6. First Report from the Select Committee on the Parliamentary Commissioner for Administration: Health Service Commissioner, p. vi at para. 4.

[3] Ibid., p. 4.

TABLE XIV

Complaints to the Health Service Commissioner from England, Scotland, and Wales, 1973–1976

	1973–4 1 Oct. '73– 31 Mar. '74	1974–5 1 Apr. '74– 31 Mar. '75	1975–6 1 Apr. '75– 31 Mar. '76
Complaints received in the year	361	493	504
Brought forward from previous year	—	119	106
Total received	361	612	610
Rejected as outside jurisdiction	203	354	360
Discontinued after partial investigation (or withdrawn)	16	24	17
Investigated	23	128	128
Complaints upheld in whole or in part	Not recorded	68	67
Carried forward to the following year	119	106	105

Source: Health Service Commissioner's Annual Reports.

were of course subsidiary to her main complaint which was that the treatment had been wrong and had caused her brother's death. Since this was a matter of clinical judgement the Commissioner could not give any view of this aspect of the case and although the complainant agreed that the Commissioner's investigator had shown every courtesy and care in interviewing her about her complaint, in the privacy of her own home, she was deeply dissatisfied with the outcome of the investigation. Nor can it have been a very satisfactory outcome to the consultant who, one may reasonably assume, would have preferred to have his decision regarding treatment tested before the Commissioner's skilled medical adviser.

It has long been recognized that the internal procedures in Health Service hospitals for investigating complaints against medical and nursing staff are very unsatisfactory. There is no uniformly applied system and such committees of inquiry as are appointed to investigate the most serious kinds of complaint against medical staff are not statutory tribunals and are not therefore subject to the scrutiny of the Council on Tribunals which has, since 1958, acted as a watch-dog of the composition and operation of statutory tribunals. The Department of Health and Social Security appointed a broadly based committee chaired by a barrister, Sir Michael Davies, to consider this question. The Committee included among its membership Sir John Richardson, a leading consultant physician who in 1974 became President of the General Medical Council, two other medical men, three university social scientists, expert in the area of inquiry, representatives of interested voluntary associations, of hospital administrators, and of nursing staff, and two well-known journalists specially interested in Health Service questions.

The Michael Davies Committee reported in October 1973 recommending three main lines of reform.[1] First, it suggested that there should be a national Code of Practice for dealing with suggestions and complaints about hospital services which should be uniformly applied by health authorities in all hospitals. This Code should include provision of a booklet for all patients, on entering hospital, telling them how to make a complaint. Second, it recommened that there should be a standard procedure for internal inquiries into complaints including provision for a hearing at which the complainant would himself be present accompanied, if he wished, by a friend to help represent him. Third, for the most serious types of complaint, which could involve litigation, there should be independent Investigating Panels which would be subject to the scrutiny of the Council on Tribunals.

The report was not immediately implemented by the Department of Health and Social Security, indeed after three years the report had still not been implemented. The main reason for delay was strong opposition from the medical profession to the recommendations in the report. Eventually, the Secretary of State for Social Services asked the Select Committee on the Parliamentary Commissioner to undertake a special inquiry into the jurisdiction of the Health Service Commissioner, in the light of the Davies Committee's proposal for Investigating Panels. What it was being asked in effect to do was to take evidence and recommend which would be the better alternative: to extend the jurisdiction of the Health Service Commissioner to allow him to consider complaints about clinical judgement, or to set up Investigating Panels on the lines suggested by the Davies Committee. The Select Committee was asked by the Secretary of State to undertake this inquiry on 9 February 1976 and although it accepted the commission with some reluctance, since members of the Committee were not certain that they were an appropriate body for this kind of inquiry, they felt that they could not refuse since 'an essential feature of the inquiry would be an examination of one of the major statutory limitations on the jurisdic-

[1] Department of Health and Social Security. The Welsh Office, *Report of the Committee on Hospital Complaints Procedure* (H.M.S.O., 1973).

tion of the Health Service Commissioner'.[1] The Select Committee began its inquiry in the summer of 1976 by inviting evidence from the Department of Health and Social Security, the Health Authorities, the Community Health Councils, doctors' and nurses' organizations, and voluntary bodies like the Patients' Association. The Committee was given the services of a special adviser and two assistants to help in the inquiry.[2]

It is appropriate to consider at this point what light the Health Service Commissioner's reports already throw on which would be the more effective method of examining complaints against hospital staff in clinical questions. One case which he summarized in his Report for 1975–6 illustrated very well some of the strong points of the Ombudsman style of investigation. A man had complained to him that he had been improperly detained in a psychiatric ward of a general hospital and there given electro-convulsive therapy (E.C.T.) without his consent. The complainant told the Commissioner that he had twice declined to sign the consent form for E.C.T. but on the second occasion his hand had been guided by an attendant. He was then too weak from the drugs which had been administered to him to resist, but he snatched at the form afterwards. The Commissioner examined the consent form and found that the signature did not particularly resemble the patient's usual signature and that the form had been torn and repaired. He also noted that the form should have been signed by a charge nurse confirming that the nature, effect, and risks of E.C.T. had been explained to the patient, but this part of the form had been left blank. The Commissioner concluded, in studiedly moderate but nevertheless firm words that it seemed to him that the nurses 'had gone further than was appropriate in getting the complainer to sign the form against his real wishes'.[3] The Commissioner asked the Health Board (the hospital was in Scotland) to review its procedures and instructions to staff, and he noted in his report that the Board had made arrangements to ensure that consent for E.C.T. was obtained only by medical

[1] H.C. 282 of 1975–6. First Report from the Select Committee on the Parliamentary Commissioner for Administration: Health Service Commissioner, pp. vi–vii at para. 7.

[2] The Select Committee has now reported suggesting that the Health Service Commissioner should no longer be prevented from investigating cases which involve clinical judgement. *First Report from the Select Committee on the Parliamentary Commissioner for Administration, 1977–8: Independent review of Hospital Complaints in the NHS*, H.C. 45 of 1977–8 (M.S.).

[3] H.C. 528 of 1975–6. First Report of the Health Service Commissioner, p. 15 at para. 4.

staff, and had altered the consent form so that it was obvious that only a doctor was allowed to explain E.C.T. and obtain consent.

A number of the advantages of the Commissioner's kind of investigation are illustrated by this case. First, the power that the Commissioner enjoys to require that all the documents be shown to him, or to his investigator, enabled him to scrutinize the actual consent form and verify, to his satisfaction, the complainant's account. A tribunal in this instance would probably have been able to examine the consent form, but there is less certainty in the tribunal procedure that all the relevant documents will be produced for it. The Commissioner's investigator is able to see all the relevant documents in the files and records. Second, this incident which clearly had occurred in a highly charged emotional situation, in which the nurses argued that they were acting in the best interests of a very disturbed man, was investigated with the minimum of fuss. Tribunal proceedings would have been much more cumbersome, possibly more protracted, and probably would have caused more anguish to the parties. Third, the Commissioner received a follow-up from his investigation in the shape of evidence from the Health Board that it had changed its instructions to staff and modified the consent form. A tribunal arrives at a finding and allocates blame, where it thinks appropriate, but it is not able itself to follow up its findings by ascertaining whether procedures are changed to minimize the possibility of a similar incident in future.

There are two further points in favour of the Commissioner procedure which are not illustrated by this case. The first is that the Commissioner can apply uniform standards in his investigations whereas tribunals, particularly when there are a great many of them, apply a multiplicity of standards. Variations can in theory be corrected by provision for appeal, but appeal systems are rarely altogether satisfactory. Certainly, as we shall see, the provisions for appeal from the administrative tribunals in the family practitioner sector, the Service Committees, are not adequate. Second, the Health Service Commissioner is accountable for his recommendations whereas tribunals are not accountable for their findings in as full a sense. The Commissioner's recommendations are embodied in his results reports which are now published in quarterly volumes and can be scrutinized by the Select Committee. Similarly, a complainant who is dissatisfied by one of the Commissioner's case reports can complain to the Select Committee.

The case against the Commissioner's method of investigation has been made (in letters to the Patients' Association) by some dissatisfied complainants to the Commissioner. They criticize the fact that the complainant is not allowed to see the statements given to the Commissioner by hospital personnel, and therefore the complainant is not able to challenge the accuracy of the evidence given by hospital staff, as he would be able to do in tribunal proceedings. They have also criticized the fact that the Commissioner does not disclose the identity of hospital personnel and that there is no right of appeal from the Commissioner's findings (other than complaint to the Select Committee).

There is substance in these points. What they seem to indicate is that the advantages which we have suggested are inherent in the Commissioner's investigating procedure are more than outweighed if the complainant does not have confidence in the determination and acumen of the Commissioner and his investigators. It is therefore for the Commissioner to show in his reports that his investigators are fair-minded, but also penetrating, and that they do not tolerate obstruction or special pleading on the part of hospital staff.

By and large, they have given this impression. The Health Service Commissioner's annual reports have, in the author's view, been much more informative than the Parliamentary Commissioner's annual and quarterly reports are. There are a number of reasons for this. First, the Health Service Commissioner did not, until December 1976, attempt to give the text of all his reports as the Parliamentary Commissioner does. He gave a selection of summarized reports and he made the selection in a way which illustrated the scope of his investigations and their effectiveness. Second, each of the summaries was headed in black type with a title such as 'Failure to provide an adequate dental service' or 'Failures in nursing care, and delay in dealing with complaints' which helped the reader to find the summaries which were most interesting to him. In December 1976 the Health Service Commissioner decided to publish the 'anonymized' texts of all his reports, at intervals throughout the year, in much the same way as he does as Parliamentary Commissioner.[1] This has certain advantages in making possible a comprehensive review of his investigations, but it is to be hoped that the Health Service Commissioner will not now modify the form of his annual

[1] H.C. 21 of 1976–7, First Report of the Health Service Commissioner, gives the first collection of 'anonymized' texts of his reports.

report but will continue to provide the same kind of informative summaries as he has in the past.

A third reason for the Health Service Commissioner's reports being, on the whole, more informative than those of the Parliamentary Commissioner may be his wider terms of reference. Since he can report on the failure of a service, or the failure to provide a service, he is able to make rather broader criticism and more far-reaching recommendations than are always open to the Parliamentary Commissioner. Thus in a case which he summarized in his first report, covering the period from October 1973 to the end of March 1974, the Health Service Commissioner investigated a complaint from a man requiring nose surgery who had been waiting eighteen months for treatment and who also complained that the hospital failed to make an appointment for the consultant to review his condition, when he told them that this was deteriorating. When the Commissioner's investigator called for the admission records in ear, nose, and throat cases at the hospital, he found that some patients had been waiting over six years for admission. He found that a major cause of these delays was the refusal by the Regional Hospital Board to agree to the appointment of an additional consultant, on the grounds that other specialities needed to be given higher priority in the region. The Commissioner then made three sets of recommendations in his report. He suggested, first, that more information should be given by the hospital to patients about the length of time they might be kept waiting for admission, and what they should do to get urgent action if their condition deteriorated. Second, he suggested that the Hospital Management Committee should make more satisfactory admission arrangements in the hospital, and he was informed of the proposals the Management Committee was making to the Regional Hospital Board with this end in mind. Third, on the wider question of the low priority being given in the region to ear, nose, and throat cases, he suggested that the Regional Board should review 'the clearly unsatisfactory situation' revealed by his investigation.[1] In this case we see, therefore, that because the Commissioner was able to report on 'a failure in the service' he was able to indicate, both in detail and on broader issues of planning and priorities, where he thought improvements could be made.

[1] H.C. 161 of 1974. First Report of the Health Service Commissioner, Annual Report for 1973–4, pp. 14–15.

The organization of the Health Service Commissioner's staff is also a strong point in enhancing his role in investigations. Here, the staff organization developed by the Parliamentary Commissioner, with its emphasis on the investigator going himself to the authority complained against, examining the files, and, where appropriate, interviewing the staff concerned, is particularly appropriate to Health Service cases. The Health Service Commissioner's staff invariably interview the staff concerned and in the great majority of cases interview the complainant too, often in his or her home. It is clearly highly advantageous that this should be done as merely sending for the documents and asking for written representations from the parties would be most unsatisfactory since Health Service complaints often involve conflicting statements about what actually occurred, and these can only be satisfactorily assessed by personal interviews. Other features of the organization of the Commissioner's staff are more open to question. His staff in April 1977 consisted of the Deputy to the Health Service Commissioner, who is of Under-Secretary rank, two Investigating Directors (of Assistant Secretary rank), and twenty investigators, some of Principal and some of Higher Executive Officer rank.[1]

The Commissioner's Deputy in April 1977 was Mr. Geoffrey H. Weston. He is a Fellow of the Institute of Health Service Administration and is on secondment from the Health Service. Of the remaining staff, nearly half were also on secondment from the Health Service and just over half from the Civil Service. The author would see an advantage in modifying the composition of the staff to include a good proportion from outside the Health Service and the Civil Service, alongside people with a Civil Service or Health Service background, whether on secondment or permanent appointment.

The question of the exclusion of the Health Service Commissioner from clinical questions, and whether it should be retained, is an issue of first importance but discussion of it should not obscure the importance of the other main exclusion from the Commissioner's jurisdiction: from considering complaints about the operation of the Service Committees which examine allegations that a general practitioner, dentist, pharmacist, or optician has behaved towards a patient in a way which is in breach of his terms of contract in the

[1] See above, pp. 140–1 for an organization chart of the Parliamentary Commissioner's and the Health Service Commissioner's staffs.

Health Service. These Service Committees are part of the Family Practitioner Committees of the Area Health Authorities (and in Scotland of the Health Boards) which since 1974 have administered the general practitioner services. The predecessors of the Family Practitioner Committees from 1911 to 1948 were called Local Insurance Committees and, from 1948 to 1974, National Health Service Executive Councils. Each Service Committee consists of one-half laymen and one-half professionals and has a lay chairman. Thus the Medical Service Committees consist of three laymen, three doctors, and a lay chairman. The recommendations of each Service Committee have to be approved by its parent Family Practitioner Committee and there is restricted provision for appeal to the Secretary of State for Health and the Social Services (in Scotland to the Secretary of State for Scotland, and in Wales to the Secretary of State for Wales), which is less restricted for professionals than it is for patients. In the more serious cases there can also be reference to the National Health Service Tribunal.

There are good features of the system of Service Committees. One is the balanced composition of the Committees with a lay chairman, although the laymen may be disguised professionals since former or even practising doctors, dentists, etc. may sit as laymen if, for example, they have been appointed to the Committee by a local authority instead of by their local professional committee. Another good feature is the informal nature of proceedings. Barristers, although they may be present to advise the parties, may not address the Committee. Finally, the Service Committees, and the Minister's appeal committees, are all statutory tribunals and are therefore under the general scrutiny of the Council on Tribunals.

There are a number of defects in the system in addition to the points we have already noted: that ostensible laymen may in fact be professionals and that there is unequal provision for appeal to the Minister. The other defects are principally these. First, the rules of procedure are sometimes imperfectly known or applied by the Service Committee chairman and members. The author was himself a member of a Medical Service Committee for eight years and on more than one occasion had to ask the chairman to call to order a barrister advising the doctor complained against, since the barrister was, against the rules of procedure, continually intervening and addressing the Committee. The Committees meet in private and there is no adequate check on how far they are following the rules of procedure in this and in other respects. Second, whereas the doctor is always assisted by a barrister, paid for out of his subscription to the Medical Defence Union (or other comparable body), patients usually have no specialized assistance. They may bring a friend or relative to the hearing, or occasionally an officer of their trade union branch, but usually they are very poorly assisted compared with the skilled assistance which the doctor invariably receives. There is a very strong case for provision for specialized assistance for patients both before and during the hearing. One possibility would be to provide for assistance to be available by the Secretary of the Local Community Health Council which since 1974 has been assigned the role of helping individual complainants as well as making representations to the Area Health Authority. Third, very few patients know about the existence of the complaints procedure. There is a strong case for requiring all doctors and dentists to display a notice in their waiting-rooms telling patients how to make a complaint, and giving the address of the local Family Practitioner Committee. Fourth, the channel of appeal to the Minister's appeal committee is obstructed by the provision in the regulations that the Minister may award costs on appeal.[1] This is a deterrent to complainants against appealing since it is assumed to mean that they may have to meet the heavy costs of barristers' fees incurred by the other party. This provision should be taken out and replaced by a statement that on appeal the Minister will pay appropriate expenses to the complainant and the respondent.

The Department of Health and Social Security is aware of some of the defects in the functioning of Service Committees and in May 1974 the Secretary of State announced in the Commons that there was to be a review of the Service Committee system. It was subsequently decided that this review should be postponed until there had been a decision on the Davies Committee's recommendations on complaints procedure in the hospitals. When this also was postponed, because of opposition from the doctors to the recommendations, and it was decided to ask the Select Committee on the Parliamentary Commissioner to make its inquiry into the possibility of extending the Health Service Commissioner's role by allowing him to look at clinical judgement, it became clear that the review of

[1] Statutory Instruments 1974, No. 455. The National Health Service (Service Committee and Tribunal) Regulations 1974, Sect. 10–(4).

the Service Committee system should proceed independently. The review began in September 1976.

Whether or not some of the defects we have noted in Service Committees are remedied, there is a strong case for allowing the Health Service Commissioner to investigate complaints about the operation of Service Committees. At present, he can investigate complaints about all other aspects of the work of Family Practitioner Committees. He can and does examine complaints about, for example, the closure of surgeries, the removal of patients from a doctor's list, or the handling of complaints about badly fitting dentures. He can also examine complaints about the informal procedure for conciliation which has been operated since 1968 by many Executive Councils (and the Family Practitioner Committees which have succeeded them) when a patient complains against a doctor. This is an alternative to the Service Committee procedure. It is therefore somewhat illogical, and baffling to the complainant, that the Commissioner can look at these other aspects of the Family Practitioner Committee system but not at the Service Committees.

The argument that Service Committees are administrative tribunals and that an Ombudsman should not investigate complaints against tribunals is not a sound one. As we have seen, some Provincial Ombudsmen in Canada can look at complaints against administrative tribunals and they do so with considerable effectiveness.[1] In fact, the Ombudsman's method of investigation is highly appropriate for examining complaints about procedural defects in administrative tribunals. The sort of things that can go wrong in Service Committees could be well exposed as a result of the Commissioner's power to call for the records of the Service Committee and interview the parties concerned. The Commissioner is much better placed than is the Council on Tribunals to investigate such complaints since he has the necessary powers and staff whereas the Council on Tribunals has neither adequate powers nor staff. It has no inspectorate of its own and tribunals are only visited sporadically by members of the Council who act on an unpaid, voluntary basis.

In the hospital sector, the Health Service Commissioner is very much concerned with the operation of internal complaints procedures. In a great many cases he has commented on the failure to provide adequate machinery for complaints. For example, in a case

[1] See above, pp. 54–5, 74–5.

which he summarized in his Report for 1975–6, he described how, after a muddle in a hospital in which a young boy had been 'lost' for four days because he had been placed in the wrong ward, the operation on him having thereby been delayed, it was agreed between the hospital administrator, the parents, and the consultant that there should be an internal inquiry. But the nature of this inquiry was strongly criticized by the Commissioner. It was not held on the lines recommended by the Department of Health and Social Security. The parents were not given the opportunity to take part in the inquiry, nor were they given a written report of its conduct or findings.[1] The Commissioner also commented on the main body of his Report for 1975–6 that on a number of occasions he had 'criticised the shallowness of the investigation of complaints by authorities and the inadequate replies sent to the complainant'.[2] In one case, for example, hospital administrators, acting on legal advice, had sent deliberately uninformative replies to a complainant, and in another the chairman of a Medical Executive Committee gave the administrator wrong information on which to base his reply to the complainant which conflicted with the true explanation given by the consultant concerned in the case.

Clearly, a central part of the Commissioner's role, as is indicated by the provisions in the Act requiring complainants to complain in the first instance to the health authority, is to check on the adequacy of the methods by which the health authorities investigate complaints. One of the principal methods by which they investigate complaints is by holding internal inquiries or, in the case of the Family Practitioner Committees, by using the Service Committee procedure. If the Commissioner is to be fully effective he must be able to examine complaints against Service Committee proceedings, as he can against other forms of internal inquiry. Equally, he must be able to look at the clinical aspects of cases as well as at the administrative aspects. The conclusion seems inescapable, therefore, that if the Health Service Commissioner is to be fully effective the two main bars on his investigation of complaints should be removed. He should be able to examine complaints concerned with clinical questions and he should be able to investigate complaints about the operation of Service Committees in the family practitioner sector.

[1] H.C. 528 of 1975–6. First Report of the Health Service Commissioner, Annual Report for 1975–6, pp. 11–12.

[2] Ibid., p. 6 at para. 14.

At present he is, in the author's view, proving reasonably effective within his limited frame of reference, but he cannot really hope to gain the full confidence of complainants unless these bars on his investigations are removed.

Strengthening the role of the Health Service Commissioner is not, of course, the whole answer to the problem of securing better machinery for complaints in the Health Service. Internal procedures need to be improved in the hospitals on the lines recommended by the Davies Committee, the Service Committees need to be improved, broadly on the lines we have recommended here, and the Community Health Councils need to be brought in much more directly into the complaints procedure. As things stand, their members are often insufficiently aware of what their role could be. When they do take up complaints on behalf of patients, they find all too often that they come up against the limitations regarding clinical judgement or Service Committees which we have seen so often create frustrations for ordinary complainants. There is a need for pressing ahead with reform on all these fronts, but the removal of the principal bars to the effectiveness of the Health Service Commissioner should be a high priority.

There is one further respect in which a widening of the Commissioner's powers should be sought. The Health Service Commissioner is excluded by Schedule 3–(3) of the National Health Service Reorganization Act from investigating complaints about 'Action taken in respect of appointments or removals, pay, discipline, superannuation or other personnel matters in relation to service under the Health Service Acts.' As we have seen, the Select Committee on the Parliamentary Commissioner for Administration has many times recommended that similar restrictions placed upon the Parliamentary Commissioner should be removed. The case for allowing complaints to the Health Service Commissioner in personnel matters is even stronger. The Commissioner has said in his Report for 1973–4 that he would be able to investigate an allegation from a member of staff that he had been victimized for complaining to the Commissioner on behalf of a patient who was not able to complain for himself.[1] He can do this under the provision in the National Health Service Reorganization Act which makes Section 9 of the Parliamentary Commissioner Act applicable to him as Health Service Commissioner. This section empowers the Commissioner

[1] H.C. 161 of 1973–4, p. 8 at para. 26.

to take court proceedings for contempt against anyone who obstructs him in the performance of his functions. But if a Health Service employee suffers victimization for any other reason, the Commissioner is not able to investigate his complaint because that is a personnel matter. This is a quite unsatisfactory situation since acts, or threats, of victimization do occur at various levels in the Health Service and it would be salutary if staff could complain to the Commissioner.

Removing these three main restrictions on the investigating powers of the Commissioner, the bars on clinical questions, Service Committee proceedings, and personnel matters, would increase considerably the volume of complaints which he examines each year. As Table XIII shows, in 1975–6 he had to decline 360 of the 504 cases he received in the year for lack of jurisdiction. A good proportion of the rejected cases fall in one of these categories, although the Commissioner has also pointed out that the largest category of rejected cases consists of complaints which have not yet been submitted to the health authority concerned. He told the Select Committee in 1975 that about one-quarter of the cases he rejects fall in this category.[1] It is probably appropriate that this limitation should be retained for most types of complaint since, as has been suggested in this chapter, the role of the Commissioner *par excellence* is to concern himself with the operation of complaints procedures, to act as an umpire when the patient or member of staff has not been able to get satisfaction from his health authority, and to have a general oversight of the working of internal complaints procedures.

If users of the Health Service were more aware of the existence of the Commissioner, the volume of complaints he receives would be greater. In 1974 the Commissioner commented in his report that he hoped that when the Secretaries of State had made up their minds about the Davies Committee recommendations and given comprehensive guidance about hospital complaints procedures, his own functions would be more widely known and understood by patients.[2] As we have seen, the Davies Committee recommendations have still not been implemented. Neither have the Community Health Councils been well organized in their role in assisting

[1] H.C. 282 of 1975–6. First Report from the Select Committee on the Parliamentary Commissioner for Administration, Minutes of Evidence, p. 2.

[2] H.C. 161 of 1973–4, p. 10 at para. 41.

patients to complain. If a real improvement in Health Service Complaints procedures is to be achieved, both these developments, as well as the widening in the powers of the Commissioner which we have suggested, are necessary.

IX

THE UNITED KINGDOM: THE LOCAL COMMISSIONERS FOR ADMINISTRATION

IN his speech before the 1964 General Eelection, outlining Labour's plans for a Parliamentary Commissioner, Harold Wilson had said that it would be necessary to limit the Commissioner to central government but that the Ombudsman principle could be extended to local government at a later stage.[1] The Parliamentary Commissioner Bill provided that the Commissioner should only have power to examine complaints against central departments or authorities, and the Government successfully resisted attempts in Commons and Lords to include local authorities in the scope of the Bill.

Government spokesmen explained that they were not rejecting the idea of local Ombudsmen but that it would be better for the system to be introduced for local government under separate legislation. The Wilson Government decided that this should await the major review of local government which was begun in May 1966 with the appointment of the Royal Commission on Local Government under the chairmanship of Sir John Maud (later made a life peer under the title Redcliffe-Maud). The Royal Commission reported in June 1969 in favour of an entirely new system of local authorities in England (apart from London which had been re-organized in 1963).

The Wilson Government accepted the proposals with some modifications and the following month the Prime Minister announced in the Commons that legislation would be introduced to set up a system of local Ombudsmen. Discussions with the local authority associations and other interested bodies would precede the introduction of legislation.[2]

[1] Speech by Harold Wilson at Stowmarket on 3 July 1964. See Stacey, *The British Ombudsman*, pp. 43 and 328.

[2] Harold Wilson's statement to the Commons was on 22 July 1969. H.C. Deb., Vol. 187, Cols. 1501–3.

The inter-party organization of lawyers, 'Justice', which, as we saw in Chapter VII, played a major part in preparing the ground for the Parliamentary Commissioner Act, had meanwhile been turning its attention to the question of local Ombudsmen. 'Justice' set up a committee in 1968 chaired by Professor J. F. Garner which in November 1969 produced a report under the title *The Citizen and his Council. Ombudsmen for Local Government?*[1] The report recommended the appointment of one chief commissioner and five or six commissioners for local administration. It suggested that these commissioners should work from a central office rather than being based in the regions because it envisaged that in some branches of government, such as education, planning, and housing, considerable numbers of complaints would involve both central and local government. Liaison between the local commissioners and the Parliamentary Commissioner would then be easier if the local commissioners had their office in a central place. The report recommended that the local commissioners should investigate complaints of maladministration by local authorities, and that the commissioners should receive complaints direct from members of the public.

Early in 1970 the Wilson Government published its proposals for local Ombudsmen as part of a White Paper on *Reform of Local Government in England* whose primary purpose was to set out the Government's proposals for reform of the structure of local government.[2] On the question of local Ombudsmen, the White Paper said that the Government proposed to set up ten or more Local Commissioners for Administration. They would not, as 'Justice' had proposed, work from one central office, but would be based in different parts of the country. They would examine complaints of maladministration by local authorities. They would not receive complaints direct from members of the public. On the analogy of the Parliamentary Commissioner system, complaints to the Local Commissioners would have to be channelled through local councillors.

[1] 'Justice', *The Citizen and his Council. Ombudsmen for Local Government?* (Stevens, 1969). J. F. Garner has been Professor of Public Law at Nottingham University since 1964. From 1950 to 1960 he was Town Clerk of Andover. His many published works on administrative and local government law include *Administrative Law* (4th edn., 1974), *French Administrative Law* (with L. N. Brown, 2nd edn., 1973) and *Law of Sewers and Drains* (5th edn., 1975).

[2] Cmnd. 4276, Reform of Local Government in England (H.M.S.O., 1970).

The Wilson Government's proposals for local government reform were still-born since, in July 1970, the Conservatives defeated Labour at the general election. The incoming Heath Government adopted a different scheme for reforming the structure of local government, but took up the plan for Local Commissioners for Administration. In May 1972 the Government presented it in a modified form in a Consultative Document.

The Document proposed nine Commissioners for Local Administration for England and one for Wales. The Commissioners would investigate complaints of maladministration by local authorities, and although complaints to them would normally be channelled through councillors, if two councillors declined to forward a complaint to the Commissioner he would be empowered to investigate it. The Commissioners would report to specially constituted representative bodies of local authorities and water authorities, and their operation would be financed by the local authorities.

When their views on the Consultative Document had been received from the associations of local authorities and from the National and Local Government Officers Association legislation was drafted in the Department of the Environment. At this stage one potentially important change was made. The decision was taken in the Department to require reference to only one councillor before a complaint could be examined by a Local Commissioner direct from a member of the public. With this change, the provisions setting up a system of Local Commissioners for England and Wales were incorporated into the Local Government Bill, 1974, which became law on the last day of the 1973–4 session of Parliament, before the general election in February 1974.

The 1974 Act provides that there shall be a body of Commissioners known as the Commission for Local Administration in England, and a body of two or more Commissioners known as the Commission for Local Administration in Wales. The Parliamentary Commissioner is a member of both Commissions in order, chiefly, to assist liaison between him and the Local Commissioners in cases which involve both local authorities and central departments. The English Commissioners are appointed by the Queen on the recommendation of the Secretary of State for the Environment, and the Welsh Commissioner on the recommendation of the Secretary of State for Wales, after consultation with the representative bodies of local authorities.

The Act does not specify the number of Commissioners to be appointed. In fact only three Commissioners were appointed for England. Lady Serota, who was designated chairman of the English Commission, had long experience as a councillor. She had been a member of Hampstead Borough Council from 1945 to 1949, of the London County Council from 1954 to 1965, and of the Greater London Council from 1964 to 1967. From 1969 to 1970 she was Minister of State for Health at the Department of Health and Social Security. The other two members of the English Commission are Denis Harrison and Patrick Cook. Denis Harrison had been Town Clerk of Sheffield until local government reorganization in April 1974. Patrick Cook had been chief executive of the English Tourist Board since 1970, and before that was Principal of the British Transport Staff College.

The Local Government Act, 1974, says that the English Commission shall divide England into areas and shall provide for one or more of the Commissioners to be responsible for each area. It does not specify whether or not the Commissioners shall have their offices in those areas. So far, the English Commission has compromised on this question. It divided England into three areas on a population basis. Lady Serota's area consists of Greater London and the south-eastern parts of England, Kent, Surrey, and East and West Sussex. Denis Harrison investigates complaints from the rest of southern England, from the West country, and from the whole of the middle part of England up to a line drawn roughly from the northern Cheshire boundary to just south of the Wash. Patrick Cook is responsible for the whole of England north and north-east of this line. His territory includes Derbyshire, Nottinghamshire, and Lincolnshire but, more surprisingly, also extends into East Anglia, since Cambridgeshire, Norfolk, and Suffolk are all within his area.

For the first year of operation, from the autumn of 1974 until October 1975, all three Commissioners were based in London. In October 1975 the Commission set up a regional office in York from which Patrick Cook operates but Lady Serota and Denis Harrison continued to work from the London office. All the initial screening of complaints, for the northern as well as for the other two regions, is also done at the London office which is in Queen Anne's Gate, close to St. James's Park, and only a short walk away from Westminster and the Parliamentary Commissioner's office.

The English Commissioners were appointed in the summer of

1974 and began to receive complaints in the autumn of that year. A Local Commissioner for Wales, Dafydd Jones-Williams, was appointed at the same time and also began to investigate complaints, from his office in Cardiff, in the autumn of 1974. Before his appointment as Local Commissioner for Wales, Dafydd Jones-Williams had been Clerk to the Merioneth County Council from 1954 to 1970 and then Circuit Administrator for Wales under the Courts Act, 1970. The Welsh Local Commission for Administration consists of himself and the Parliamentary Commissioner. It reports to a Welsh Representative Body composed of four representatives of the Welsh Counties Committee, four representatives of the Council for the Principality, on which all the district councils in Wales are represented, and two representatives of the Welsh National Water Development Authority.

The Local Government Act, 1974, closely follows the Parliamentary Commissioner Act in numerous ways. Part III of the Local Government Act provides at Section 26 that a Local Commissioner may investigate a complaint that a member of the public has 'sustained injustice in consequence of maladministration' in connection with action taken by a local authority, a police authority, or a water authority. The Act also states, at Section 34, that a Local Commissioner may not 'question the merits of a decision taken without maladministration' by a local authority or other relevant authority.

The Act also closely follows the Parliamentary Commissioner Act in saying that a Commissioner shall not investigate a complaint in a case where the complainant has a right of appeal to a tribunal, or has a remedy in a court of law, but that the Commissioner has discretion to investigate in such cases where he is satisfied that it is not reasonable to expect the complainant to have gone to a court or administrative tribunal. To these two provisions, which exactly reproduce provisions in the Parliamentary Commissioner Act, is added a third partial exclusion which is similar in kind. The Commissioner shall not investigate where a complainant has a right of appeal to a Minister of the Crown. He also has discretion to disregard this provision if he thinks it is not reasonable to expect a complainant to appeal to a Minister.

When the Act was drafted in the Department of the Environment, the intention was to give the Commissioners as full access to documents in the possession of a local authority as is provided for the Parliamentary Commissioner in having access to the files of central departments. The Act states that a Local Commissioner 'may require any member or officer of the authority concerned, or any other person who in his opinion is able to furnish information or produce documents relevant to the investigation, to furnish any such information or produce any such documents'.[1] But a decision of the Queen's Bench Division on 15 February 1977 seriously weakened the effect of this provision. Liverpool City Council had refused to disclose documents to the Local Commissioner, Patrick Cook, on the ground that the Act, at Section 32, empowers a local authority to give notice to a Local Commissioner that disclosure of a document would be contrary to the public interest. Clearly the intention was to enable the Local Commissioners to see all the documents but to enable local authorities sometimes to instruct a Commissioner not to disclose in his reports information from documents which he sees. The Lord Chief Justice, Lord Widgery, and two other judges ruled, however, that the words in the Act meant that a local authority could, in the public interest, refuse to disclose documents to a Local Commissioner and they found for Liverpool City Council. The Act will now clearly have to be amended to give the Commissioners the right of access to all local authority documents.

As with the Parliamentary Commissioner, there is a long list of matters from which the Local Commissioners are excluded; these are given in Schedule 5 of the Act. The Local Commissioners may not investigate complaints about personnel matters, including appointments or removal of staff, pay, discipline, or superannuation. They may not investigate complaints about the commencement or conduct of civil or criminal proceedings before a court of law, or about action taken by any authority in connection with the investigation or prevention of crime. They may not investigate action taken on contractual or commercial transactions by any authority, except those relating to the acquisition or disposal of land. This means that no complaint can be investigated, for example, against the bus services run by many local authorities, or about the operation of markets. In the educational sphere, they may not investigate complaints about secular or religious instruction or about the curriculum of schools or colleges. Nor can they investigate complaints about the internal management and organization of schools

[1] Local Government Act, 1974, Sect. 29-(1).

or colleges.[1] As with the Parliamentary Commissioner, any of these exempted matters may be brought within the jurisdiction of the Local Commissioners by Order in Council, proposed by the Government and subject to annulment by either House of Parliament.

Some other limitations on the Commissioners are mentioned in the main body of the Act, and not in the Schedule, and would therefore have to be taken out by full Act of Parliament. Thus Section 26–(7) provides that a Commissioner shall not investigate a complaint about the action of an authority which in his opinion 'affects all or most of the inhabitants of the area of the authority concerned'. This means, for example, that a Commissioner cannot examine a complaint against the level of rates levied by a local authority.

There is one respect in which the role of the Local Commissioners more closely resembles that of the Health Service Commissioner than of the Parliamentary Commissioner. The Local Commissioners, before investigating a complaint, must satisfy themselves that the complaint has already been made to the local authority (or water or police authority) concerned and that the local authority has had an opportunity to investigate and reply to the complaint. This provision in the Local Government Act is comparable to the provisions in the statutes governing the work of the Health Service Commissioner under which he only investigates complaints which have first been made to the relevant health authority, except where a complaint is made by a member of staff on behalf of a patient who cannot complain for himself.[2]

There are three main respects in which the powers and role of the Local Commissioners differ from those of the Parliamentary Commissioner and the Health Service Commissioner. The first we have touched on already: complainants must take their complaints in the first instance to a councillor, but if the councillor declines to forward the complaint to a Commissioner, the Commissioner has discretion to investigate it. Second, the provisions for publicity for the Local Commissioners' reports are more extensive. Third, the Local Commissioners do not report to Parliament but, in England and Wales, to the representative bodies of local and water authorities. We shall examine each of these differences in turn and consider their importance.

[1] Local Government Act, 1974, Sect. 29–(1).

[2] See above, p. 178.

We have noted that it was potentially important that the original plan put forward by the Wilson Government for only allowing access to the Commissioners through councillors was modified by two stages. The 1972 Consultative Document stated that the Commissioners could take up a complaint direct from a member of the public if two councillors had declined to forward it, and when the Bill was introduced in Parliament this had been reduced to one councillor. It therefore appeared that the system might be less restrictive than the Parliamentary Commissioner system, where access is only through M.P.s. In practice it is proving almost as restrictive.

Thus in the year ended 31 March 1977 the three English Commissioners received 2,277 complaints, in addition to 363 brought forward from 1975–6. Of these 1,449, or 64 per cent, were sent to them direct by members of the public and all had to be sent back to the individual complainant advising him to take the complaint first to a councillor. This compares with 40 per cent in the previous year. As in 1975–6, so in 1976–7, very few returned. By the end of the year 1976–7 only 247 (17 per cent) of the 1,449 complaints sent back had been referred to the Commissioners through a councillor.[1]

The Welsh Local Commissioner has had a similar experience. In fact in the year ending 31 March 1976 he received an even higher proportion of complaints direct from members of the public. Of the 302 complaints he received in the year 1975–6 more than two-thirds came direct from members of the public. He wrote back to the 112 complainants who had not approached a councillor and whose complaints were prima facie within his jurisdiction. He said in his annual report that only a small proportion of these eventually returned to him as formal complaints (i.e. were referred by a councillor). In the four cases in question he exercised his discretion to investigate the case since a councillor had declined to forward it to him.[2]

The Commissioners themselves are concerned by this high degree

[1] Commission for Local Administration in England, *Your Local Ombudsman*, report for the year ended 31 March 1976, London, 1976, pp. 12–13 and year ended 31 March 1977, pp. 11–12. The Commission has investigated, with assistance from the Centre for Environmental Studies, the reasons for this low rate of return of referred complaints. Ibid., p. 16. The Statistics in this and subsequent paragraphs have been updated to include data on 1976–7 which Frank Stacey had received but had not had time to incorporate. Minimal consequent textual alterations have been made (M.S.).

[2] Commission for Local Administration in Wales, Annual Report for the year ended 31 March 1976, pp. 12 and 14.

of 'wastage'. The English Commission reported in 1976 that one large metropolitan district council had already registered its belief that complaints should be made direct to the Local Commissioners.[1] The Welsh Local Commissioner said in his Report for 1975–6 that the effectiveness of the procedure for referral in the first instance through a councillor was in doubt and that, when further experience had been gained of the procedure, consideration should be given to whether referral of a complaint through a councillor was necessary.[2]

The provisions in the Local Government Act for ensuring that the Commissioners' reports receive publicity are in considerable contrast to the Parliamentary Commissioner Act which, as we saw in Chapter VII, only provides that the Commissioner shall send a copy of his report on an investigation to the principal officer of the department concerned, to the official named in the complaint, and to the M.P. referring the complaint. The Local Government Act provides that when a Local Commissioner has completed an investigation, he must send his report to the councillor who referred the complaint, if applicable, to the person complaining, and to the authority complained against. The Act further provides that when the local authority (or water or police authority) has received the report, it must make copies of the report available for inspection to the public, at one or more council office, for a period of three weeks. An officer of the authority must 'give public notice, by advertisement in newspapers and such other ways as appear to him appropriate, that the report will be available for inspection'.[3]

If the Commissioner finds in his report that 'injustice has been caused to the person aggrieved in consequence of maladministration', the local authority concerned is required to consider the report and to notify the Commission what action on the report it has taken or proposes to take. If the Commissioner does not receive any such notifications within a reasonable time, or if he is not satisfied with the action which the authority concerned has taken, he is instructed by the Act to make a further report, and this report too must be published by the local authority.

These provisions ensure that the Local Commissioners' reports on investigations receive publicity and cannot be ignored by the

[1] *Your Local Ombudsman*, p. 13, para. 45.

[2] Commission for Local Administration in Wales, op. cit., p. 8.

[3] Local Government Act, 1974, Sect. 30–(5).

local authority concerned. The Act does provide that a Commissioner can direct that one of his or her reports be withheld from publication. Such a direction would be issued, the Act states, in the public interest or in the interests of the complainant. Thus in his Report for 1975–6 Denis Harrison recorded that in a complaint about the custody of three children he decided that it was in the public interest, and in the interest of the complainant and the children, that his report should not be open for public inspection.[1] But this was one of only two cases so far in which any one of the Commissioners in England, Wales, or Scotland has directed that a report should not be made public. The power to issue such directives is likely to be rarely used because publicity is the chief weapon available to Commissioners to induce local authorities to act on their reports.

The Commissioners are proving commendably conscious of the need to provide publicity for their activities and reports. In April 1975 the English Commission produced a well-designed booklet describing the operation of the local Ombudsman system, including a four-page form which complainants could use in submitting a complaint to a member of their local authority. Over 400,000 copies of this booklet were distributed to local authorities, Citizens' Advice Bureaux, and voluntary organizations. The Welsh and Scottish Local Commissions distributed similar booklets but the Welsh Commissioner did not include in his booklet a form for the submission of complaints.

The Welsh Local Commissioner is particularly co-operative with the press in making copies of his reports on investigations available to them. He has arranged, with the agreement of the Representative Body, to send a copy of his report on an investigation to the press as soon as the local authority has advertised in the local newspaper that the report is available for inspection at the authority's office. Three papers which are widely read in Wales have standing orders to receive all the Welsh Commissioner's reports on investigations. These are the *Western Mail*, which is a morning paper printed in Cardiff with a readership throughout Wales but predominantly in South and Mid Wales, the *South Wales Echo*, which is an evening paper published by the same firm in Cardiff, and the *Liverpool Daily Post*, which has a considerable circulation in North Wales. The *South Wales Evening Post*, which is published in Swansea, has

[1] *Your Local Ombudsman*, p. 37 at para. 9.

a standing order to receive all the Welsh Commissioner's reports on authorities in the two country areas in south-west Wales: West Glamorgan and Dyfed.

The English Local Commission is less liberal in supplying case reports to the press. The Secretary to the Commission sends brief details of a Commissioner's report, which has been announced as open to inspection at a local authority's office, to the newspapers and radio stations in the locality concerned. He does not, as the Welsh Commissioner does, send them a full text of the reports nor does he supply all reports to any newspaper on a standing order basis. There are two explanations for this different practice. The first is that there are literally hundreds of local newspapers in England and several regional papers; each one would only be interested in, at most, a handful of reports in any year. There are also special problems in securing press publicity for the Commissioner's reports in the London area. Lady Serota pointed out in her Annual Report for 1975–6 that in the Greater London area no single local newspaper has a very wide geographical circulation. The local papers, which appear generally on a weekly basis, each circulate in a relatively restricted part of London, often based on only two or three London boroughs. Publicity from one of the Commissioner's reports therefore only reaches readers in the immediate locality where an investigation has taken place.[1]

A second explanation for the greater reticence shown by the English Commission in making the Commissioners' reports available to the press lies in the more cautious attitude of the English Representative Body on this question, compared with the Welsh Representative Body. The Welsh Local Commissioner consulted his Representative Body and gained its approval for the liberal practice which he follows in publicizing his reports. The attitude of the English Representative Body has in general been more restrictive in relation to the publicity for case reports.

This inevitably raises the question of whether or not the Representative Bodies provide an effective back-up for the Local Commissioners. But before we tackle this major issue it is appropriate to make an interim assessment of the impact which the Commissioners are making in taking up complaints against local authorities. Table XV compares the complaints received and reports issued by the three English Commissioners in the years 1975–6 and

[1] *Your Local Ombudsman*, 1976, p. 24.

1976–7, their first two full years of operation. In both years, the disappointing feature is the high number of complaints which were not accepted for investigation. In 1976–7, out of 2,277 complaints received during the year, and 363 carried forward from the previous year, no less than 1,671 were not accepted for investigation by a Commissioner. The main reasons for non-acceptance were either that the complaint had not been submitted through a councillor, or that the complaint gave no indication that injustice had been caused to the complainant by maladministration on the part of the authority. In 1976–7, no less than 1,153 complaints were not accepted on these latter grounds: 895 were rejected on the basis of the information given in the complaint and 258 after informal inquiry with the local authority concerned.[1]

The Commissioners do not give examples of complaints which they have not investigated because the complaint does not indicate that there has been maladministration on the part of the authority, but they say that such complaints often indicate disagreement with a decision made by the authority. The application of the dual provisions in the Local Government Act, 1974, which limit the Commissioners to investigating complaints of injustice caused by maladministration, and inhibit them from questioning the merits of a decision taken without maladministration in the exercise of a discretion, can, however, be studied by scrutinizing the text of their reports on completed investigations.[2]

Analysis of all the case reports of the English, Welsh, and Scottish Commissioners to date shows the Commissioners identifying a great many types of maladministration. Some of the principal kinds they have found include: unjustifiable delay, misleading advice given to a complainant, failure to consider the evidence properly, inaccurate or incomplete presentation of the facts to a council committee, failure to consult with other authorities where this might have influenced the decision, failure to communicate with the complainant, failure to give a complainant sufficient notice to appear before a council sub-committee, inadequate information provided to members of the public concerned (including failure to make known the criteria on which an education department was

[1] *Your Local Ombudsman*, 1977, p. 21; cf. *Your Local Ombudsman*, 1976.

[2] I am greatly indebted to the English, Welsh, and Scottish Commissioners who kindly made available to me copies of all their case reports and to my Research assistant, Mr. Peter James, who did a great deal of the preliminary analysis of the reports.

TABLE XV

English Commission for Local Administration, 1975–1976, and 1976–1977

Complaints received and reports issued

	1975–6	1976–7
Complaints		
Complaints carried forward from previous year	93	363
Complaints received during the year	2,249	2,277
Not accepted for investigation	1,749	1,671
Withdrawn–grievance settled informally	65	62
Under consideration at year end	363	647
Reports issued		
Maladministration and injustice found	49	107
Maladministration found but no injustice to complainant	3	8
Maladministration not found	47	74
Total of reports issued	99	189

Source: Your Local Ombudsman, 1976, p. 60; *Your Local Ombudsman*, 1977, pp. 22, 24.

allocating school places), failure to inform a complainant of alternative procedures open to him, failure to advertise an amended planning application, failure to honour an undertaking given to the complainant.

It is clear, therefore, that the Commissioners are classifying as maladministration a great many faulty procedures which are detrimental to the complainant. But virtually all these categories are procedural. The only example which could be said to go beyond the procedural is the category 'failure to consider the evidence properly'. This can be compared with Sir Alan Marre's interpretation of maladministration where he concluded that a reasonable man could not have arrived at the decision on the evidence available.[1] The Local Commissioners have not, however, taken the further step of widening the concept of maladministration which we saw the Parliamentary Commissioner has taken by finding, in a number of major reports such as the Court Line or the asbestosis cases, simply that there has been a failing on the part of the government department concerned.

[1] See above, p. 157.

They have, it seems, felt themselves to be more bound by the precise terms of the statute than Parliamentary Commissioners have in recent years felt themselves to be. Thus we find Patrick Cook concluding, in a report on an investigation of a complaint against Cambridgeshire County Council, that he could not say whether or not a decision to refuse an application for a discretionary further education award was an arbitrary decision because 'it is not for me to question the merits of decisions taken without maladministration by the Council, who devise their own policy and procedures for discretionary awards'.

It is perhaps reasonable to suggest that the statutory limitations placed on the Local Commissioners, although couched in precisely similar terms to those placed on the Parliamentary Commissioner (limitations to investigate maladministration and not to consider the merits of a discretionary decision taken without maladministration), are proving more restrictive on them than they are on the Parliamentary Commissioner. One reason for this may be that whereas the Parliamentary Commissioner has had the Commons Select Committee to encourage him to take a broad interpretation of his powers, the Local Commissioners report to the representative bodies and they are representative of the authorities rather than of the citizen.

We have already examined the composition of the Welsh Representative Body.[1] The English Representative Body consists of three representatives of the Association of County Councils, three representatives of the Association of District Councils, three representatives of the Association of Metropolitan Authorities, one representative of the Greater London Council, and two representatives of the National Water Council. The men and women who are appointed as representatives tend to be senior councillors and office-holders in the local authority associations. Sir Robert Thomas, for example, is chairman of the Association of Metropolitan Authorities and a leading member of the Greater Manchester Council. The advantage of having such people on the Representative Body is that they can provide valuable liaison between the Commissioners and councillors in the local authority associations. The disadvantage is that the Representative Bodies may tend to look at the work of the Commission in a rather defensive way. Under the Act, the Representative Body has the right to add its comments to

[1] See above, p. 199.

the Commission's annual report and several of its comments which preface the English Commission's Report for 1975–6 are defensive in tone. Thus to the Commission's suggestion, which we have already noted, that the method of access to the Commissioners might be reconsidered because of the large number of complainants who do not refer their complaint through a councillor, the Representative Body offered an emphatic negative: 'It is a fundamental feature of the system that complaints should be handled by members in the first instance, and there is no evidence that any change is needed. . . . If there were absolute open access to the Commission, the Commission could be overwhelmed with complaints, some of a frivolous nature.'[1]

We should note here that it was open to the legislators to make the Local Commissioners responsible to Parliament. Several of the national Ombudsmen we have studied in this book can examine complaints against local authorities. Ombudsmen in Sweden, Denmark, and Norway have such powers as does the French Médiateur. All are responsible to their national Parliaments.[2] The powers of the Scandinavian Ombudsmen to examine complaints against local authorities are incomplete. Thus the Swedish Ombudsmen can examine complaints against local administrators but cannot examine complaints against councillors. The Danish Ombudsman cannot examine complaints against some local services where the central government does not have a co-ordinating role. But the 1975 Ombudsmen Act in New Zealand which empowers the national Ombudsmen to examine complaints against local authorities does not impose any such limitations. The Act provides that Parliament shall appoint one or more Ombudsmen, specifying that one of the Ombudsmen shall be appointed as Chief Ombudsman. The original Ombudsman, Sir Guy Powles, was appointed Chief Ombudsman in 1976 and two additional Ombudsmen, Mr. G. R. Laking and Mr. A. E. Hurley, were also appointed. Mr. Hurley, who was stationed in Auckland, had as his main task investigating complaints against local authorities in the northern half of New Zealand. Mr. Laking was stationed in Wellington and investigated complaints against local authorities in the southern half of the country, as well

[1] *Your Local Ombudsman*, 1976, p. 4.

[2] Of the Canadian provincial Ombudsmen studied in this book, the New Brunswick Ombudsman was in 1976 given power to examine complaints against local authorities. See above, p. 85.

as dealing with some complaints against central departments. The Chief Ombudsman specializes in complaints against central departments as well as exercising a general co-ordinating role in the team of three Ombudsmen. In April 1977 Sir Guy Powles retired after fourteen years in office as Ombudsman and one as Chief Ombudsman. He was succeeded as Chief Ombudsman by Mr. Laking and Mr. Lester Castle was appointed as Ombudsman alongside Mr. Hurley. The New Zealand Ombudsmen apply the same criteria in investigating complaints against local authorities as against central departments. In particular, they investigate complaints that actions (or omissions to act) by local authorities have been 'unreasonable, unjust or improperly discriminatory'.

Since the population of Britain is so much larger than that of New Zealand it was probably right to establish local Ombudsmen in Britain quite distinct and separate from the Parliamentary Commissioner. But although the Local Commissions for Administration are separate they could still have been made responsible to Parliament and their activities could have been backed up by a House of Commons Committee. The aim was to make the Commissioners responsible neither to Parliament nor to individual local authorities as the Ombudsmen for Zurich, Jerusalem, Haifa, and certain American cities are.[1] Instead the Local Commissioners in England and Wales report to bodies which are representative of all the local authorities against whom they investigate complaints. But although they report to the Representative Bodies they are not accountable to them. In law they are appointed by and are accountable to the Queen. Does this mean then that they are accountable, in practice, to the Secretary of State for the Environment? If so, he is accountable to Parliament and it would be appropriate for the House of Commons to receive the reports of the Local Commissioners and take an interest in their activities, by appointing a committee with similar powers to those of the Select Committee on the Parliamentary Commissioner.

The Scottish Local Commissioner is in a different position again. Under the Local Government (Scotland) Act, 1975, he submits his annual report to the designated body which arranges for publication. The designated body does not have the right to comment on the

[1] In the United States, Atlanta City, Georgia, Daytona City, Ohio, Detroit City, Michigan, Jackson County, Missouri, Jamestown City, New York, and Wichita City, Kansas, each has its own Ombudsman.

report nor does it have the duty to transmit the Commissioner's recommendations or conclusions to local authorities. The designated body is the Commission for Local Authority Accounts in Scotland. This is an independent appointed body set up under the Local Government (Scotland) Act, 1973. Its members are appointed by the Secretary of State for Scotland and its main functions are to audit the accounts of Scottish local authorities and to hold hearings, where necessary, on matters reported from the audit. The Commission has no parallel in England and Wales. The chairman of the Commission is Tom Fraser who was an Under-Secretary of State for Scotland from 1945 to 1951 and Minister of Transport in the Wilson Government from 1964 to 1965. Other members of the Commission include a former County Clerk, two former City Chamberlains (Treasurers), a chartered accountant who has specialized in local authority audit, and an academic with local government interests.

The Scottish Local Commissioner, Robert Moore, does not therefore have statutory machinery for consultation with representatives of local authorities but to what is, in effect, an independent regulatory body. Robert Moore mentioned in his report on his first period of office, from 1 January to 31 March 1976, that he felt the need for such machinery and that he had approached the convention of Scottish Local Authorities to discuss how best this gap might be filled.[1] There is one other respect in which the provisions of the Act, the Local Government (Scotland) Act, 1975, differ from those in Part III of the Local Government Act, 1974. There is no Scottish Commission for Local Administration. The Scottish Commissioner, unlike the Welsh Commissioner, does not have a special relationship with the Parliamentary Commissioner who, as we saw, is a member of the Welsh and English Commissions. The Scottish Commissioner stands on his own and reports to the designated body. There is one other curious difference between the position of the Scottish Commissioner and that of the English and Welsh Commissioners. The Scottish Commissioner was appointed on a half-time basis. This is not mentioned in the statute. Scotland has a population of more than 5 million; Wales of around 2,700,000. The Welsh Commissioner with a staff of comparable size reported in 1976 that he was hard pressed to deal with the volume of com-

[1] Report of the Commissioner for Local Administration in Scotland for the year ended 31 March 1976, p. 4 at para. 10.

plaints he was receiving and that more staff would be needed.[1] It is to be expected that the Scottish Commissioner, who has only been in office since 1 January 1976, will receive a comparable, if not greater, volume of complaints and it is to be hoped that the Scottish Office will, at an early date, review its decision to appoint him on only a half-time basis.

There is a further point to be considered in assessing the back-up arrangements at present provided for the Local Commissioners in Britain. The Representative Body in Wales has so far proved more supportive to the Welsh Local Commissioner than the English Body has been to the English Commissioners. We saw above that the Welsh Representative Body approved the Welsh Commissioner's proposal to make his case reports readily available to the press.[2] In its Annual Report for the year ended 31 March 1976 the Welsh Local Commission put on record its appreciation of the help given to it by the Representative Body. The Commission said that it was gratifying that such a good relationship had been established between the Commission and the Representative Body. This it attributed largely to the understanding and enlightened attitude of the chairman of the Representative Body, Lord Heycock, and of its Corresponding Secretary, Haydn Rees.[3] Lord Heycock is Leader of the West Glamorgan County Council and prior to reorganization had for long been a leading figure on the old Glamorgan County Council. He is a railwayman and a Labour life peer.

Any such relationship, however, has two sides, and a great deal of credit should also go to the Welsh Local Commissioner, Dafydd Jones-Williams. The fact that, as the former Clerk to Merioneth County Council, he was known personally by the Chief Executives of many Welsh local authorities clearly eased his path, as did his decision to choose his staff from men with local government experience. The Secretary of his office, Hywel F. Jones, was previously Chief Financial Officer of the Afan District Council in South Wales. One investigator was Clerk and Treasurer to the Llanelli Water Board before being appointed to the Welsh Commissioner's staff and before that again had been in the Cardiganshire Treasurer's Department. The other investigator had previously been an administrative assistant in the Education Department of West Glamorgan County Council.

[1] Commission for Local Administration in Wales, p. 17. [2] See above, p. 204–5.
[3] Commission for Local Administration in Wales, p. 8.

The Welsh experience shows that the relationship between a Commission for Local Administration and its Representative Body can be good. But there may be special circumstances in the Welsh case. The smaller population of Wales, as compared with England, and its greater homogeneity clearly help to improve good relations between the Commission and the Representative Body when there is goodwill on both sides. But the reservations we expressed earlier about the Representative Body acting as the back-up for the Commissioners' activities remain. Clearly, the Representative Bodies have a useful role in assisting liaison between the Commissioners and the associations of local authorities. They should continue to have this role and should therefore receive and discuss the Commissioners' annual reports. There is a strong case, however, for the Commissioners' annual reports also being scrutinized by the relevant legislature: in England by a committee of the House of Commons and in Scotland and Wales by committees of the Scottish and Welsh Assemblies, if established under the legislation for devolution.

We have tended to concentrate so far on some of the features of the Local Commissioner system which are most open to criticism: in particular on the effects of limiting access to the Commissioners and on some of the disadvantages of making the Representative Bodies the only back-up for the Commissioners' work. It is appropriate now to consider the extent to which the Commissioners are finding maladministration in the cases which they investigate. Table XVI shows that in the year 1976–7 in 107 of their reports on investigations the English Commissioners found instances of maladministration which had caused injustice to the complainant: Lady Serota in 27 cases, Patrick Cook in 42, and Denis Harrison in 38. The majority of these cases, were complaints about planning or housing: 33 out of 107 in each case. Education came next with 12 cases. The proportion of housing complaints where maladministration with injustice was found increased from 11 out of 49 in 1975–6 to 33 out of 107 in 1976–7, while the proportion of planning cases declined from 60 to 30 per cent.

The predominance of planning cases was most marked in Denis Harrison's area where 18 out of 38 cases in which he found maladministration involved planning. In Patrick Cook's area 13 out of 42 were planning cases; in Lady Serota's area 2 out of 27, a lower proportion than in the previous year, when it had been 11 out of 22.

The high proportion in Denis Harrison's area can perhaps be explained by the fact that there is only one metropolitan county in his area; the West Midlands County. In Patrick Cook's area there are five metropolitan counties: Greater Manchester, Merseyside, South Yorkshire, West Yorkshire, and Tyne and Wear. Lady Serota's area is dominated by the Greater London Council. The hypothesis is that in the conurbations there is a lower proportion of owner-occupiers, and that there it is likely that housing cases will bulk larger than planning cases since the majority of housing complaints come from the tenants of council flats and houses. In the light of this, the proportionate increase in housing in 1976–7 is interesting. The widening of the range of complaints must also be noted.

TABLE XVI

English Commission for Local Administration, 1975–1976 and 1976–1977

Reports issued by the English Commissioners in which they found maladministration causing injustice

	Planning		Housing		Education		Other*		Totals	
	1975–6	1976–7	1975–6	1976–7	1975–6	1976–7	1975–6	1976–7	1975–6	1976–7
Lady Serota	11	2	6	17	4	1	1	7	22	27
Denis Harrison	9	18	2	7	1	1	0	12	12	38
Patrick Cook	9	13	3	9	2	10	1	10	15	42
Totals	29	33	11	33	7	12	2	29	49	107

* In 1975–6, the 2 other cases were one against a Water Authority and one against a Legal Department. In 1976–7, the 29 other cases included complaints about Social Services (3), land (7), highways (4), environmental health (3), rating matters (1), drainage (1), amenity (7), fencing (2), water (2). (M.S.).

Source: Your Local Ombudsman, 1976, pp. 26, 38, and 50; *Your Local Ombudsman*, 1977, pp. 30, 34, 39.

The high proportion of planning cases[1] may be partly explained by the complex method of approaching the Commissioners; through a councillor or direct if turned down by a councillor. The more well-to-do owner-occupier is more likely to understand this procedure and make use of it. If the law were amended to provide for

[1] It should be noted that of complaints made in 1976–7, planning cases outnumbered housing by 708 to 535 and, in addition, there were 125 land complaints. If land is added to planning in cases where maladministration with injustice was found the total is 40, compared with 33 housing cases (M.S.).

direct access to the Commissioners we might expect to see the proportion of complaints concerned with housing, social services, and other areas rising more sharply. But it is all to the good that the Commissioners are receiving a considerable flow of complaints about planning matters. The efforts made in recent years to secure greater involvement of citizens in planning matters have been considerable. Local government reorganization, under the 1972 Local Government Act, brought decision-making in planning nearer to the people by making the district councils the planning authorities in the approval of local plans, whereas previously only the counties and county boroughs had planning functions. This development was welcome in that it made it easier for the individual householder to inspect plans of developments which might affect him. The Act also gave to parish councils the right to see all planning applications in their area. The complaints on planning matters which go to the Local Commissioners are in some cases complaints by householders about planning permission being delayed, and in some cases by neighbours about permission being granted despite objection, or without consultation. The power to complain to the Local Commissioners is a reinforcement of the power of citizens in influencing the planning process.

The high proportion of cases in which the Commissioners find maladministration in the complaints which they investigate should be noted. In the year 1975–6 the English Commissioners completed investigation and reported upon 99 cases and in 1976–7 upon 189. In 49 of the 99 in 1975–6 and in 107 of the 189 in 1977–8 they found that there had been maladministration and injustice to the complainant. In 3 cases in 1975–6 and 8 in 1976–7 they found maladministration but no injustice.[1] This high proportion should be considered against the background of the very large number of cases which were not accepted for investigation by the Commissioners: 1,749 in 1975–6 and 1,671 in 1976–7. Cases are subjected to a double scrutiny before the investigating process begins. First, as we saw above, cases in which no indication is given in the complaint of maladministration having occurred are not accepted for investigation. Second, the fact that the vast majority of complaints come through councillors must mean that in some instances councillors advise complainants that maladministration is not involved and that there is no point in pursuing the complaint.

[1] See above, Table XV, p. 207.

The extent to which local authorities are providing redress when the Commissioners find injustice in consequence of maladministration varies considerably. In Wales, the Commissioner has found maladministration in 16 of the cases which he has investigated since he began to receive complaints in 1974. In no case has he as yet had to issue a second report indicating that the authority has not provided appropriate redress. The situation is less good in England. In the year 1975–6 the English Commissioners issued six second reports because the local authority had not yet provided redress. The English Commission stated in its annual report that by 31 March 1976, 'the Local Commissioner had expressed satisfaction in three of those six cases, had expressed partial satisfaction in two of them and was not satisfied in the remaining case'.[1] In 18 cases the Commissioners were satisfied with the local authorities' response to their first report and in 23 cases the local authority concerned was still considering the Local Commissioner's findings at the end of the year.

The English Commission pointed out in its Report for 1975–6 that the remedies expected from local authorities fall into two broad categories. The first is a review of procedures by the authority to try to see that similar maladministration does not occur again. The second is provision of tangible redress to a complainant by, for example, a changed decision in his favour or the payment of compensation. A scrutiny of the Commissioners' reports reveals numerous cases in which the local authority has informed the Commissioner that it is reviewing procedures on lines indicated by the Commissioner's investigation. The English Commission noted in its Report for 1975–6 that it must then rely on the local authority to fulfil its promise.[2] The only sanction is publicity and the hope that once the issue has been brought to the attention of the council and local opinion there will be sufficient pressure on the authority to live up to its promises. The Commissioners have themselves no means of following up this kind of remedy and monitoring the performance of the authority concerned.

On the provision of a tangible remedy, numerous instances can be found of local authorities providing such a remedy as a result of the Commissioner's investigation. The Welsh Commissioner reported in 1975, for example, that Arfon Borough Council had

[1] *Your Local Ombudsman*, 1976, p. 17 at para. 70.
[2] Ibid., pp. 17–18 at para. 73.

wrongly advised a complainant about the procedure for securing an improvement grant for work at his house. It had failed to inform him that he needed to complete the work by an early deadline if he was to secure a grant at a higher rate. As a result of the Commissioner's investigation the Council decided to pay the complainant the difference between the lower-rate grant which he had already received and the grant at the higher rate. Of several English cases in which the complainant has received a tangible remedy, one may cite a case investigated by Lady Serota in Kensington and Chelsea. Her investigation found that as a result of a delay in dealing with an application for planning permission the complainant had to pay £720. This sum was remitted to the complainant by the local authority.

A number of problems are, however, associated with the provision of a tangible remedy. The first is, as the English Commission says, that 'authorities do not always have power to make payments even where a payment is the logical remedy for injustice'.[1] Sanction to make such a payment can be sought from the Secretary of State for the Environment under Section 161 of the Local Government Act, 1972, and this sanction removes the possibility of proceedings by the District Auditor against the local council concerned. But it does not seem at all appropriate that local authorities should have to seek permission to provide compensation in this way.

The second main problem arises when the local authority does not agree that compensation to the complainant is called for. Denis Harrison, for example, concluded in a report issued on 19 March 1975 that a complainant had suffered injustice in consequence of maladministration by the West Oxfordshire District Council. As a result of an avoidable delay in dealing with his planning application for an extension to his house, the work had cost him a great deal more than was originally anticipated owing to the rise in cost of building materials in the intervening period. He had also incurred additional costs through storage of furniture and further legal expenses. On 25 November 1976 Denis Harrison made a second report saying that the local authority had reviewed its procedures. The Council had instituted a system of post-committee meetings at which an officer of the planning department, and the committee clerk, 'determine their responsibilities for carrying out the resolutions of the committee. Action is then taken and monitored on a

[1] Ibid., p. 18 at para. 78.

progress sheet.'[1] But the Council had not agreed to provide any financial compensation to the complainant. The Commissioner said that he hoped the Council would give further consideration to making an *ex gratia* payment to him. Eventually, in the spring of 1977, the Council made an *ex gratia* payment of £150 to the complainant, after obtaining sanction under Section 161 from the Secretary of State.

The English Commission is clearly not happy about the absence of any provision in the 1974 Act giving the Commissioners power to enforce remedies when a local authority is not co-operative. In its Report for 1975–6 it pointed out that in Northern Ireland, when the Commissioner for Complaints finds that a complainant has suffered injustice in consequence of maladministration, the complainant can secure redress by going to the County Court which will award damages to him on the basis of the Commissioner's report. The Commissioner for Complaints was set up by the Commissioner for Complaints Act (Northern Ireland), 1969. He investigates complaints against local authorities and a number of statutory agencies in Northern Ireland, including hospital management committees and the Northern Ireland Housing Trust.[2]

The English Local Commission said that it was too early to judge whether some such provision would be needed if the local Ombudsman system were to be fully effective. But it was 'bound closely to watch the way in which authorities respond to findings which are only made after most careful investigation'.[3] The Commission said it would obviously wish to discuss the subject with the Representative Body in the light of experience.

The Representative Body gave a dusty answer to this suggestion. In its comments on the Commission's Report for 1975–6 it said that it felt there was no case for treating the Commission for Local Administration differently from the Parliamentary Commissioner. It considered it was 'fundamental that the present system should continue whereunder a Local Commissioner suggests a course of action to remedy an injustice, leaving the final decision to the individual authority. The effective sanction is public opinion.'[4] But

[1] Commission for Local Administration in England, *Investigation 80H Complaint against the West Oxfordshire District Council. Further report*, (London, 1975), p. 2.

[2] See J. F. Garner, 'Commissioner for Complaints Act (N.I.) 1969', *Northern Ireland Legal Quarterly* (autumn 1970), 353–6.

[3] *Your Local Ombudsman*, 1976, pp. 18–19 at para. 79.

[4] Ibid., pp. 4–5.

the Parliamentary Commissioner has the Select Committee to back up his reports and will summon senior civil servants to account for any failure to implement recommendations in his reports. Furthermore, in a decentralized service even the back-up provided by such a committee is liable to be less effective since the Chief Executive or elected Leader of a local authority is not responsible to the House of Commons.

We argued earlier that there should be such a committee to receive the reports of the English Commission (and committees of possible future Welsh and Scottish Assemblies to receive reports of the Welsh and Scottish Commissioners) and it could have a useful role in publicizing cases where a local authority is not implementing a Commissioner's recommendations.[1] But a local authority might well be prepared to defy a Commons Select Committee whereas a senior civil servant cannot do so unless he is backed up by the Government which is answerable to the House of Commons. Therefore the case for legislation to enable a complainant to get a court order to secure compliance with a Local Commissioner's recommendation is a very strong one. Recourse to the courts in this way would probably be infrequent, as indeed it is in Northern Ireland. As things stand, the occasions when a local authority refuses to act in the light of a Commissioner's findings are relatively rare. But it would provide an effective reinforcement to the Commissioners' power to investigate and report.

Despite its defects, the system of Local Commissioners in Britain has many strong points. One is that the system is already enabling the exposure of civil liberty cases in which an individual has suffered by arbitrary action by a local authority. One such case was reported on by Denis Harrison in December 1976. He found that the complainant had suffered injustice in consequence of maladministration in that a social worker employed by Hertfordshire County Council had secured the complainant's compulsory admission to a mental hospital without making a thorough preliminary assessment of the condition and circumstances, or ascertaining that there were friends who could have vouched for her degree of mental balance and ability to care for her seven-year-old daughter. After the complainant had been detained for observation in the hospital for seventy-two hours she was discharged, and during this period

[1] If devolution legislation is not enacted, the Committee of the House of Commons should receive reports of the Scottish and Welsh Commissioners.

no adequate steps were taken by the social worker to ensure that her daughter was cared for. The social worker who was instrumental, with a general practitioner, in securing the complainant's compulsory admission to hospital had never before seen the complainant and had not interviewed her friends or neighbours. In the Commissioner's own conclusion, in his report, the social worker had little background information about the complainant apart from reports by police and neighbours about her alleged disturbed behaviour and information provided by the general practitioner who had not in fact seen her for several months.[1]

This was a complicated case for which the Local Commissioner's investigator carried out a thorough and painstaking investigation interviewing the complainant, her husband, her solicitor, her ex-husband, the social worker named in the complaint and other officers of the Council, friends and neighbours, doctors, police officers, and the former headmistress and class teacher of the complainant's daughter.[2] The thoroughness of the investigation and the clarity of the Commissioner's findings are equally impressive. It is also significant that the complainant's original complaint to the County Council had produced an equivocal reply from the Chief Executive in which he argued that he was in no position, and not qualified, to substitute his own judgement for that of the social workers involved in the case, although he did admit, by inference, that they should have proceeded with more deliberation.[3]

The importance of an investigation such as this by a Local Commissioner lies not only in its demonstration of the way his investigations can uncover a failure in administration which had not been properly exposed by the authority's own review of the case, but also in its likely effect on standards of administration in that authority and in other authorities. This is what Sir Alan Marre called the 'tonic' effect of his investigations as Parliamentary Commissioner. The knowledge that the Parliamentary Commissioner can investigate makes civil servants more keenly aware that they must try to achieve as fair and humane standards as possible in decision-making and administration, and a similar effect can follow from the activities of the Local Commissioners.

Another effect of the Commissioner's powers to investigate which

[1] Commission for Local Administration in England, *Investigation 1030H. Complaint Against Hertfordshire County Council* (London, 1976), p. 31.

[2] Ibid., p. 2.

[3] Ibid., p. 28.

is not shown up by the statistics of investigations completed is the redress provided informally, in some cases, to complainants without an investigation being started by a Commissioner. For example, the English Commission noted in its Report for 1975–6 that of 180 complaints referred back to complainants, because they had not come through a councillor, 25 were, as far as the Commission knew, settled amicably between the complainant and the council concerned.[1]

Another good feature of the Local Commissioner system in Britain is the thoroughness of the investigation procedure. The Hertfordshire case which we have described was one of perhaps exceptional complexity involving more interviews than the average investigation would entail. But in the great majority of cases the Commission's investigator goes to the local authority concerned, examines the files, interviews the officer, or officers, concerned in the complaint, and also interviews the complainant and anyone else involved in the complaint. In very few cases has the investigation been conducted merely by correspondence and scrutiny of documentary evidence, although this is clearly appropriate in some cases.

The staffing of the Commissions, and in particular the staffing of the English Commission, is less open to criticism than is the staffing of the Parliamentary Commissioner's office. Whereas we saw that the Parliamentary Commissioner has always been appointed from within the ranks of the higher Civil Service and all his staff are civil servants on temporary secondment from their departments, only one of the three English Local Commissioners was formerly a local government officer and the staff of the Commission have a variety of backgrounds. The Secretary of the English Commission, Michael Hyde, was previously Secretary of the Eastern Electricity Board. The Commission has three Assistant Secretaries, each of whom is a Director of Investigations. Of these three, two were previously local government officers and one was formerly an administrator with the Electricity Council. There are eleven full-time investigators whose previous employments were as follows: two former senior police officers, one former company director, one former journalist, one former deputy hospital secretary, one former colonel in the army education corps, one former planning inspector with the Department of the Environment, one planner from a London borough, one former officer from the Race Relations Board, one from the Social

[1] *Your Local Ombudsman*, 1976, p. 13.

Science Research Council, and one from a London borough housing department.

The Scottish Commissioner and his staff also have a variety of backgrounds, or a varied earlier career, not confined to the world of local government. The Scottish Commissioner, Robert Moore, began his career in local government. During and after the Second World War he was Town Clerk of the Burgh of Port Glasgow. In 1948, on the founding of the Health Service, he was appointed Secretary of the Scottish Eastern Regional Hospital Board. From 1960 he held a key post in training Health Service administrators in Scotland and for some years was also a Lecturer in Administrative Law at St. Andrews University. The bulk of his previous career had therefore been in Health Service Administration, but he has also had considerable local government and some academic experience. The Secretary of the Commissioner's office, who is also Chief Assistant to the Commissioner, has been Head of Business Studies at Falkirk Technical College. The Senior Investigator was formerly an investigator on the Parliamentary Commissioner's staff, at his Edinbrugh office. At that time he was a civil servant on secondment from the Department of Employment. Finding great interest in the work of an Ombudsman's office he decided to make this his career rather than return to the Department of Employment. He therefore applied for and secured the post of Senior Investigator with the Scottish Local Commissioner.

The Welsh Local Commissioner and his staff, however, as we have seen, all have local government experience.[1] The Welsh Local Commissioner's office is therefore the odd man out, in this respect, in the three countries of Great Britain. We suggested that one of the reasons for the good relations which the Welsh Commission has enjoyed with the Welsh Representative Body may be that all its staff have local government experience. Is this therefore a reason for modifying the view that we have earlier put forward that it is desirable for an Ombudsman's staff to have a variety of backgrounds and not be drawn only from serving, or former, civil servants, in the case of an Ombudsman concerned with central government, or from former local government officers, in the case of a local Ombudsman's staff? This is a difficult question, but, on balance, we would maintain our view. The advantages to be gained in having a staff of

[1] See above, p. 199.

varied background outweigh the possibly short-term advantages of a staff drawn entirely from the ranks of local authority or water authority administrators.

Another criticism which we make of the Parliamentary Commissioner's office is that he does not have a lawyer on his staff and is dependent for legal advice on one of the Government's own legal advisers, the Treasury Solicitor. This criticism does not apply to the English or Welsh Local Commissions or to the Scottish Commissioner. One of the English Commissioners, Denis Harrison, is a solicitor with a law degree and two of the Assistant Secretaries on the English Commission's staff are also qualified solicitors. The Welsh Local Commissioner and the Scottish Commissioner are both qualified solicitors with law degrees.

The local Ombudsman system in England and Wales has only been operating for just over two years, and in Scotland for only a year. It is therefore not possible in concluding this chapter to make a full assessment of the strong and weak features of the system. Already, however, some of the defects in the legilsation are clear. We have seen that providing for access only through councillors, or direct if a councillor does not forward the complaint, is a severe limitation. It means that the Commissioners are not nearly as widely used as they would be if there were direct access. The legislation should be amended to enable a citizen to complain either direct to a local commissioner or through a councillor. In this way, the role of councillors in assisting complaints would be maintained while at the same time access to the Commissioners would be improved for the majority of potential complainants.

Confining the Local Commissioners to maladministration also severely reduces the number of complaints which they can investigate. In the year ended 31 March 1976 the English Local Commission rejected 783 of the 2,249 complaints it received on the ground that the complainant did not refer to his complaint to any 'specific act of maladministration or injustice'.[1] In the year ended 31 March 1977, the comparable figure was 895 out of 2,277.[2] In the majority of these cases the Commission reported that the complaint was basically against the merits of a decision or action. If the Commissioners were empowered, like the Canadian provincial Ombudsmen, to investigate complaints about unreasonable decisions

[1] *Your Local Ombudsman*, 1976, p. 14 at para. 51.
[2] *Your Local Ombudsman*, 1977, p. 21.

they would be able to examine a good proportion of these complaints which are at present not investigated. The argument for limiting the Commissioners to maladministration is as unsound as it is for the Parliamentary Commissioner. The Local Government Acts should be amended to enable the Commissioners to investigate and report on unreasonable decisions, actions, or omissions by local authorities.

Several other restrictions placed upon the Commissioners by the Local Government Act, 1974 (and on the Scottish Commissioner by his Act) are modelled on restrictions placed on the Parliamentary Commissioner and have as little justification. The Local Commissions are not able to examine complaints from employees of local authorities in personnel matters, just as the Parliamentary Commissioner is not allowed to examine such complaints from civil servants. None of the other Ombudsmen we have studied, except the French Médiateur, is restricted in this way. We have also seen that the Select Committee on the Parliamentary Commissioner has several times reiterated its view that the Parliamentary Commissioner should not be so restricted. The exclusion of personnel matters in local government from the Local Commissioners' remit is equally indefensible.

Similarly, their exclusion from commercial and contractual transactions (except land transactions), which is also modelled on the Parliamentary Commissioner's exclusion from these areas, is not in the public interest. Finally, the exclusion of the Local Commissioners from complaints about the curricula and the internal administration of schools is very hard to justify. There can be examples of unreasonable and arbitrary action in schools, and there seem to be no better grounds from excluding the Commissioners from investigating complaints about them than from investigating complaints about the administration of social service departments or housing.

If the legislation were changed to allow direct access to the Commissioners, to enable them to consider unreasonable actions or decisions, and to enable them to consider complaints in personnel matters, about commercial or contractual transactions, and about the internal administration of schools and colleges, the number of cases investigated each year by the Commissioners would increase considerably. This increased case-load would need to be met in part by the appointment of more investigators in the Welsh and

Scottish Commissioners' offices and by the appointment of more staff and an additional Commissioner for England. We have seen that the Heath Government's Consultative Document in 1972 proposed nine Commissioners for England but, in fact, only three have been appointed. Patrick Cook and Denis Harrison have to cope, at present, with far too extensive areas. Patrick Cook's 'northern' region extends into East Anglia and Denis Harrison's 'western' region includes not only the whole of southern England and the south-west but also the whole of the western Midlands and part of the eastern Midlands. There is a strong case for the appointment of a fourth Commissioner covering the Midlands region, with his office either in Birmingham or Derby (either is a good centre for road and rail communications for the Midlands). Patrick Cook's northern region, centred on York, would then be more compact. Denis Harrison's region could cover the whole of south-western, south central, and southern England. How far it should extend into south-east England is a matter which should be determined by the relative case-load. There is a case for Lady Serota's area continuing to include Kent as well as Greater London unless her relative case-load would then be too high.

The additional case-load should not mean the abandonment, or severely curtailed use, of the present method of investigation in which the investigator visits the authority, examines files, and interviews the complainant and officials complained against. This is one of the best features of the system and is particularly appropriate in a complicated case like the Hertfordshire social services case which we described earlier. It would be possible to deal with some of the increased volume of cases by correspondence but for a high proportion of complaints against local authorities the 'face-to-face' personal investigation is certainly the best method.

Finally, we have seen that there is at present ineffective back-up for the Commissioner's reports. We have suggested that the English Commission should report to Parliament as well as to the English Representative Body and that the Welsh Commission should report to the Welsh Assembly and the Scottish Commissioner to a Scottish Assembly, if these are established under devolution legislation. The House of Commons and the Welsh and Scottish Assemblies could then reinforce the Commissioner's activities and press for implementation and, where necessary, reforms. Even so, it would be desirable to enact legislation which, on the pattern of the

Northern Ireland Commissioner for Complaints Act, 1969, would allow complainants to have compensation awarded to them by the county courts on the basis of a report by a Local Commissioner.

The agenda for reforms in the Local Commissioner system is already a long one. But the defects to which we have pointed in the legilsation should not obscure the fact that the new system has some excellent features. The morale of the Commissioners and their staff is high and they have already made a considerable impact.

X

CONCLUSION

In this book we have given special emphasis to a comparison of Ombudsmen in Sweden, Denmark, Norway, Canada, France, and the United Kingdom. But the Ombudsman idea has, in the last ten years in particular, been developing on a worldwide scale. It is appropriate then to begin this chapter by surveying those developments in the establishment of Ombudsmen systems which have not as yet been touched on in this book. We must first acknowledge a major omission in our discussion of Scandinavian Ombudsmen. Finland has had an Ombudsman since 1919. The Ombudsman's powers are similar to those of Swedish Ombudsmen and Finland, like Sweden, also has a Chancellor of Justice.

The similarity with Sweden is not accidental. Finland was part of Sweden until ceded to Russia in 1809. The Swedish office of Chancellor of Justice was carried over into the Grand Duchy of Finland and continued in being through the period of Tsarist rule. When Finland became an independent state after the Russian Revolution the office of Chancellor of Justice was retained and an Ombudsman was also established, under the new Constitution approved in 1919. The Ombudsman is elected by Parliament for a four-year term. He has jurisdiction over all branches of government, both central and local. He can prosecute all officials, including judges, for breaches of legality. In fact, his jurisdiction is wider than that of the Swedish Ombudsmen since he can prosecute Ministers and local councillors, although he has done so only on rare occasions. The Swedish Ombudsmen, as we have seen, do not prosecute Ministers or elected members of local authorities.

The Finnish Ombudsman has wide powers to see official files and documents and has special responsibility to look at the welfare of people in detention in prisons or mental hospitals, or under military discipline. As in Sweden, letters sent by prisoners to the Ombudsman must be forwarded to him uncensored. There is no limitation on the number of letters which a prisoner in Finland may send to the Ombudsman and every such letter is sent by official mail; the prisoner does not have to pay postage.

The Ombudsman can carry out inspections of all official premises but concentrates on inspections of prisons, other closed institutions, and units of the armed forces. Even then, the task of inspection is a big one and the Ombudsman has, in recent years, selected certain issues or procedures for special consideration in inspections. Thus he has concerned himself particularly with the treatment of juvenile delinquents and the procedure for determining the mental condition of people accused before the courts. Finland has a population of around 4,700,000. By 1971 the case-load of the Ombudsman had become heavy and in that year Parliament enacted legislation for the appointment of an Assistant Ombudsman. Since the Chancellor of Justice is also active in investigating citizens' complaints, Finland now in effect has three Ombudsman style officials.[1]

A partial omission from our study has been the New Zealand Ombudsman. But since all the Canadian provincial Ombudsmen have been set up with powers similar to those of the New Zealand Ombudsman, we have given considerable space to discussion of the key provisions in his statute as well as outlining recent developments in the widening of his jurisdiction to include local authorities, and the appointment of two additional Ombudsmen in 1975.[2] The New Zealand statute has also provided the model for the establishment of Ombudsmen in Australia. Developments at state level began there later than in Canada but have proceeded at an even faster rate. Western Australia appointed an Ombudsman in 1971, South Australia in 1972, Victoria in 1973, Queensland in 1974, and New South Wales in 1975. Tasmania is the only Australian state which does not now have an Ombudsman. Australia still does not have an Ombudsman at federal level.

Developments in the United States began two years earlier than in Australia. Hawaii, in 1969, was the first state to set up an Ombudsman. But relatively few states have since followed the Hawaiian

[1] The fullest study of the Finnish Ombudsman in English is Mikael Hiden, *The Ombudsman in Finland: The First Fifty Years*. (Institute of Governmental Studies, Univ. of California, Berkeley, 1973). See also W. Gellhorn, *Ombudsmen and Others* (Harvard U.P. and Oxford U.P., 1967), Ch. 2.

[2] See above, pp. 52, 54–5, 60, 70–1, 78–9. The most recent study of the New Zealand Ombudsman is Larry B. Hill, *The Model Ombudsman. Institutionalizing New Zealand's Democratic Experiment* (Princeton U.P., 1976).

example. Nebraska appointed an Ombudsman in 1971, Iowa in 1972, and Alaska in 1975. Only four out of fifty states in the United States therefore have an Ombudsman. Why then have developments been so much slower than in Canada or Australia? This requires some explanation particularly since there has been considerable interest in the Ombudsman idea in the United States amongst academics and lawyers. Some of the principal academic authorities in the study of Ombudsman systems are American and the American Bar Association has for many years had an Ombudsman Committee. Dr. Bernard Frank, as its chairman and latterly as chairman of a Committee of the International Bar Association, has done a great deal to disseminate information about progress in the adoption of Ombudsman systems by means of a newsletter sent out from his office in Allentown, Pennsylvania.

At a conference in 1967 of the American Assembly, which is a non-partisan institution concerned with the discussion of public issues, the theme of the conference was the relevance of the Ombudsman idea to American government and the obstacles to its adoption present in the American system.[1] There seems little doubt that the American system of checks and balances does place greater difficulties in the path of those who are attempting to set up an Ombudsman than is present, for example, in a parliamentary system. In Britain, or in an Australian state or Canadian province, when the Government decides to set up an Ombudsman it normally has a majority in the legislature and can secure support for the necessary legislation. When an American State Governor wants to introduce an Ombudsman he must persuade the majority in both Houses of the state legislature (all but one of the States are bicameral) to approve the measure. In many cases, he is not able to secure such support and for this reason several State Governors have set up 'Executive Ombudsmen'. These are officers with an Ombudsman function but responsible to the Governor, not to the legislature. An American study in 1973 identified four states where executive officers had been allocated a complaint function and were capable of being classified as Executive Ombudsmen.[2] These were Colorado, Illinois, Oregon, and Pennsylvania. Other states in which Executive Ombudsmen

[1] See S. V. Anderson (ed.), *Ombudsmen for American Government* (Prentice Hall, 1968).

[2] A. J. Wyner (ed.), *Executive Ombudsmen in the United States* (Institute of Govern mental Studies, Univ. of California, Berkeley, 1973).

have been established are Florida, Kentucky, Montana, New Jersey, and North Carolina. There are also, as we have seen earlier, a number of American cities which have Ombudsman style officers handling complaints about local services.[1]

There is therefore more interest in, and more development of, Ombudsman style institutions in the United States than is apparent from a mere head count of State Ombudsmen responsible, in the classical style, to the legislature. The German Federal Republic is another federal country in which there has been relatively little apparent development in Ombudsman institutions but where an increasing interest in the Ombudsman idea may well presage more rapid development in the future. West Germany has had an Ombudsman for the Armed Forces since 1957.[2] There has been no further development at federal level but in 1974 one of the ten states, Rhineland-Pfalz, set up an Ombudsman. In Italy an Ombudsman was appointed for the region of Tuscany in 1975. He is Dr. Italo de Vito who had been Prefect of Florence and Commissaire for the region of Tuscany from 1971 to 1975. In 1977 the region of Liguria also appointed an Ombudsman. There the Regional Council chose a former judge, Dr. Domenico Riccomagno, as Ombudsman. Both Dr. de Vito and Dr. Riccomagno are known as 'Civic Defenders' but they have the functions of classical Ombudsmen, providing direct access to complainants and investigating complaints against all regional authorities. But none of the other eighteen regions of Italy as yet has an Ombudsman and there is no Ombudsman at national level.

A country in which there has been more rapid development is Israel. An Ombudsman was appointed at national level in 1971 and two of the principal cities in Israel, Jerusalem and Haifa, also have an Ombudsman. A country in which there has been much discussion of proposals for Ombudsmen is Switzerland. As yet no Ombudsman has been established at federal or cantonal level, but Zurich has had its own Ombudsman for city affairs since 1971.

The Ombudsmen we have discussed so far are all in developed countries with parliamentary or presidential systems of government. There have also been a number of Ombudsmen established in Third World countries. Thus Tanzania set up a collegiate form of Ombudsman in 1966 known as the Permanent Commission of Inquiry. Guyana established an Ombudsman in 1967, Mauritius

[1] See above, p. 210. [2] See above, p. 46–50.

in 1970, Fiji in 1972, and Zambia in 1973. India has established three Ombudsmen at state level: in Maharashtra in 1971, and in Bihar and Rajasthan in 1973.

The problems which Ombudsmen in these countries face are to some extent comparable with, and to some extent different from, the problems faced by Ombudsmen in the developed countries. We shall therefore confine our comparisons to Ombudsmen in developed countries. Here the most satisfactory comparisons can be made between the Ombudsmen to which chapters have been devoted in this book, because in each case the Ombudsmen or their senior officers have been interviewed by the author (in some cases both the Ombudsmen and their senior staff) and a first-hand study made of the documentary material available. In the case of the other Ombudsmen in the developed countries, the author is dependent on secondary sources. But two generalizations can be made with some certainty about Ombudsmen in developed countries, including both those given special study in this book and those briefly surveyed in this final chapter. First, out of all the developed countries or states in federal countries which have Ombudsmen systems there are only two which do not permit a member of the public to take his complaint direct to the Ombudsman. These are the United Kingdom and France. Second, among all the Ombudsmen in developed countries, there is only one, and that is the United Kingdom Parliamentary Commissioner, who is confined to investigating complaints of maladministration. The British Local Commissioners are also, of course, in the same situation. All other Ombudsmen have powers, like those of the New Zealand Ombudsman, to report on unreasonable action by public authorities or, like the Médiateur, to report on failures in the public service.

Now, confining ourselves to the Ombudsmen specially studied in this book, we can proceed to some more developed comparisons. It is clear that when access to an Ombudsman is limited to approaching him through a parliamentarian, as in the United Kingdom or in France, the volume of complaints which he receives is much less than when there is direct access. Such an Ombudsman is less well known by the general public than an Ombudsman to whom there is direct access. There can, however, be considerable variation within both indirect access systems and direct access systems, in the degree to which Ombudsmen are conscious of the need to gain publicity for their activities, if they are to maximize their availability to the aggrieved citizen. Thus we have seen that the French Médiateur is much more publicity-conscious than the British Parliamentary Commissioner. We suggested above that the style of the British Parliamentary Commissioner's office was set more on the lines of an internal 'administrative audit' than of the classical Ombudsman's office accessible to the public and open to the public gaze. This concept also fundamentally affected the staffing of his office. The Parliamentary Commissioner's office and the Health Service Commissioner's office (which in fact overlap) are the only national Ombudsmen's offices which are entirely staffed by civil servants or Health Service staff. Of the local Ombudsmen's offices in Britain, only the Welsh Local Commissioner's office is entirely staffed with former local government officers and even they are not local government officers on secondment. The English Local Commissioners and the Scottish Commissioner have staff like those of the Ombudsmen in the other countries we have studied: with a variety of occupational backgrounds and none of them on secondment from local authorities or government departments.

The Parliamentary Commissioner and the British Local Commissioners are distinguished from all the other Ombudsmen we have studied in being limited to investigating complaints that individuals have suffered injustice in consequence of maladministration. We have seen that by subtle stages, and with the encouragement of the Select Committee, Parliamentary Commissioners have widened the interpretation of maladministration.[1] But the limitation is still unfortunate in its effects. The wider interpretation which Parliamentary Commissioners have placed on the term is not widely appreciated or understood. The term is anyway so imprecise that it makes it hard to predict whether or not the Parliamentary Commissioner will find maladministration. Its narrowly procedural meanings are clear enough, but there is a grey area—for example, interpretation of evidence in an unreasonable way, 'failings' in administration which constitute maladministration—where there is much uncertainty.

The alternative formulation which we found is used by all the Canadian provincial Ombudsmen is 'unreasonable action or decision'. This is a better phrase from almost every point of view. It gives the Ombudsman the function which the ordinary person expects him to have. It is unreasonable decisions on the part of the

[1] See above, esp. pp. 156–61.

administrator which the aggrieved citizen wants to see reversed. The concept of maladministration is baffling to him and particularly frustrating when there is an implication from a Parliamentary Commissioner's or Local Commissioner's report that the decision may have been unreasonable but that it was not maladministration. The fear expressed by British Ministers during debates on the Parliamentary Commissioner Bill that to allow the Parliamentary Commissioner to report on unreasonable decisions would be to give him too much power is shown to be unfounded. Ministers argued that to give him this power would lead to 'government by Parliamentary Commissioner', rather than government by Ministers. This is to misconceive the role of an Ombudsman which is to act as an independent critic of the Executive, not to substitute his decision for that of the Ministers. The exercise by Ombudsmen in the Canadian provinces of power to criticise unreasonable decisions clearly in no way detracts from the power of Ministers. There are strong grounds for suggesting that the powers of the Parliamentary Commissioner should be extended to enable him to report on unreasonable actions or decisions by departments. The powers of Local Commissioners should be widened in a similar way. Restriction to maladministration is proving even more limiting for the Local Commissioners than for the Parliamentary Commissioner.[1]

Another distinctive feature at present of the British Parliamentary Commissioner, as compared with the other Ombudsmen we have studied, is the formidable list of areas of government from which he is excluded. One of the most criticized exclusions, from investigating complaints against hospitals, has been partially remedied by setting up a Health Service Commissioner but his effectiveness is much reduced since he is excluded from looking at clinical matters and from investigating complaints against general practitioners.[2] Of the areas from which the Parliamentary Commissioner is still excluded, the exclusion which is least justifiable is from personnel matters in the Civil Service. All the national and provincial Ombudsmen we have studied, except the French Médiateur, are able to examine such complaints. The Select Committee on the Parliamentary Commissioner has on three occasions recommended that the Parliamentary Commissioner should be able to investigate complaints from civil servants in personnel matters. Action to remove this

[1] See above, pp. 206–8, 213–5, 223–4.
[2] See above, pp. 179–81, 187–90.

exclusion is long overdue, and the exclusion of Local Commissioners from investigating complaints by local government employees in personnel matters should also be removed.

The exclusion of the Parliamentary Commissioner from investigating complaints from members of the armed forces in personnel matters is also unusual. The Swedish and Danish Ombudsmen have such powers and in Norway there is a special Ombudsman for the Armed Forces.

Several other exclusions should be looked at again. The Royal Commission on Standards of Conduct in Public Life recommended in 1976 that the Parliamentary Commissioner should be able to examine complaints about the commercial and contractual transactions of government departments, and the exclusion of the Local Commissioners from investigating complaints about these aspects of local government is equally undesirable. The Parliamentary Commissioner is also excluded from examining complaints against nationalized industries whereas the Scandinavian Ombudsmen, the French Médiateur, and the Canadian provincial Ombudsmen can all examine complaints against state-owned industries. Again there seems no good reason for maintaining this exclusion. A committee of 'Justice' has recently investigated this question and recommended that a Nationalized Industries and Agencies Commissioner should be set up to examine complaints against nationalized industries.[1] The 'Justice' Committee suggested that he should examine complaints which had not been resolved through the existing system of consultative councils. It also recommended that the consultative councils should be strengthened and improved.

Another area from which British Ombudsmen are excluded is from considering complaints about the operation of administrative tribunals. Here again comparison with Scandinavian countries and the Canadian province shows that this exclusion is unnecessary and doubtfully desirable. The Scandinavian and Canadian Ombudsmen are able to examine complaints about procedural failings in administrative tribunals and we have seen in a number of instances what effective use can be made of this power.[2] We have seen that there is a strong case for the Health Service Commissioner being given

[1] 'Justice', *The Citizen and the Public Agencies. Remedying Grievances* (Justice, 1976). The chairman of the Committee was Professor J. F. Garner. Research for the study was carried out by Dr. Philip Giddings of Reading University and Dr. Wyn Grant of Warwick University.

[2] See above, pp. 11, 54 and 74.

power to examine complaints about the operation of Medical and Dental Service Committees and the other administrative tribunals in the Health sector.[1] His exclusion from this area is particularly hard to justify since he has a major role in considering the adequacies of complaints procedures in the hospital service. The exclusion of the Parliamentary Commissioner from examining complaints about the operation of other administrative tribunals is equally unnecessary. The existence of the Council on Tribunals is not a sufficient reason for not making the Parliamentary Commissioner an alternative channel for complaint. The Council on Tribunals has a very small staff and is dependent on its unpaid, voluntary membership to carry out spot checks on the operation of tribunals. The Parliamentary Commissioner, with his power to see all the documents and his ability to send an investigator to interview the complainant and the staff or members of a tribunal, would be able to carry out a much more effective investigation into a complaint about procedural unfairness in a tribunal than the Council on Tribunals can. This is not to say that the Council on Tribunals does not have a distinctive and important role. It does. Its role is to keep a continuous oversight of the whole field of administrative tribunals and inquiries, and their operation, and to give its views on the composition and powers of new tribunals. Its role would be complementary to that of the Parliamentary Commissioner if he were also to be given power to investigate complaints against administrative tribunals.

An almost obsessive shunning of provision for alternative channels of complaint is in fact a feature of the British Parliamentary Commissioner system, under present legislation. It is not found to anything like the same extent in, for example, the Swedish Ombudsman system. In Sweden the aggrieved citizen often has a choice of several different channels of complaint and the fact that he has already used one channel does not necessarily debar him from using another. Indeed, when a ctizen has complained to an Ombudsman and received a finding in his favour he can use the Ombudsman's report as evidence in a court of law. This is the same principle which is operated under the Northern Ireland Commissioner for Complaints Act and we saw that there is a strong case for new legislation to enable a complainant in Britain to use a report from a Local Commissioner, after investigation of his complaint, as

[1] See above, pp. 187–90.

evidence in a court of law to secure redress against a local authority which is unwilling to act upon the Commissioner's report.[1]

While there are then numerous ways in which the British Ombudsman system needs to be improved, there are several strong points in the system of which we will single out three in particular. First, the Parliamentary Commissioner, the Health Service Commissioner, and the Local Commissioners all use, as a matter of course, much more thorough investigating procedures than are normally used by other Ombudsmen. William B. Gwyn has shown in a paper prepared for the International Ombudsman Conference at Edmonton, Alberta, in September 1976 that the majority of Ombudsmen normally depend on the government department itself to review a case when a complaint is referred to them by the Ombudsman. In relatively few cases does the New Zealand Ombudsman, for example, himself go to the department, or send his investigator to the department, to interview officials and examine files in the department.[2] In Britain this is the normal procedure and we have seen that its use is particularly appropriate in Health Service Commissioner cases and in many Local Commissioner cases. If, as we have suggested, access to Ombudsmen in Britain were to be made easier and some of the limitations placed upon their investigations removed, there would be a much larger flow of complaints to the Ombudsmen. For a good many complaints, less thorough methods of investigation would then have to be used. But it would be important to retain the thorough method of investigation for as high a proportion of complaints as possible, and particularly for cases where there was a substantial disagreement between the complainant and the government department, local authority, or health authority about what in fact had occurred.

A second strong point in the British system is that Ministers are not exempt from scrutiny by the Parliamentary Commissioner, as they are, for example, in New Zealand where the Ombudsman can investigate the advice given to Ministers but not the action of the Minister himself. In a number of cases, of which the Sachsenhausen and Court Line cases are perhaps the most important, the role of the Minister has rightly come in for criticism by the Parliamentary

[1] See above, p. 219.

[2] William B. Gwyn, 'A Comparative Study of the Investigative Methods of Ombudsmen' (cyclostyled paper prepared for the International Ombudsmen Conference, Edmonton, Alberta, September 1976).

Commissioner. Similarly, the Local Commissioners are able to criticize the actions of elected members of local authorities as well as of officials.

A third strong point of the Parliamentary Commissioner system in Britain is the active support given to the Parliamentary Commissioner by the Commons Select Committee. All national or provincial Ombudsmen are responsible to their legislature and many report to a committee of the legislature. But none has a committee which takes such an active interest in the work of the Ombudsman as is taken by the Commons Select Committee on the Parliamentary Commissioner. We have seen that the Select Committee has played an important part in encouraging the Parliamentary Commissioner to widen his interpretation of maladministration, and has given him most effective backing when he has met resistance from government departments to implementing recommendations in his reports. The position of the Local Commissioners for Administration is relatively weaker because they do not have such a committee to reinforce their findings. We have suggested that a Commons Committee should receive the reports of the English Local Commissioners and should inquire into failure on the part of local authorities to implement the Commissioners' recommendations. This Committee would not replace but would complement the Representative Body of local authorities which has a different role in promoting liaison with the Commissioners. If the Scotland Bill and the Wales Bill become law, the Scottish and Welsh Local Commissioners should report to Committees of the newly created Scottish and Welsh Assemblies. If the Bills do not become law, they should report to the Commons Committee.[1]

Another sound feature of the system in the United Kingdom, as it has developed since 1967, is the provision of a variety of Ombudsmen. In a unitary country with a large population it is appropriate to have, as in Britain, a number of 'functional' Ombudsmen dealing with different areas of government. Thus we have a Parliamentary Commissioner concerned with the central departments, a notionally separate Health Service Commissioner, concerned with health authorities, and Local Commissioners receiving complaints against local authorities and water authorities. The 'Justice' proposal for an Ombudsman for the nationalized industries would create a fourth

[1] The data relating to the devolution bills in this and the subsequent paragraph have been brought up to date by Wyn Grant (M.S.).

specialized Ombudsman. In federal countries, on the other hand, it is appropriate, as in Canada and Australia, for the Ombudsmen to deal with all aspects of government below the federal level. Similarly, in small unitary states an 'all-purpose' Ombudsman, or Ombudsman's office, is appropriate. If Scotland and Wales achieve their own Assemblies they will acquire an intermediate status between federalism and unitary government. In this situation, it would be appropriate for any Ombudsman established by the Scottish assembly to deal with matters within its legislative competence, also to deal with complaints against local authorities in Scotland. The Parliamentary Commissioner would continue to investigate complaints against United Kingdom services in Scotland and Wales. Similarly, the Health Service Commissioner would investigate complaints against the health authorities in Scotland and Wales, but he could report to the Scottish and Welsh Assemblies.[1] In England the existing system of a separate Parliamentary Commissioner, Health Service Commissioner, and Local Commissioners would continue.

Whereas there is a good case for continuing with the present variety of Ombudsmen, because in a country with a large population a unified Ombudsman's office would become an unwieldy and impersonal organization, the present system does involve problems of co-ordination. Shortly after retiring from the posts of Parliamentary Commissioner and Health Service Commissioner, Sir Alan Marre said in an interview that in his view it was confusing to members of the public not only that there are a number of different Commissioners but that the method of access is different to each of them.[2] Before his retirement he had told the Select Committee on the Parliamentary Commissioner that it should consider how in the long term 'a more co-ordinated total system, more directly related

[1] The Scotland Bill, unlike the original Scotland and Wales Bill, does not propose the creation of Assembly Commissioners for the investigation of complaints against the new Scottish administration and its officials; however, the Scottish Assembly would be able to legislate on this matter. The investigation of maladministration in local government and the Health Service is within the legislative competence of the proposed Scottish Assembly. There might be a case for any Assembly Commissioner in Scotland taking over the functions of the Local Commissioner, making only three sets of Commissioners in that country. Under the Wales Bill, the Welsh Assembly would acquire certain functions at present exercised by the Secretary of State in relation to the Local Commissioner; principally, the designation of the Commissioner, the appointment and functions of the Representative Body, and powers restraining the disclosure of information and documents contrary to the public interest.

[2] In an interview to *C.H.C. News*, April 1976. See also above, p. 175.

to the interests of members of the public, could be brought about'.[1]

For the reasons we have already given, it would not, in our view, be desirable to set up one unified Ombudsman's office. But better co-ordination could be provided in two main ways. First, the Parliamentary Commissioner should act as a channel of complaints to other Commissioners, or to other agencies handling complaints, when a complaint reached him which was outside his jurisdiction. This function would be assisted by the second main change which would promote co-ordination, that is providing for direct access to all Commissioners by members of the public. Not only would there then be no difficulty in each Commissioner sending on a complaint to the appropriate Commissioner, since he would not have to ask the complainant to take his complaint to an M.P. or a councillor, but Citizens' Advice Bureaux and other information offices could play a much more important role than at present in channelling cases to an Ombudsman. Bureaux would no longer have to tell complainants that they must go to their M.P. or councillor but would be able to assist complainants directly in formulating their complaints and forwarding them to the Commissioner.

One of the difficulties for many potential complainants is that a complaint must be made in writing to a Commissioner. Even Ombudsman systems like the Quebec system which allow complaints to be made initially by telephone require the complaint proper to be made in writing. Linking in the Citizens' Advice Bureaux with the Commissioner system in Britain would enable Bureaux staff to help the person who finds difficulty in putting his complaint in writing to draft his initial complaint or supporting letter to his complaint, if Commissioners were to allow the initial complaint to be made by telephone. In this way, access to Ombudsmen in Britain by the less socially and educationally advantaged sections of the population should be greatly improved. Providing for direct access to all Ombudsmen in the United Kingdom, then, appears to be the key reform which would make it possible for Ombudsmen to be widely known and used by members of the public. At the same time, the link with elected members and representatives should be preserved by also allowing Members of Parliament, Assembly members, local councillors, and community health councillors to forward complaints on behalf of members of the public.

[1] H.C. 480 of 1976–7. Second Report from the Select Committee on the Parliamentary Commissioner for Administration, p. vii at para. 7.

SELECT BIBLIOGRAPHY

COMPARATIVE WORKS

FRIEDMAN, K., 'The Public and the Ombudsman: Perceptions and Attitudes in Britain and in Alberta', *Canadian Journal of Political Science*, x, No. 3 (Sept. 1977), 497–525.

GELLHORN, W., *Ombudsmen and Others: Citizens' Protectors in Nine Countries* (Harvard U.P. and Oxford U.P., 1967).

GWYN, W. B., 'A Comparative Study of the Investigative Methods of Ombudsmen' (cyclostyled paper prepared for the International Ombudsman Conference, Edmonton, Albert, Sept. 1976).

ROWAT, D. C., *The Ombudsman Plan. Essays on the Worldwide Spread of an Idea* (McClelland and Stewart, 1973).

—— (ed.), *The Ombudsman. Citizens' Defender* (Allen and Unwin, 1965).

WEEKS, K. M., *Ombudsmen Around the World: A Comparative Chart* (Institute of Governmental Studies, Univ. of California, Berkeley, 1973).

SWEDEN

BEXELIUS, A., 'The Ombudsman for Civil Affairs', in D. C. Rowat (ed.), pp. 22–4.

LUNDVIK, U., 'Comments on the Ombudsman for Civil Affairs', in D. C. Rowat (ed.), pp. 44–50.

RUDHOLM, S., 'The Chancellor of Justice', in D. C. Rowat (ed.), pp. 17–22.

The Swedish Parliamentary Ombudsmen (Stockholm, 1976) (pamphlet in English on the operation of the Ombudsmen's office).

The Swedish Parliamentary Ombudsmen, summaries in English of Annual Reports since 1972.

The Swedish Parliamentary Ombudsmen, summary in English of Report for the period 1 January 1976 to 30 June 1976.

DENMARK

HURWITZ, S., 'The Scandinavian Ombudsman', *Political Science* (New Zealand, 1960), 121–42.

—— *The Ombudsman. Denmark's Parliamentary Commissioner for Civil and Military Administration* (Det Danske Selskab, Copenhagen, 1962).

—— *The Ombudsman* (Det Danske Selskab, Copenhagen, 1968).

LERHARD, M. (ed.), *The Danish Ombudsman 1955–1969. Seventy-Five Cases from the Ombudsman's Reports*, trans. Reginald Spink (Schultz, Copenhagen, 1972).

FOLKETINGETS OMBUDSMAND. English version of part of Annual Report for 1975.

NEILSEN, N., 'The Danish Ombudsman', *Administration* (Dublin, 1973), 355–64.

PEDERSEN, I. M., 'Denmark's Ombudsmand', in D. C. Rowat (ed.), pp. 75–94.

NORWAY

OS, A., 'The Ombudsman for Civil Affairs', in D. C. Rowat (ed.), pp. 95–110.

RUUD, A., 'The Military Ombudsman and his Board', in D. C. Rowat (ed.), pp. 111–18.

SINDING-LARSEN, T., 'The Storting's Ombudsman for Public Administration' (cyclostyled, Oslo, 1977).

THUNE, S., 'The Norwegian Ombudsmen for Civil and Military Affairs' (cyclostyled, Oslo, 1970).

FINLAND

HIDEN, M., *The Ombudsman in Finland: The First Fifty Years* (Institute of Governmental Studies, Univ. of California, Berkeley, 1973).

KASTARI, P., 'Finland's Guardians of the Law, The Chancellor of the Justice and the Ombudsman', in D. C. Rowat (ed.), pp. 58–74.

CANADA

ANDERSON, S. V., *Canadian Ombudsman Proposals* (Institute of Governmental Studies, Univ. of California, Berkeley, 1966).

FRIEDMANN, K. A., 'Canadian Ombudsmen' (cyclostyled paper prepared for the International Ombudsman Conference, Edmonton, Alberta, Sept. 1976).

MCBRIDE, J. J., 'Nova Scotia Ombudsman', *Dalhousie Law Journal* (1975), 182–200.

NORTHEY, J. F., 'The Manitoba Ombudsman Act 1969', *Manitoba Law Journal* (1970), 206–12.

WEIR, A. B., 'The Legislative Ombudsmen', *Alberta Law Review* (1976), 256–65.

BACCIGALUPO, A. and E. GROULX, 'Protecteur du citoyen dans la province de Quebec', *Revue Administrative* (1972), 640–6.

BACCIGALUPO, A., 'Protecteur du citoyen et la societé québécoise', *International Review of Administrative Sciences* (1975), 128–34.

BACCIGALUPO, A., 'Le protecteur du citoyen', *Recherches sociographiques* (Quebec, 1975), 353–73.

LEGISLATIVE ASSEMBLY OF QUEBEC, Public Protector Act, 1968.

PUBLIC PROTECTOR, Annual Reports, published from 1969 (Quebec).

MANITOBA OMBUDSMAN ACT, 1969.

PROVINCE OF MANITOBA, Annual Report of the Ombudsman, published from 1970 (Winnipeg).

NEW BRUNSWICK OMBUDSMAN ACT, 1967.

PROVINCE OF NEW BRUNSWICK, Annual Reports of the Ombudsman, published from 1968 (Frederictown).

ONTARIO OMBUDSMAN ACT, 1975.

PROVINCE OF ONTARIO, Annual Reports of the Ombudsman, published from 1976 (Toronto).

MALONEY, A., Speech on 'The Powers of the Ombudsman and their Judicious use' (cyclostyled text of proceedings of the International Ombudsman Conference, Sept. 1976).

ALBERTA OMBUDSMAN ACT, 1967.

PROVINCE OF ALBERTA, Annual Reports of the Ombudsman published from 1968 (Edmonton).

REPORT OF THE SELECT COMMITTEE of the Legislative Assembly to Review Legislation on the Ombudsman Act (Alberta, May 1977).

SASKATCHEWAN OMBUDSMAN ACT, 1972.

PROVINCE OF SASKATCHEWAN, Annual Reports of the Ombudsman published from 1973 (Regina).

NOVA SCOTIA OMBUDSMAN ACT, 1970.

PROVINCE OF NOVA SCOTIA, Annual Reports of the Ombudsman, published from 1971 (Halifax).

NEWFOUNDLAND PARLIAMENTARY COMMISSIONER (OMBUDSMAN) ACT, 1970.

PROVINCE OF NEWFOUNDLAND, Annual Reports of the Ombudsman, published from 1975 (St. John's).

FRANCE

BARBET, M., 'De l'ombudsman au Médiateur', in *Aspects nouveaux de la pensée juridique. Recueil d'études en homage à Marc Ancel* (Éditions A. Pedone, 1975), vol. i, pp. 231–42.

BROWN, L. and P. LAVIROTTE, 'Mediator: a French Ombudsman?', *Law Quarterly Review* (1974), 1–26.

CHAPUISAT, L., 'Médiateur français ou L'Ombudsman sacrifié', *International Review of Administrative Sciences* (1974), 109–29.

KLEIN, R., 'Ombudsman into Médiateur', *Political Quarterly* (1976), 92–4.

MESCHERIAKOFF, A., 'Le Médiateur: un ombudsman français?', *Bulletin de l'Institut international d'administration publique* (1973), 7–51.

—— 'Le Médiateur deux ans après', *Bulletin de l'Institut international d'administration publique* (1975), 45–70.

Pierot, R., 'Médiateur: rival ou allié du juge administratif?', *Mélanges offerts à Marcel Waline. Le Juge et le droit public* (Librairie générale de droit et de jurisprudence, Paris, 1974), vol. ii, pp. 683–99.

Pinay, A., 'Quelques réflexions sur l'institution du Médiateur', *Revue Administrative* (1973), 615–19.

Verrier, P., 'Le Mediateur', *Revue du Droit Public et de la Science Politique en France et à l'Étranger* (1973), 941–84.

Loi numéro 73–6 du 3 janvier 1973 instituant un médiateur.

Loi numéro 76–1211 du 24 décembre 1976 complétant la loi numéro 73–6 du 3 janvier 1973 instituant un médiateur.

Rapport annuel du Médiateur, published (in French) from 1973 (Paris).

THE UNITED KINGDOM:
THE PARLIAMENTARY COMMISSIONER FOR ADMINISTRATION

Cohen, L. H., 'The Parliamentary Commissioner and the "M.P. Filter" ', *Public Law* (1972), 204–14.

Friedmann, K. A., 'Commons, Complaints and the Ombudsman', *Parliamentary Affairs* (1967), 38–47.

Gregory, R., 'Court Line, Mr. Benn and the Ombudsman', *Parliamentary Affairs*, xxx, No. 3 (Summer 1977), 269–92.

—— and A. Alexander, 'Our Parliamentary Ombudsman. Part I. Integration and Metamorphosis', *Public Administration* (1972), 313–31.

—— 'Our Parliamentary Ombudsman. Part II: Development and the Problem of Identity', *Public Administration* (1973), 41–59.

—— Gregory, R. and P. Hutchesson, *The Parliamentary Ombudsman. A Study in the Control of Administrative Action* (Allen and Unwin, 1975).

Gwyn, W. B., 'The British P.C.A.: "Ombudsman or Ombudsmouse?" ', *Journal of Politics* (1973), 45–69.

'Justice', *The Citizen and the Administration. The Redress of Grievances* (Stevens, 1961).

—— *The Citizen and the Public Agencies. Remedying Grievances* (Justice, 1976).

—— *Our Fettered Ombudsman* (Justice, 1977).

Marre, Sir A., 'Some Reflections on an Ombudsman', *Social and Economic Administration* (1975), 3–12.

Marshall, G., 'The British Parliamentary Commissioner for Administration', *Annals of the American Academy of Political and Social Sciences 377* (May 1968), 87–96.

—— 'Maladministration', *Public Law* (1973), 32–44.

—— 'Parliament and the Ombudsman', in A. H. Hanson and B. Crick (eds.), *The Commons in Transition* (Fontana, 1970), 114–29.

—— 'Parliament and the Redress of Grievances: the Parliamentary Commissioner in the 1970's', in S. A. Walkland and M. Ryle, *The Commons in the Seventies* (Fontana, 1977), 222–37.

MITCHELL, J. D. B., 'Administrative Law and Parliamentary Control', *Public Law* (1973), 360–74.

STACEY, F., *The British Ombudsman* (Clarendon Press, 1971).

WHEARE, K. C., *Maladministration and its Remedies* (Stevens, 1973).

Parliamentary Commissioner Act, 1967.

Annual Reports of the Parliamentary Commissioner for Administration from 1967.

Special Reports of the Parliamentary Commissioner for Administration from 1967.

Quarterly volumes of results reports of the Parliamentary Commissioner for Administration from 1972.

Reports of the House of Commons Select Committee on the Parliamentary Commissioner for Administration from 1968.

THE UNITED KINGDOM:
THE HEALTH SERVICE COMMISSIONER

KLEIN, R., 'The Health Service Commissioner: no cause for complaint', *British Medical Journal* (1977), 248.

ROBB, B., *Sans Everything* (Nelson, 1967).

Cmnd. 4557, Report of the Farleigh Hospital Committee of Inquiry, H.M.S.O., London, 1971.

Department of Health and Social Security. The Welsh Office, *Report of the Committee on Hospital Complaints Procedure* (H.M.S.O., 1973).

National Health Service Reorganization Act, 1973.

Reports of the Health Service Commissioner from 1974.

THE UNITED KINGDOM:
THE LOCAL COMMISSIONERS FOR ADMINISTRATION

CHINKIN, C. M. and R. J. BAILEY, 'The Local Ombudsman', *Public Administration* (1976), 267–82.

COHEN, L. H., 'Local Government Complaints: the M.P.'s Viewpoint', *Public Administration* (1973), 175–83.

COOK, P., 'The Work of the Commission for Local Administration in England', *Public Administration Bulletin* (1975), 68–71.

DRAKE, C. D., 'Ombudsmen for Local Government', *Public Administration* (1970), 179–89.

ELCOCK, H. J., 'Opportunity for Ombudsman: The Northern Ireland Commissioner for Complaints', *Public Administration* (1972), 87–93.

GARNER, J. F., 'Commissioner for Complaints Act (N.I.) 1969', *Northern Ireland Legal Quarterly* (Autumn 1970), 353–6.

'JUSTICE', *The Citizen and his Council. Ombudsmen for Local Government?* (Stevens, 1969).

POOLE, K. P., 'The Northern Ireland Commissioner for Complaints', *Public Law* (1972), 131–48.

Local Government Act, 1974.

Local Government (Scotland) Act, 1975.

Annual Reports of the Commission for Local Administration in England from 1975.

Annual Reports of the Commission for Local Administration in Wales from 1975.

Annual Reports of the Commissioner for Local Administration in Scotland from 1976.

OTHER COUNTRIES

New Zealand

HILL, L. B., *The Model Ombudsman. Institutionalizing New Zealand's Democratic Experiment* (Princeton U.P., 1976).

KEITH, K. J., 'The Ombudsman and "Wrong" Decisions', *New Zealand Universities Law Review* (1971), 361–93.

NORTHEY, J. F., 'New Zealand's Parliamentary Commissioner', in D. C. Rowat (ed.), 127–43.

POWLES, SIR G., 'Aspects of the Search for Administrative Justice with Particular Reference to the New Zealand Ombudsman', *Canadian Journal of Public Administration* (1966), 133–57.

—— 'The Office of Ombudsman in New Zealand', *Journal of Administration Overseas* (1969), 287–92.

Australia

DISNEY, J., 'Ombudsmen in Australia', *Australian Quarterly* (1974), 38–55.

SAWER, G., 'The Ombudsman and Related Institutions in Australia and New Zealand', *Annals of the American Academy of Political and Social Sciences*, 377 (1968), 62–72.

United States

ANDERSON, S. V. (ed.), *Ombudsmen for American Government* (Prentice Hall, 1968).

FRANK, B., 'Nebraska public counsel—the ombudsman', *Cumberland–Samford Law Review* (1974), 30–58.

—— 'State ombudsman legislation in the United States', *University of Miami Law Review* (1975), 397–445.

GELLHORN, W., *When Americans Complain, Governmental Grievance Procedures* (Harvard U.P., 1966).

WYNER, A. J., *The Nebraska Ombudsman: Innovation in State Government* (Institute of Governmental Studies, Univ. of California, Berkeley, 1974).

—— (ed.), *Executive Ombudsmen in the United States* (Institute of Governmental Studies, Univ. of California, Berkeley, 1973).

Israel

ELMAN, P., 'The Israel Ombudsman', *Israel Law Review* (1975), 293–323.

HIRSCH, J., 'The Genesis of the Israel Public Complaints Commissioner', *Public Administration* (Jerusalem, 1972), 119–28.

KERBER, N. M., *L'Ombudsman israélien* (Éditions A. Pedone, 1975).

India

GUPTA, B. K., 'Ministerial responsibility and the proposed Lokpal: do they go hand in hand?', *Journal of the Indian Law Institute* (1974), 387–98.

Tanzania

OLUYEDE, P., 'Redress of grievances in Tanzania', *Public Law* (1975), 8–26.

NORTON, P. M., 'Tanzanian Ombudsman', *International and Comparative Law Quarterly* (1973), 603–31.

INDEX